Power of Our Stories Won't Stop: Intergenerational Truth-Telling as Civic Democratic Practice

We need a bold new vision for how we think about education so that we can address the question, "how do we wish to live together?" These essays encourage us to interrogate how we know "what we know" so that we can imagine a more deeply interconnected—and genuinely inclusive—future.
—Stephen Seng-hua Mak, Assistant Head of School for Program and Innovation, PreK–12. The Berkeley Carroll School

If there was ever a time for an intergenerational conversation, it is now. Youth crave political insight, and elders are eager to be in dialogue with them. This anthology moves us in a direction to better understand how to make the world we all desire to live in.
—Ula Y. Taylor, Professor, University of California Berkeley, Department of African American Studies, 1960 Chair of Undergraduate Education

The insightful contributors to this anthology paint a tapestry, not one that points to the easy understandings, but one that invites us to wrestle with hard truths. Ideas come in the form of autobiographical narrative, retelling of Movement history, and pedagogical lessons. They weave together a book that asks us to rethink Asian American experiences in relation to Blackness, to colonial histories, to gender and sexuality. We hear multiple generations of activists, artists, storytellers, and ordinary people sharing their stories that connect us and challenge us towards more complex understandings of the world.
—Diane C. Fujino, Professor, Asian American Studies, University of California, Santa Barbara

For youth in particular, intergenerational truth-telling is absolutely vital to both historical understanding and to building a future democracy for all. This powerful and inspiring anthology charts a compelling path forward in this critically important work; as such, it deserves the widest possible audience.
—Waldo E. Martin, Jr., Alexander F. and May T. Morrison

POWER OF OUR STORIES WON'T STOP

Intergenerational Truth-Telling as Civic Democratic Practice

Editor: Hellena Moon
Assistant Editor: Madeleine Moon-Chun
Educational Partner: Anthony Downer II

Eastwind Books of Berkeley

Power of Our Stories Won't Stop:
Intergenerational Truth-Telling as Civic Democratic Practice

Editor: Hellena Moon
Assistant Editor: Madeleine Moon-Chun
Educational Partner: Anthony Downer II

Copyright © 2023 by Hellena Moon

Published by:
EASTWIND BOOKS OF BERKELEY
Berkeley, California
USA

www.AsiaBookCenter.com
email: eastwindbooks@gmail.com

All rights reserved. No part of this book may be used or reproduced in any manner without written permission from the author and publisher.

Eastwind Books of Berkeley is a registered trademark of
Eastwind Books of Berkeley

Published 2023. First Edition
Printed in the United States of America

For more information or to book an author event,
contact www.AsiaBookCenter.com

Cover Design: Cheryl Truong

ISBN: 9781734744071 (Paperback)

ISBN: 9781734744088 (Ebook)

10 9 8 7 6 5 4 3 2 1

Front cover artwork: Drawings of Jamie Foxx (his role of Walter McMillian in Just Mercy), Asian American girl, and the Asian American boy were done by Madeleine Moon-Chun. "The Girl in Prayer," by Julyann Moon.

Front cover photo: Students block Sather Gate at UC Berkeley during the Third World Liberation Strike of 1969.

DEDICATION

To

Professor Ramsay Liem

And to educators who desire to *teach* truths

And to their students who desire to *learn* truths

We all have a responsibility to create a just society

—Bryan Stevenson

TABLE OF CONTENTS

Foreword: Andrea Young, Executive Director of the
    ACLU of Georgia   xviii
Introduction: What I Wish I Had Known in High School Now That I know
    What I know, Hellena Moon   xxiv

PART ONE:
THEORIES OF LIBERATION

1 Third World Studies: A Conversation. Gary Y. Okihiro   2
2 Listening to Truths: Democracy & Its Neighbor, Fascism.
    Hellena Moon   20
3 Are Queers Dangerous? What I wish I Had Known about the
    Intersections of Race, Gender, Class, and Sexuality in High School.
    Sig/Sara Giordano   49
4 A Politics of Our Time: Reworking Afro-Asian Solidarity in the Wake of
    George Floyd's Killing. Yuichiro Onishi   80

PART TWO:
PRACTICING & SHARING STORIES OF LIBERATION

5 can't stop, won't stop: The Tradition of Black Education as the Practice
    of Freedom. Anthony Downer II   100
6 Music, Math, and Malcolm X: My Intellectual Journey of Truth. Douglas
    Henry Daniels   125
7 Who Am I? Madeleine Moon-Chun   129
8 In the Hour of the Dragon: Nationalism, Feminism, and a Korean
    American Identity. Elaine Haikyung Kim   131
9 What I Wish I Had Known When I Was in High School: A Brief
    Reflection. Ramsay Liem   138
10 My Dearest Ancestors, Children, & Future Generation. Judy W. Yu   150
11 Why Trying to Fit in Is the Problem. Moon-Ho Jung   157
12 Liberation Through Identity: "We Are Lucky to Be Free". Takeru
    Nagayoshi   169

PART THREE: GENERATIONAL STORIES, CONVERSATIONS, & HEALING TRAUMAS

13 Ebony in the Ivory Tower, Adia Butler & Dr. Lee Butler   174
14 Creative Expressions: An Interview Between a Teenager and His Mom. Kyle Little and Lahronda Welch Little   178
15 "Centering" Yourself Before You Log On: Black Girls, The Enneagram, and Self-Care in the World of Social Media. Christal Bell & Danielle Buhuro   190

PART FOUR: LEADERSHIP, MORAL BRILLIANCE, & COMMUNITY ENGAGED LEARNING

16 Two Leaders Who Are Students of Relationships: A Conversation. By Lori Klein and Jonathan Klein   204
17 How Do We Teach Moral Brilliance? Nathan Reddy and Nadinne Cruz   216
18 Fighting Racism with Solidarity: #knowyourBIPOChistory. Akemi Kochiyama   229
19 Speaking Up and Speaking Out: Living at Full Volume. Allegra Lawrence Hardy   240
20 *Teh Bà Ta Hkèh Poo:* Sharing Stories. By Nathan Reddy, Eh Tha Yooi Lee, and Hserkaw Ler   245
21 Out Here: Writing with the Unhoused. Christie Towers   260

PART FIVE: FICTIONS AS TRUTH-TELLING

22 Walter McMillian: Defeating the Powerful Hands of Death. Madeleine Moon-Chun   274
23 Life In a Three-Day Loop. Leenah Safi   282
24 Dreams That Hold Power. Madeleine Moon-Chun   294
Afterword: Teaching and Learning Through *Konbit.* Cécile Accilien   296

Contributors

Cécile Accilien (she/her), PhD, is professor of African and African Diaspora Studies in the Interdisciplinary Studies Department at Kennesaw State University (Georgia). She is Vice President of the Haitian Studies Association. Her work includes the co-edited volume, *Teaching Haiti: Strategies for Creating New Narratives*. Her forthcoming monograph is titled, *Bay Lodians: Haitian Popular Film Culture*.

Christal Bell (she/her), MDiv (Garrett-Evangelical Theological Seminary), DMin (Payne Theological Seminary), is a preacher, public speaker, Christian educator, published writer, and Chaplain. Reverend Dr. Christal currently serves as the Director of Christian Education for the Fourth Episcopal District which includes Indiana, Illinois, Chicago, Michigan, Canada, and India Conferences. Dr. Christal specializes in Pediatric Chaplaincy at Advocate Children's Hospital in Oaklawn, IL. She provides spiritual care and leadership in the areas of grief and bereavement for families.

Danielle Buhuro (she/her) received both her MDiv and DMin from the Chicago Theological Seminary. Reverend Dr. Buhuro is passionate about issues of race, gender, and sexuality. She serves as Executive Director and lead CPE Supervisor of Sankofa CPE Center, LLC. She is also the Director of Movement Chaplaincy for Faith Matters Network. Dr. Buhuro is editor of the book, *Spiritual Care in an Age of #BlackLivesMatter: Examining the Spiritual and Prophetic Needs of African Americans Living in a Violent America*. She is currently a PhD student studying social media identity, violence, and pastoral theology. Dr. Buhuro has also served on the national board of directors of ACPE: The Standard for Spiritual Care & Education. She facilitates numerous workshops nation-wide on African American Pastoral Care and African-centered psychology.

Adia Robinson Butler (she/her) is a 2022 summa cum laude graduate of Ithaca College with a BA in Writing. She is committed to equity and justice in the world. She is the daughter of Dr. Lee Butler.

Lee H. Butler, Jr. (he/him), PhD, is the father of Adia Robinson Butler. He is Vice President of Academic Affairs and a professor at Phillips Theological Seminary, Tulsa, OK. Committed to equity and justice, his publications include *A Loving Home*; *Liberating Our Dignity, Saving Our Souls;* and *Listen My Son*.

Nadinne Cruz (she/her) is an immigrant from the Philippines, where her college volunteer experiences with peasants' rights inspired her work as a pioneer of service-learning in the United States. She was the director of Stanford's Haas Center for Public Service, where she founded the Public Service Scholars Program and taught community organizing for the Program in Urban Studies.

Douglas Henry Daniels (he/him), PhD, was born in Chicago and received his A.B. in Political Science from the University of Chicago. He received his M.A. and PhD in History from University of California, Berkeley. His first job as a professor was at the University of Texas, Austin, and in 1979, he was hired in Black Studies and History at the University of California, Santa Barbara. He has published books on Black San Francisco, a biography of saxophonist Lester "Pres" Young, and a history of the Oklahoma City Blue Devils. He is currently completing a history of the Berkeley civil rights movement.

Anthony Downer II (he/him) is an abolitionist educator-organizer, Equity Coordinator in City Schools of Decatur, Georgia, Lead Learner of Liberation Learning Lab, and host of *dat way: conversations on education and liberation*. Anthony taught high school social studies in Atlanta and Gwinnett County. He was raised and resides in Norcross. He is an educational partner to this book project.

Sig/Sara Giordano (they/them), PhD, is an activist-scholar working as an Associate Professor at Kennesaw State University specializing in feminist science studies in the Department of Interdisciplinary Studies. Their areas of interest are the politics and ethics of science with a focus on critical science literacy and the democratization of science.

Moon-Ho Jung (he/him), PhD, is Professor of History and the Harry Bridges Chair in Labor Studies at the University of Washington. He is the author of *Menace to Empire: Anticolonial Solidarities and the Transpacific Origins of the US Security State* (2022) and *Coolies and Cane: Race, Labor, and Sugar in the Age of Emancipation* (2006).

Elaine H. Kim (she/her) (B.A., University of Pennsylvania, M.A. Columbia University, PhD University of California at Berkeley) is Professor *Emerita* of the Asian American and Asian Diaspora Studies Program of the Ethnic Studies Department at UC Berkeley. She is the recipient of a Rockefeller Fellowship, a Fulbright Fellowship, an Honorary Doctorate from the University of Massachusetts Boston, and an Honorary Doctor of Laws from the University of Notre Dame. She wrote, edited, and co-edited ten books, the earliest of which was *Asian American Literature: An Introduction to the Writings and Their Social Context* (1982) and the most recent of which is *Fresh Talk/Daring Gazes: Conversations on Asian American Art* (2003). She co-edited *East to America: Korean American Life Stories* (1996), *Making More Waves: New Writing by Asian American Women* (1997), *Dangerous Women: Gender and Korean Nationalism* (1998), and *Echoes Upon Echoes: New Korean American Writing* (2003).

Jonathan Klein (he/him) is the consummate real estate professional, bringing an unparalleled wealth of expertise and experience in all areas of residential and commercial construction, property management, organizational management, operations, finance, maintenance, and development: https://kleinpropertymanagement.com/.

Lori Klein (she/her) is a chaplain at Stanford Health Care and Montage Health Care. Rabbi Klein co-authored an essay titled, "Spiritual Care in the Shadow of Loss and Uprising." It appears in *Postcolonial Practices of Spiritual Care: A Project of Togetherness during COVID-19 and Racial Violence* (edited by Hellena Moon and Emmanuel Lartey, Wipf and Stock, 2022).

Akemi Kochiyama (she/her) is a writer, scholar-activist, and doctoral candidate in the PhD Program in Cultural Anthropology at the Graduate

Center of the City University of New York. She is co-director of the Yuri Kochiyama Solidarity Fund and co-editor of *Passing It On: A Memoir by Yuri Kochiyama*.

Allegra Lawrence-Hardy (she/her), a graduate of Spelman College and Yale Law School and co-founder of Lawrence & Bundy, a nationally recognized litigation firm, has profoundly impacted the lives of those in her community through her leadership and commitment to working for the next generation of leaders. Her extensive community involvement and board leadership extend to many of Atlanta's long-established organizations, including Zoo Atlanta, Alliance Theater, Girl Scouts of Greater Atlanta, and Children's Museum of Atlanta, among others, and educational institutions, including St. Anne's Day School, the Paideia School, her alma mater, Spelman College, and Emory University. She also is a recipient of a number of legal distinctions, including Top 100 Georgia Super Lawyers, Top 50 Female Georgia Super Lawyers, Benchmark Litigation Stars, and Best Lawyers in America.

Hserkaw Ler (he/him) is twenty-two years old. He was born in Tham Him refugee camp located on the border of Thailand. His favorite hobbies include playing soccer and going on walks. He is currently attending college in hopes of providing a better life for his family.

Ramsay Liem (he/him), PhD, is professor emeritus of psychology, Boston College, and an affiliated faculty member at BC's Center for Human Rights and International Justice. His interests include the intergenerational transmission of historical trauma and the social and historical contexts of Asian American identity formation and movement building. He directed the oral history project "Korean American Memories of the Korean War" and was the project director for the multi-media exhibit, *Still Present Pasts: Korean Americans and the "Forgotten War"* (www.stillpresentpasts.org). He co-directed the award-winning documentary film, "Memory of Forgotten War" (https://www.mufilms.org/films/memory-of-forgotten-war/) that traces the lives of Korean American war survivors through the years preceding, during, and following the Korean War. Ramsay Liem is also a founding member of the Asian American

Resource Workshop in Boston and works with several organizations devoted to peace and reunification in Korea.

Kyle Little (he/him) is a scholar-athlete and junior in high school. He runs cross country and track and field, and he participates in the school drama club. Through social media (especially YouTube), Kyle offers social commentary on fashion trends, sports, and music. As an aspiring actor, he hopes to one day be featured in a Netflix series. Currently, he manages the audio/visual system at his mother's church.

Lahronda Welch Little (she/her), PhD, Kyle's mother, is an interdisciplinary and transdisciplinary scholar with expertise in soteriology through a religion and public health lens. Her research interests include womanist discourse, spirituality, and interreligious/intercultural encounters. She is assistant professor in the practice of spirituality and health. She is also the director of the Women in Theology and Ministry certificate program at the Candler School of Theology at Emory University.

Hellena Moon (she/her), PhD, is an educator, community volunteer, and parent. She has degrees from Boston College (BA), Harvard University (A.M.), Harvard Divinity (M. Div.), and Emory University (PhD). She is the author of two co-edited books with Dr. Bishop Emmanuel Y. Lartey: *Postcolonial Images of Spiritual Care: Challenges of Care in a Neoliberal Age* (2020); *Postcolonial Practices of Care: A Project of Togetherness during COVID-19 and Racial Violence* (Wipf & Stock, 2022). She is also the author of *Liberalism and Colonial Violence: Charting a New Genealogy of Spiritual Care* (Wipf & Stock, 2022).

Madeleine Moon-Chun (she/her) is a high school student at The Paideia School (Atlanta, Ga). She likes writing poetry, drawing, and all other forms of art. She also loves ballet, running, swimming, and biking. She is a junior editor and teen consultant to this book project.

Takeru Nagayoshi (he/him) "TK" is the 2020 "Massachusetts Teacher of the Year," whose work and voice have been featured in places such as "This American Life," "The Smithsonian," and the Federal Reserve Bank.

An education advocate and facilitator, he leads training around the country on topics ranging from teacher leadership to education policy, and to curriculum and pedagogy. He is currently an adjunct professor at Northeastern University.

Gary Y. Okihiro (he/him), PhD, is professor emeritus of international and public affairs at Columbia University. He is currently visiting professor of American studies and Ethnicity, Race & Migration at Yale University. He is author of twelve books, including *Third World Studies: Theorizing Liberation* (2016) and *The Boundless Sea: Self and History* (2019). He received the Lifetime Achievement Award from the American Studies Association and the Association for Asian American Studies. He also received an honorary doctorate from the University of the Ryūkyūs, Okinawa.

Yuichiro Onishi (he/him), PhD, teaches in the Department of African American & African Studies and Asian American Studies Program at the University of Minnesota, Twin Cities. He is the author of *Transpacific Antiracism* (NYU Press 2013) and co-editor of *Transpacific Correspondence* (Palgrave 2019).

Nathan Reddy (he/him) is currently getting his master's in educational psychology at the University of Virginia. He wants to learn how service-learning and action research can be used as a tool for Asian American college students to develop their own identity and foster a sense of purpose in their lives.

Leenah Safi (she/her), MDiv, carries her Syrian heritage and US upbringing with her into the field of pastoral theology. She has served as a university chaplain and is currently a PhD student at the Chicago Theological Seminary with special interests in Islamic education, moral injury, and the cultivation of religious leadership.

Christie Towers (she/her) is a chaplain for the MANNA Community, a community of unhoused and unstably housed individuals, at the Cathedral Church of St. Paul, Boston. She is currently pursuing her Master of Divinity

(MDiv) at Boston University's School of Theology and holds an Master of Fine Arts (MFA) in Poetry from the University of Massachusetts, Boston.

Eh Tha Yooi (she/her) was born in Ratchaburi, Thailand and lived in Tham Hin Refugee Camp for seven years before moving to the US in 2007. Her family first settled in Georgia then moved to Ithaca New York later in the year. She graduated in May of 2022 with a BS in Science. After graduation, she moved to Chapel Hill, NC to work at Transplanting Traditions Community Farm as the Americorp VISTA Equity & Outreach Coordinator.

Andrea Young (she/her), JD, is the Executive Director of the 22,000 member American Civil Liberties Union (ACLU) of Georgia. She is a life-long advocate for civil and human rights. The ACLU of Georgia is a trusted, ethical, nonpartisan defender of our civil liberties: opposing threats to civil liberties; combating voter suppression; supporting criminal justice reform; protecting freedom of speech, immigrant rights, and women's rights, especially reproductive freedom. Young is the author of *Life Lessons My Mother Taught Me*; co-author of *Andrew Young and the Making of Modern Atlanta*, and co-editor with former Atlanta Mayor Andrew Young in *An Easy Burden: Civil Rights and the Transformation of America*. Young has been recognized as Georgia Trend's 100 Most Influential Georgians and Atlanta Magazines' 500 Most Powerful Atlantans. She is a board member of the National Center for Civil and Human Rights.

Judy W. Yu (she/her), EdD, is founding director of REACH and a faculty member at Queens College, where she utilizes critical multicultural education and theory to conduct research and practice on the challenges of curriculum and instruction to create educational change. Throughout her career, Dr. Yu has developed critical Asian American studies curriculum with K–12 students.

Foreword

Andrea Young
Executive Director of the ACLU of Georgia

When I was a student at Swarthmore College, I took a course by an amazing professor—Kathryn Morgan. Dr. Morgan taught her students to use primary sources—letters and oral histories—to reclaim the history of people of color and women. We were invisible in traditional history texts in the 1970s. One of the most popular professors on campus– the liberal Swarthmore "powers that be" refused Dr. Morgan tenure until her students expressed their outrage at the injustice. Black students, feminists, and LGBTQ students worked together in one of my first experiences with intersectionality. Through Dr. Morgan, we all learned techniques for revealing suppressed history—and we were forever changed.

A great society should not fear the truth of its history. We should teach about race and racism the same way we teach about math or chemistry: as accurately as we can. As a kid, I learned about the fight for freedom and democracy in the Revolutionary War and about how Thomas Jefferson penned those immortal words, that all men are created equal. The silence on the rights of women, the fact that Jefferson owned other human beings, people who were sold to pay his debts, the lands stolen from the Indigenous people of the Americas—I only began to learn in college. The many paths of refugees of American imperial wars and other immigrants from Asia, Africa, Latin America, the Middle East, I learned from my own self-study and work in progressive movements.

If we are going to build Dr. Martin Luther King's Beloved Community, we must face the reality of our history. We have to understand the many perspectives that the members of our diverse community bring to the American story.

Would I love it if my granddaughter could learn that the people I most admire were perfect? Yes, but that would not be the truth. Franklin Roosevelt led us out of the Great Depression and to victory in World War II. But he also had Japanese Americans taken from their homes and incarcerated in internment camps during the war. That teaches volumes about the prejudices of his time but also how much progress we've made since, that we couldn't imagine doing that today. I want our children to learn things I never learned in school, like about the massacre in Tulsa of Black people (1921) who'd done everything right and prospered for it, or the lynching of Italian Americans because they weren't considered "white enough." I want them to learn about the bombing of the Temple and the Atlanta Student Movement's non-violent marches to end segregation in stores and lunch counters.

I want my granddaughter to be free to discuss in school the stories of her ancestors who endured generations of slavery and emerged founding schools and churches. I want her to be free to share the pain and triumph of her great-grandmother's journey from her birth in a segregated Alabama and the Chair of the International Year of the Child appointed by President Carter.

In then Governor Jimmy Carter's Inaugural Address in 1971, he said, "I say to you quite frankly that the time for racial discrimination is over. Our people have already made this major and difficult decision, but we cannot underestimate the challenge of hundreds of minor decisions yet to be made. Our inherent human charity and our religious beliefs will be taxed to the limit. No poor, rural, weak, or black person should ever have to bear the additional burden of being deprived of the opportunity of an education, a job or simple justice."

What are the lived experiences behind President Carter's powerful statement of purpose and course correction? What other prejudices must we relinquish? Who are we as an American people? What has been our journey?

These are questions we must answer to move toward a future where every person present in the United States feels a sense of inclusion and belonging. This volume of essays, reflecting diverse perspectives and lived experiences makes an important contribution to that future.

Additional Notes on Andrea Young's Bio:

Andrea Young has devoted her career to promoting policies to defend and extend civil and human rights. She served as Legislative Assistant to Senator Edward Kennedy contributing to significant civil rights and international policy including the Martin Luther King Holiday Act and

South Africa sanctions legislation; She worked with the United Church of Christ in global mission and advocacy; served as Chief of Staff for the first woman to represent Georgia in Congress, and as Vice President for External Affairs for Planned Parenthood of Metropolitan Washington. As Vice President of the National Black Child Development Institute, Young led a school readiness initiative.

Acknowledgements

"Knowing is Not Enough"

I would like to thank the many educators in my life who have taught me truths in education.

This book has truly been a collaborative effort. I wish to sincerely thank the many people who have been involved in helping in the stages of this book coming together. I want to offer deep gratitude to Professor Harvey Dong (University of California, Berkeley), who suggested the names of prospective contributors, provided much support, and offered great ideas. I am grateful that I found a publishing home for this anthology with Eastwind Books of Berkeley. The title for this book was inspired by Professor Dong's edited anthology, *Power of the People Won't Stop: Legacy of the TWLF at UC Berkeley*.

I want to thank Mr. Anthony Downer for his role as consultant and educational partner in this project. His activist work and deep intellectual commitments to anti-racist education and fugitive pedagogy are outstanding. His work, intellect, and energy are unmatched. He has been a constant source of feedback for this project. His social media channels helped shape the ideas for parts three and four of the book. He invites people of different generations to be in conversation with one another, uplifting youth voices as equal scholars. Thank you for your educational partnership in the project, Anthony.

I also want to thank my family in this book endeavor: my daughter, Madeleine Moon-Chun, was a junior editor of this book project. She read and did the first-round edits for many of the chapters in the anthology. She also provided feedback on the short story by Leena Safi. Most importantly, she was an excellent conversation partner about almost all the topics in this book. Madeleine showed me the importance of expanding this book's framework to be as capacious as possible. She reminded me that we need "big feet" to walk on this journey of liberation—together with as many people as possible. I also want to thank my son, Benjamin Moon-Chun, who is deeply passionate about making the world a more justice-oriented, feminist space. He has the kindest, most compassionate heart that anyone could have. Thank you for your loving goodness, my sweet. I am grateful that I have a loving partner, Elbert Chun, who is equally passionate about raising two justice-oriented children: our most important project together and gift to each other.

I want to offer deep gratitude to the many contributors to this book project, who have generously sacrificed their time to contribute to this project for high school students. I thank my students and the many other students who desire to learn truths in their education.

I met Professor Ramsay Liem when I was an undergraduate student at Boston College. I took his very first course offered in Asian American identity, and it truly changed my life! I don't think many students would say that a single class could change their life, but his course taught me to insert "myself" into the readings and to do the deep critical thinking when reading history or a book. The tools I gained in his class helped me to see that such critical thinking is needed at every level. I have bothered him much over the past thirty years—and I thought the one way to repay him was to put together this book project in his honor. It was a small project in comparison to all he has given me and his students.

Professor Liem's tireless work on behalf of human rights is admirable and deeply inspirational. In that regard, I wanted to honor him by donating all proceeds/royalties from the book to Bryan Stevenson's Equal Justice Initiative's (EJI), Legacy Museum, in Montgomery, Alabama. The donation will be made "in honor of Professor Ramsay Liem, Professor *Emeritus*, Boston College." This book is dedicated to your teaching truths, listening to students' stories, and helping pave the path for others to do justice work.

Professor, thank you, for that invaluable gift.
Hellena

Reprints

The content of Allegra Lawrence Hardy's chapter, "Speaking Up and Speaking Out: Living at Full Volume," was originally offered as words of inspiration to the next generation of leaders when she was honored by Atlanta Girls' School with the Full Volume Award, October 28, 2022.

Hellena Moon's chapter, "Listening to Truths: Democracy and Its Neighbor, Fascism," was a revision of a previously written chapter titled, "Shepherding as Method & Practice: The Banality of the Shepherding Paradigm," in *Liberalism and Colonial Violence: Charting a New Genealogy of Spiritual Care*. Hellena Moon. Eugene, OR: Wipf & Stock Publishers, forthcoming 2022.

Madeleine Moon-Chun's flash fiction story, "Dreams That Hold Power," won the Gold Key Award for flash fiction and was first published in the 2021 Regional Scholastic Writing Award magazine. I want to thank the Alliance for Young Artists and Writers for their generosity in allowing its republication here.

Madeleine Moon-Chun's chapter, "Walter McMillian: Defeating the Powerful Hands of Death," was written for her humanities class in 2022 (taught by Kendall Tappan-O'Connor).

Gary Okihiro previously published his chapter, "Third World Studies: A Conversation," in *Postcolonial Practices of Care: A Project of Togetherness During COVID-19 and Racial Violence*. Hellena Moon & Emmanuel Lartey, Eds. We thank the editors of Wipf & Stock for allowing this publication to be reprinted here.

An earlier version of Yuichiro Onishi's, "A Politics of Our Time: Reworking Afro-Asian Solidarity in the Wake George Floyd's Killing," was published in *Unmargin* (Unmargin.org), in June 2020. He has revised it for this book.

Nathan Reddy's chapter, "*Teh Bà Ta Hkèh Poo*: Sharing Stories," was previously published in *Community Works Journal* on the following website: https://magazine.communityworksinstitute.org/teh-ba-ta-hkeh-poo-sharing-stories/.

Introduction
What I Wish I Had Known in High School
Now That I know What I know

Hellena Moon

Grammars of Truth-Telling

Grammar and grammatical rules change in accordance with societal practices, cultural changes, and a community's language adaptations to those changes. Grammar adapts to such changes in language that people find are no longer relevant. Other practices in society change similarly—evolution is happening before our very eyes. Literally, we can *see* life forms changing and predict its patterns, as biologist Jonathan Losos has described, debunking Stephen Jay Gould's argument of the unpredictability of evolution.[1] Evolutionary biologist Simon Conway Morris also supports the theory of rapid evolutions and has proposed a "theory of evolutionary convergence," which is "the recurrent tendency of biological organization to arrive at the same 'solution' to a particular 'need.' Perhaps the best-known example is the similarity between the camera-like eye of the octopus and the human eye [or that of any other vertebrate]."[2]

Sadly, these revised hypotheses of evolution and scientific interrogations are not taught in many public schools. Evolution is usually avoided altogether. According to a recent study, only one third of biology teachers in public schools even teach evolution in accord with national recommendations set by leading scientific authorities in the field.[3] In addition, 13% of the teachers teach their students that "creationism [is] a valid scientific alternative to modern evolutionary biology."[4] While the study showed that there has been an increase in teachers spending more time on evolution and a decrease in teaching "alternative" theories such as creationism as a scientific perspective, it is deeply alarming that we are still teaching myths and fables as a scientific perspective in schools. It is disappointing that we teach myths as truths in any subject. Truths, as well as evolving "grammars" and theories in science and the humanities, need to be

---
1 Losos, *Improbable Destinies*.
2 Morris, *Life's Solution*, xii.
3 Plutzer, et al., "Teaching Evolution."
4 Plutzer, et al., "Teaching Evolution."

taught. Schools should not be isolated bubbles of denial, where students are kept ignorant and sheltered from truths.

This book project is about creating new grammars—teaching truths about our society—for high school students. And like the rules for grammar, many rule changes happen because society has adapted to the practices and realities of society. The community dictates and academia has had to pivot and be relevant to what is going on in the community. Practices precede theory. At the same time, the theories and histories taught in public high schools tend to be those that foreground white cultural supremacy. The reality of people's lives and the stories told by the minoritized community (sexually, epidermically, economically, religiously, and other marginalized communities) reveal truths that are not taught in schools.

This book project underscores the importance of teaching truths and seeks to cultivate new—and revise outdated—grammars of truth-telling to facilitate communication between academia and the public, as well as academics and high school students. Some of the theories undergirding this project might be new or unfamiliar to high school students. The contributors strive to situate the writing in a way that can be digestible and, more importantly, interesting. In this book, there are stories that tell meta-truths about US imperialism, structural racism, sexism, homophobia, democracy, et al. There are also auto-truths (self-truths and personal stories) that are woven into—and corroborate—the meta-truths.

The project grew out of my conversations with college students I have taught who have bemoaned, "why do we have to wait until we get to college to learn truths?" I have many students who have come to my classes with very little knowledge about Asian and Asian American history. After studying colonialism in Korea, the Korean War, US occupation of South Korea, histories of US imperialism, militarism, and colonialism in Asia, etc., many students have written in their papers, "wow, I wish I had learned [such and such] in my high school. Why do they not teach this?" "I feel like we don't really learn truths until we get to college!"

Mid-semester, one white student (who grew up in a southern part of Georgia) mentioned how important these histories were because of her own patriotism and love for the United States—that knowing these histories would make her a better citizen and be better equipped to engage in political conversations that could help craft and implement humane policies. While I never raised critical race theory (CRT) in the class, she stated in her paper why CRT was so important to learn in high school! She stated she would be happy to speak on a panel to support CRT if there were any opportunities to do so. She, a young white woman, saw these histories as empowering her, not making her feel shamed or embarrassed as the conservative narrative script has been saying. Even if she were to feel embarrassed, should "feelings" preclude us from teaching truths?

Professor Ramsay Liem shares the same sentiment in his twenty-one years of teaching Asian American Studies and Psychology at Boston College. His students would also say, "why are we not taught this in high school?" During the pandemic, I have heard many Asian American high school students on various zooms here in Georgia similarly lament that they want to learn their histories (the counterstories to the dominant malestream white US history they are learning).

After I had heard some of the high school students (at my children's school) express their desire to learn about Asian American history, I invited Gary Okihiro to speak with them via a Zoom session. The students were thrilled to have him engage them directly. Soon thereafter, I asked Professor Liem if he would be interested in a Zoom talk with the high school students at my children's school. He then emailed me a draft of his own personal story, "what I wish I had known in high school now that I know what I know," to share with the Asian American high school students. This book project grew out of that essay, which is featured in the book.

Such conversations as these during the pandemic gave me the idea to collect sentinel stories of truths as an anthology for high school students (but also for college students and educators). The project morphed into a more capacious project (beyond Asian American identity) as the twin pandemics of COVID-19 and racial violence revealed the need for ongoing solidarity work for dismantling the structures that uphold white supremacy. Education *can be tools for liberation*. The students are genuinely desirous to learn truths in history. If college students—who are being exposed to liberative epistemologies and decolonial historiographies—are motivated to engage in the ongoing work of resistance against forms of oppression and become better citizens, why should we/do we wait to teach truths until college? Scholars, activists, and changemakers share stories that they felt were either life-changing or were revelations they felt were important to share with youth today. And youth share their stories. In doing solidarity and justice work, we have much to learn from intergenerational conversations.

Sharing Our Counterstories: Praxis Work

This book envisions how sharing truths (and one's own story—or family stories) is a necessary step for cultivating critically thinking young people who can better participate in our society and promote a healthy democratic society. The book uses a restorative justice framework of sharing truths as a first step to healing from the harms of various forms of trauma. I highlight what Professor Ramsay Liem has critically reflected that "knowing is not enough." Professor Liem fears for the social polarization that is dividing our society. He writes,

> Ignacio Martín-Baró—Salvadoran Jesuit murdered in 1989 along with several brothers, housekeeper, and her daughter by the Salvadoran, US trained military—wrote that the worst effects of war (not to diminish the torture and killing of innocents) was "social polarization." Such polarization reduces all social discourse and interaction to 'you are either with us or against us,' which eliminates all human authenticity. I fear that is where we are and heading even more so.
>
> In that context, I think of the [prospective] book as a subtler, more natural way to comment on what we are told through mainstream education and everyday experience and its limitations. To ask people to reflect on what they wished they had known at an earlier time in their lives—especially if those folks are of different ages and hence different periods in the past—is indirectly to expose and critique the dominant and mainstream narratives that we have all been mired in, but perhaps unaware of. This would engage the volume in the current culture wars but through the lived experiences of a variety of people rather than a purely academic critique.
>
> We want to find ways to turn a static volume into an ongoing praxis of work-shopping this kind of self-reflection with students, colleagues, community groups, etc.[5]

---

5 Email exchanges with Professor Ramsay Liem November 12–17, 2021.

While I acknowledge Derrick Bell's "permanence of racism" and Jennifer Hochschild's symbiosis thesis, I argue that we can "chip away" at the structural oppressions via truth-telling work and constructions of new forms of knowledge that offer a more liberative journey. I argue that we can have a more capacious path of liberation, and this book is one structure/platform for that liberative vision.

These stories constitute what in critical race theory are called counterstories.[6] Counterstorytelling is critical writing that interrogates and deconstructs the validity of accepted premises or myths that dehumanize and criminalize a group of people, especially ones held by the majority, such as "yellow peril," "Black criminality," or "Muslim terrorism."[7] Through the power of—and the desire to create—images in social media, tweets, etc., we have seen dangerous myths and propaganda that have resulted in killings of innocent people and irreparable injuries to communities. Revisionist critical historiographies, such as the 1619 Project that rewrite the mythic narratives of US history and the #BlackLivesMatter movement that challenge statistical data on police brutality against Black bodies, are counterstories.

The stories collected in this anthology are testimonies to the importance of counterstories and forms of truth-telling, which are necessary to cultivate critical thinking skills as bulwarks against the precarities of an abuse of power that can arise in a democracy. The greatest threat to a democracy is democracy itself, as the fascists were so well-aware and used flawed ideologies as methods of destroying democracies. Methods for truth-telling can be histories, personal histories, conversations, and fictional stories. I have included a sampling of each of these. As Professor Ramsay Liem had stated, "we want to find ways to turn a static volume into an ongoing praxis of work-shopping this kind of self-reflection with students, colleagues, community groups, etc." We—the contributors and I—hope that the stories you read will inspire you to write your own counterstory, share it with others, and have conversations with people in your community (schools, churches, mosques, synagogues, temples, libraries, etc.). According to bell hooks,

---

6 Crenshaw, et al., *Critical Race Theory*.
7 Delgado and Stefancic, *Critical Race Theory*, 50.

To a grave extent, people of color who self-segregate are in collusion with the very forces of racism and white supremacy they claim they would like to see come to an end. Racism will never end as long as the color of anyone's skin is the foundation of their identity.[8]

The framework of ethnic studies sometimes keeps us gazing at our own navels, not engaging with other community's stories, and eliding the overall structural oppressions. While ethnic studies has been liberative in helping us learn about our own histories, we have ignored the ways in which our bodies—and our histories—are connected and how we have to keep those connections with others vibrant and robust. The US story—as Andrea Young has emphasized—is a kaleidoscope of diverse voices and perspectives. That US story involves a cosmopolitanism framework. Cosmopolitanism is not just about being the worldly traveler. It is not multiculturalism, as I explain in the next section.

Third World Liberation Front (TWLF) & W. E. B. DuBois

In 1968, there was a student strike at San Francisco State University, demanding liberation for—and desiring to connect with the struggles and oppressions of—peoples in the Third World. The students demanded a Third World studies curriculum as a discursive marker of peoples here and abroad that outlined the desires and struggles of the pioneer of Black liberation, W. E. B. Du Bois. While Du Bois is well-known for race relations, his life trajectory of liberation for all forms of human oppression and exploitation are less highlighted. He firmly believed that human beings needed to be in solidarity and work together to address forms of oppression and suffering. He is the global citizen whose work continues to inspire us today.

Professor of African history and ethnic studies Gary Okihiro stated that the project of the student strikes was never accomplished. We never did get Third World studies. Instead we got ethnic studies and Black studies, which was a strategic plan by administrators because they knew there would be less power when the students (and resources) were divided. As Cornel West and others have stated, "whites throw out the breadcrumbs from the table and the people of color fight over it."

---

8 hooks, *Belonging*, 77.

A part of the ongoing intergenerational work of solidarity, then, is to address the admonition of Du Bois and the color line: "The problem of the twentieth century is the problem of the color-line—the relation of the darker to the lighter races of men in Asia and Africa, in America and the islands of the sea."[9] He later revised his understanding of "the color line," after his visit to Poland in 1952 (Warsaw Ghetto) and realized the intersections between imperialism, capitalism, discrimination against non-Christians, as well as forms of violence against women that complexified his earlier understanding of racism and colonialism.[10] He witnessed what Carl Schmitt would later describe as the "doubled world" of the neoliberal global order that was in process during the lifetime of Du Bois.[11] Du Bois understood the intersectionality of oppressions (religion, gender, culture, class), as he lamented the deaths of Jews, the oppression of the disabled, the young, and widows. In a letter, Du Bois urged his friend, Gabriel D'Arboussier, to encourage others to "reassess and reformulate the problems" of such braided oppressions that continue to uphold forms of white supremacy. He states,

> In the first place, the problem of slavery, emancipation and caste in the United States was no longer in my mind a separate and unique thing as I had so long conceived it. It was not even solely a matter of color and physical and racial characteristics, which was particularly a hard thing for me to learn, since for a lifetime the color line had been a real and efficient cause of misery.... No, the race problem in which I was interested cut across lines of color and physique and belief and status and was a matter of cultural patterns, perverted teaching and human hate and prejudice, which reached all sorts of people and caused endless evil to all men. So that the ghetto of Warsaw helped me to emerge from a certain social provincialism into a broader conception of what the fight against race segregation, religious discrimination and the oppression by wealth had to become if civilization was going to triumph and broaden in the world.[12]

This quotation is of particular importance because it reflects an expansion and complexification of the original definition of the DuBoisian

---

9   Du Bois, *The Souls of Black Folk*, 9.
10 Du Bois, "The Negro and the Warsaw Ghetto," 45–46
11 Slobodian, *Globalists*, 10.
12 Du Bois, "The Negro and the Warsaw Ghetto."

color-line. He included oppression beyond that of epidermal discrimination, one that included disability, culture, gender, religion, class, and age. Du Bois revised his earlier thinking to acknowledge that the "problem of the color-line" as he initially imagined it existed in the United States, did not manifest itself identically across the world. While the "color line" was used by many as a reference to the racial problem in the United States, Du Bois saw racism as a problem cutting across much of the world in Asia(s), Africa, and the islands of the sea. He saw race intertwined and on a spectrum that included other forms of hate and prejudice. I hope we can be closer to the emancipatory vision of W. E. B. DuBois for humanity

The students of the TWLF demanded to have truths taught and spoken in the classrooms. They also envisioned that the work being done in classrooms would reach out into the communities, and vice versa. The students saw that the community was a laboratory of learning. At the same time, we do not need to wait until college to have our young people know truths. That is why the question, "What I wish I had known in high school," is a crucial one for this book project. The insertion of our story within the dominant malestream history may help us be closer to solving the problem of Derrick Bell's "faces at the bottom of the well"—of getting everyone out of the well without assimilation and proximity to the neoliberal white, heterosexual, able-bodied subject.[13]

Democracy & Cosmopolitanism

Teaching truths in education is an important component of effective global participatory citizenship (citizenship broadly understood as what historian Dipesh Chakrabarty refers to as citizenly practices). A framework of a renewed cosmopolitanism can be a bulwark to multicultural nationalism(s) or religious ethnocentrism. That is, we need to create new language around what is occurring (whether desired by the old vanguard or not) in the world. The growing visibility of pluralism in education needs to be addressed, using new epistemologies. A cosmopolitan framework for education means redefining its identity in the plural and hybrid. This 'new' cosmopolitanism is not a renewed hegemony of privileging a culture or group. We can have a "robust" pedagogical cosmopolitanism that calibrates and interrogates the problems of what political theorist

---

13 Bell, *Faces*.

Michael Walzer refers to as "thick" identities (religious or cultural nationalism) versus the "thin" (too watered down, generic, zero commitment to an identity). This idea of Walzer is itself problematic and points to Samuel Huntington's concerns that Western civilization is in danger of being "diluted or tainted by other cultures.[14] A renewed cosmopolitanism can avoid the problems of the Eurocentric assumptions extant in the old understanding of a cosmopolitan framework of citizenly practices.

To participate as a global, cosmopolitan citizen in the twenty-first century, not only do teachers need to be equipped with the tools to teach from a meta-lens of global awareness; they also need to engage in deep scrutiny in the interrelations of global events and trends as it has impacted US society on the communal and individual level. There is an intimacy of our transpacific/transatlantic histories and our personal stories. The stories in this book show the interwoven connections between the meta-stories and our personal histories. The problem of not teaching truths in education is an outgrowth of the larger problem of failing democratic systems and why I emphasize the need for a framework of global participatory citizenship.

The old cosmopolitanism is a smokescreen for universalism, Enlightenment, and Western hegemonic thought. It is the idea of historicism—the Eurocentric idea of Western superiority and the interpretation of history as a linear, stadial process whereby Asian and African cultures must "pass" through certain economic and cultural stages to become "civilized" like their white counterparts.[15] Cosmopolitanism—imbricated with historicism—was the pinnacle of the worldly, enlightened, secular-but-Christian European liberal modern subject. Cosmopolitanism was a hope and prescriptive for third world countries to unfold and become like the *imago dei* (image of god) of its white counterparts. While cosmopolitanism opposed forms of nationalism (whether ethnonationalism or religious nationalism), cosmopolitanism in its old form was white supremacy cloaked as universalism in disguise.

My understanding of cosmopolitanism eschews the universalism and historicism of white cultural superiority. What I want to highlight of the new cosmopolitanism is its primary attachment to humanity (Bruce

---

14 Huntington, *The Clash*.
15 Chakrabarty, *Provincializing Europe*.

Robbins).[16] It sees the importance of interrogating and negating the historicism of the old model. A renewed postcolonial cosmopolitanism sees movement, diasporic communities, and variegated practices as part of twenty-first century life. Cosmopolitanism embraces the pluralities and complexities of beliefs, practices, and ideas—and the ongoing shifts and changes of daily life. UC Berkeley professor John Lie refers to this new cosmopolitanism as "modern peoplehood." It understands the historicism, racism, sexism, and homophobia of our world have been part of the mythmaking and fear to perpetuate projects of white European cultural superiority that the counterstories in this anthology strive to undo.

DEI Masks White Supremacy

Many schools (K–12, universities, professional schools, etc.) are using the semblance of DEI (diversity, equity, and inclusion), when in certain ways, DEI actually upholds white supremacy. DEI departments have been receiving a lot of funds, yet many schools end up just reshuffling their staff and not actually make the systemic, staff, or curricula changes needed to dismantle cultural, epistemological, or ideological forms of white supremacy. Whites benefit from DEI—as we have witnessed in the aftermath of the racial violence towards people of color during the 2020–2022 COVID-19 pandemic. We see who (or what) has benefited most from DEI: the university endowment. In her work on whiteness and white privilege, Robyn Wiegman notes, "...seldom has whiteness been so widely represented as attuned to racial equality and justice while so aggressively solidifying its advantage."[17]

Is DEI truly doing anti-racist work of dismantling the supremacy of white culture or white epistemologies at your institution? Or is it a way to promote the school's DEI façade, while the actions needed to bring about systemic change—and transforming the institutions or the curricula—are far from reality? We need to circumscribe the window-dressing of DEI; instead, we need to highlight the lack of structural changes that continue to privilege white European colonial practices and histories in our schools. DEI, then, is a veneer to maintain and solidify white privilege in K–12 schools, universities, and the corporate world.

---

16 Robbins, *Cosmopolitanisms*.
17 Wiegman, "Whiteness Studies," 121.

Chapters

This anthology underscores how counterstories and voices across generations—the Silent generation, the Boomers, Generation X, the Millennials, the Generation Zs, and Generation Alpha—can come together to practice truth-telling, share our histories with one another and in our communities, and engage in justice work to have a healthy democratic society. Through their personal stories, the contributors of this book are cultivating a paradigm of liberation for youth that teaches them the history of oppressions, nationalist/imperialist/colonialist struggles, and feminist and sexuality liberation movements. It is intergenerational wisdom at its best. We foreground the importance of critical thinking as central to democratic practices. Packaged myths taught in high schools are forms of political propaganda tools that erode democratic practices.

The counterstories and histories in the anthology help widen the cracks and fissures within the dominant narrative that will allow for healing the wounds (of individuals, communities, and of our nation), as well as for social transformation. We hope that these stories create space for deep conversation (in the classrooms, in churches, in book clubs, homes, etc.) and for the emergence of more forms of truth-telling work. The work of truth-telling commences the path to healing. It is the work of restorative justice. In her foreword, Andrea Young, Executive Director of the ACLU of Ga (American Civil Liberties Union of Georgia), underscores the importance of hearing, telling, and teaching truths and honest perspectives in schools.

Part One: Theories of Liberation

In this chapter, "Third World Studies: A Conversation," Professor Gary Okihiro shares a powerful chapter about Third World studies, not as a place, but as a condition and cause. By that, he discusses his methodology of furthering our discursive work of liberation. That is, we need to have more conversations of truth-telling and the struggles that support emancipatory practices from the powers of oppression and exploitation. His chapter provides us with a theoretical framework, as well as historical context, for the founding of Third World studies.

My chapter (Hellena Moon), "Listening to Truths: Democracy & Its Neighbor, Fascism," explores the model of governing which we endeavor to practice today, democracy. In truth, as many of us are aware, democracy can easily slip into fascist rule because of the very nature of democracy itself. I explore the observations of one person in particular, Alexis de Tocqueville, precisely because he was a white aristocrat (who believed white people were superior) who echoed his concerns of the primogeniture of critical race theory and interest convergence today. In other words, he observed the brutality and ugliness of systemic racism extant in America and argued that racism and its harms did not benefit white people. He also warned of the dangers of concentrated power that the people unwittingly gave their leaders (i.e., the shepherd) and how critical unthinking would destroy us. Soft tyranny would lead to political passivity.

In their chapter, Professor Sig/Sara Giordano, "Are Queers Dangerous? What I Wish I Knew about the Intersections of Race, Gender, Class, and Sexuality in High School," shares the cutting-edge feminist science research they have been doing. Their work helps us to better understand the ongoing epistemological truths that have been manipulated in science and in the interconnected disciplines of history, gender studies, and philosophy. Their chapter focuses on how our understandings of queerness as a challenge to white, capitalist, heteronormative structures have helped to build activist communities where critical biology lessons are shared and developed. It was in activist communities that they first learned that gender and sex were not "naturally" binary categories. It was also in activist community where they learned about how important eugenic science was—and is—to how inequalities are justified based on ideas of better and worse genetic traits and types of people.

Some of the most important biology lessons Professor Giordano learned happened beyond biology classrooms—in women's studies classrooms and in activist workshops and informal relationship building where books and knowledges were shared among comrades. They wish they—and others—knew what they know now about sexuality when they were in high school. Throughout the chapter, Professor Giordano points out the importance of community engaged learning for bolstering their own academic work and for helping unearth "truths" regarding sexuality, racial capitalism, reproductive justice, and malestream heterosexuality to maintain forms of white supremacy.

Truth-telling can be discomfiting because it helps us to locate pieces of the oppressor—our complicity with white cultural supremacy—in all of us. At the same time, it is liberating if we choose to dislodge the piece of oppressor in us by engaging in the civic practices to repair the harms that myth-learning have caused. Our fixed mindset of sexuality and gender are part of the colonial matrix of power—controlling our sex lives is the colonization of our bodies and our sexuality. Professor Giordano provides a fascinating historiography of bio-socio-political constructs that have circumscribed our epistemologies, beliefs, and practices.

In his chapter, "A Politics of Our Time: Reworking Afro-Asian Solidarity in the Wake of George Floyd's Killing," Professor Yuichiro Onishi pointedly sees the absolute necessity for Black-Asian solidarity in our time. There is a clear history where Asians were pitted against the Black community. In scrutinizing history, however, we see that there was some intentional divisiveness (divide and conquer strategies) that was used to build anti-racist sentiments and animosity. Despite the politics and "messiness" of race," Onishi pleads for all of us to know truths in history and to care for each other—to engage in more cosmopolitan projects that address anti-imperialism and anti-war projects that directly impact our communities and our relationships with one another.

Part Two: Practicing and Sharing Stories of Liberation[18]

The question of "who is represented and how" might be raised as the reader engages in the stories in this section. I want to underscore the problem of the single voice to represent any community. We have repeatedly been told about the "dangers of the single story," and I want to remind us of that in the stories that follow. My intention in collecting these stories has been to practice narratives of truth-telling and the power of narrative, as well as the hidden meta-histories within each story. We can be inspired by the trailblazers who navigated the foundations of Black and ethnic studies in some of the contributors' stories—at a time when it was unthinkable. Some of these individual stories shaped what is Black and ethnic studies today, and the other stories are from the voices of those who follow their generation.

In Anthony Downer's chapter, "can't stop, won't stop: The Tradition of Black Education as the Practice of Freedom," he shares his own story

---

18 Thank you to Madeleine Moon-Chun for reading the stories in this section. She helped with the organization of the chapters in this section.

of academic excellence and intellectual/ activist journey that shaped his Black brilliance. By "brilliance," I not only refer to Anthony's academic [brilliance] but also his moral commitment to teaching the works of Black activists and intellectuals in the ongoing struggle for justice and liberation. His own liberation journey has shaped the moral and intellectual minds of numerous young people who are the scholars of his essay.

Carter Woodson argued that Black teachers had to teach truths furtively. They would have a book on their lap and read from that unofficial classroom text, but if someone walked into the classroom, they knew to look up and read from the standard curriculum on their desk.[19] Carter Woodson described this as "the subversive art of Black teaching."[20] Harvard Professor Jarvis Givens refers to the tradition of teaching truths despite a threat of harm to the Black community as fugitive pedagogy.[21] He describes fugitive pedagogy as a "protracted struggle"[22] of "African Americans' physical and intellectual acts that explicitly challenged antiblack protocols of educational domination; actions that often took place in discreet or partially concealed fashion."[23] Givens argues that "Black education was a fugitive project from its inception."[24] Downer encourages us to share our stories with friends, family, and the larger community so that we keep truths alive as a practice of democracy. He describes his own personal story and the work needed to build an inclusive, representative school system. He argues that we need a pedagogy of intellectual, moral, and political inspiration. He shares his own learnings, readings, and teachings with us.

In his chapter, "Music, Math, and Malcom X: My Intellectual Journey of Truth," Professor Douglas Henry Daniels tells the story of how he attended the University of Chicago. He reminds us that he was accepted into a premier institute at a time when Black students "were not really welcome" at the University of Chicago. His academic journey is a fascinating one; his research interests are diverse and innovative. His essay

---

19   Givens, *Fugitive Pedagogy*.
20   Givens, *Fugitive Pedagogy*.
21   Givens, *Fugitive Pedagogy*. See Gibson's article, "Fugitive Pedagogy," where I first read about the work of Jarvis Givens. Accessed April 2022. https://www.harvardmagazine.com/2022/03/features-fugitive-pedagogy-jarvis-givens.
22   Givens, *Fugitive Pedagogy*, 15.
23   Salomon, "Dr. Givens's Talk."
24   Givens, *Fugitive Pedagogy*, 3.

personalizes a piece of history —it describes his intellectual journey (especially for those of us who do not know him personally) in a way that is very humbling and humble. He makes it sound so matter-of-fact when I am sure his journey was/is not common. He is a pioneer and paved a path for many when the tools were so limited. This short chapter invites us to engage more of his scholarship and story.

David Palumbo-Liu writes the term, Asian/American, using the solidus, "/" to denote the distinction between "Asian" and "American," while also constituting a fluid movement between the two.[25] Both "Asian" and "American" are unsettled meanings in Asian American discursive historiography. Like Lisa Lowe, Palumbo-Liu argues that the boundaries that have been constructed between the two terms are not as solid and distinct as once assumed. "Asian/American" also underscores the inclusion/exclusion of how Asian/Americans can be seen as either/or in terms of our identity. We exist on a yellow peril spectrum. "Asian/American" also denotes the interculturality and hybridity of our identity. Whether here in the United States, or in "Asia," we are affected by the dynamics of both Asian and US cultures, as well as the cultures of the Americas and their respective and intermingled modern histories. Asian/American also delineates multiple border crossings, traversing back and forth, not just geographically, but also intellectually, historiographically, discursively, and spiritually.

Legal scholar Robert Chang sees the identity category, "Asian American," as a placeholder for how we can be "American" without being defined in opposition or in relation to the white imaginary of what the term, "American," conjures.[26] "Asian American" is a binary or a taxonomy. He argues that while it is more liberative than the racial epithet, "Oriental," it still circumscribes our identity in relation to the dominant white Christian subject as normative and is a taxonomy of hierarchy. How can these stories contest or address the taxonomy or the temporal placeholder identity of Asian American? High school student, Madeleine Moon-Chun, ruminated on this identity of "Asian American" when she was a junior high student. She offers her own "placeholder identity" of

---

25 Palumbo-Liu, *Asian/American: Historical Crossings*.
26 Chang, "Toward an Asian American."

being "Asian American" with her own placeholder story. Now, as a high schooler, she states, it is much more complex.

Despite the sixty+ years' difference between Madeleine and Professor Elaine Kim, their experiences of racism and othering are sadly similar. Professor Kim, first Asian American woman to receive tenure at UC Berkeley, is a founding member of ethnic studies, as well as Asian American and Asian diaspora studies at Berkeley. She was part of the Third World Liberation Front (TWLF) protests and has been passionate about "creating that which does not exist." Her philosophy has been, "If it is not there already, create it." Her chapter, "In the Hour of the Dragon: Nationalism, Feminism, and a Korean American Identity," describes her early childhood, followed by events that have shaped her pioneering work.

Just as Madeleine described her own unsolicited criticisms by people in Korea and comments of marginalization on her school playground, Kim mentioned her attacks for not fitting the stereotype of the small Asian woman (and was told by Koreans that her feet were too big), to which Madeleine responded, "mom, her feet are big metaphorically and she should be so proud. No one could ever fill her shoes or even walk in her footsteps. She has 'big feet,' and she should be honored." Professor Kim's shoes are too big for anyone to even attempt to walk in her footsteps. She did not even have a roadmap, and she managed to walk the journey that shaped Asian American feminism, literature, and community activism. Not many people could fill the shoes of the pioneers in the field of ethnic and Black studies. I hope that Madeleine's generation can continue doing the pathbreaking work Professor Kim (and others in this anthology) did and create "that which does not exist," have "big feet," and "be proud."

Professor Ramsay Liem's chapter, "What I Wish I Had Known When I Was in High School: A Brief Reflection," was the story that launched this book project. I first asked Professor Liem to share his story, "what I wish I had known," with some high school students at my children's school. They had just started an Asian American Alliance student group, and I heard their lamentations of "why do we not get to learn our stories," as a clarion call for a book that collected such stories—not just for Asian American students but for all of us as our histories are interwoven. In his chapter, therefore, he directly addresses the Asian American students and hopes that they, too, engage in the project of discovering and sharing truths about their own history.

Judy Yu, former student of Professor Liem, describes her passions for teaching justice, truth, and marginalized histories in her chapter, "My Dearest Ancestors, Children, & Future Generations." Dr. Yu narrates her history and the reasons that motivated her to become the activist scholar that she is today. She uses counterstories in her teaching to "validate our ancestral histories and lived experiences" as an integral kaleidoscopic piece of US history. Dr. Yu and I were in the first Asian American class that Professor Liem taught at Boston College. I recall her energy, passion, and commitment for learning our histories, and I see that she is no less passionate today.

The next chapter, "Why Trying to Fit in Is the Problem," is written by Professor Moon-Ho Jung. Learning truths and critical thinking skills in college and graduate school awakened new possibilities in challenging the myths that fed Professor Jung's learning. Like Professor Okihiro, Jung questions the limitations of an ethnic studies model. He critiques the nationalism within ethnic studies, which he argues focuses more on patterns of migration/ immigration to the US. Asian American history in US high school textbooks might focus on the Chinese and the California Gold Rush or the building of the first transcontinental railroad. These are "saccharine versions of history," he states. Instead, he argues we need to focus our critiques on US imperialism and violence in Asia, as well as violence towards Asian Americans. He, too, argues that Black-Asian solidarity is key to dismantling forms of white supremacy.

Professor Jung articulates how anti-Asian racism was crucial to the formation of US empire and used as a justification for the claims of US sovereignty across the Pacific. He reiterates the importance of seeing past the veneer of polite racism to look at the ways in which people of color have been used as tools for white supremacy. He mentions that people of color are put into key leadership roles to do the dirty work of reproducing white supremacy—this is a DEI strategy used today—and further privileging white identity.

I conclude this section with an uplifting narrative by Massachusetts Teacher of the Year: 2020, Takeru (TK) Nagayoshi. In, "Liberation through Identity: We Are Lucky to Be Free," he shares his revelatory conversation with his mom when he told her he was gay. She expressed to him that he has just unlocked the confines of heteronormative society and stated, "you are so free to define yourself, unlike others who have to live within the molds of heteronormative society." He was told by his mother that he is more liberated to be who he wants because there was not a model for how queer folk might live. Professor Giordano shared in their chapter about the power of imagination and the "worlds that queers are building within this one," as well as the unlimited power of the proliferation of "queer experiments" through transformative truths in high school biology classes. Similarly, TK use the gift of "liberation through identity" which his mother bestowed, as he envisions new and creative ways of being in community with others. He inspires us to re-explore education via this model of post-pandemic life: education and many aspects of our society do not have to function the way it currently does. What transgressive reforms or revolutions might occur to optimize our ways of being together and engaging in imaginative problem-solving for a healthier society? The transformative power of our imagination—when we liberate ourselves from the confines of myth—is unlimited.

Part Three: Generational Stories, Conversations, and Healing Traumas

In this section, we have generational conversations between father and daughter, between chaplains working on spiritual care in the digital age, and between mother and son. We hope that families, friends, neighbors, and teachers/students can have conversations such as these and engage in the self-care practices that Professors Buhuro and Bell have offered.

Father and daughter, Adia and Professor Lee Butler, share their anecdotes and perspectives about growing up Black in predominantly white academic spaces in their chapter, "Ebony in the Ivory Tower." This chapter documents, in part, the struggle for identity, alienation, and acceptance in spaces that were not built for Blackness, let alone accepting Black people in any form. Adia and Dr. Lee Butler take the lead in sharing the journey to eventually overcoming those struggles, moving forward in spite of them. Much has changed, shown through the glimpse into the past of her father's perspective, but much has stayed the same, shown through the daughter's very recent experience as a child growing up in the twenty-first century.

Dr. Lahronda Little and Kyle Little share a mother-son conversation in their chapter, "Creative Expressions: An Interview Between a Teenager and His Mom." The chapter is a coming-of-age interview on how creative expression opens the way to affirmation and fulfillment. Kyle describes how he came to act (or how acting came to him). They discuss how creative expressions, such as the performing arts, provide positive outlets for self-actualization. Since finding his passion for drama and content production, Kyle has increased his confidence socially and academically. He takes on more challenges with the hope of learning more about himself and those around him rather than for accomplishment. For Kyle, artistic endeavors begin and end from a place of joy. As a parent, particularly as an African American parent, Dr. Little is comforted and inspired as she observes her son's processes of honing his skills while also practicing self-compassion.

Chaplains Danielle Buhuro and Christal Bell discuss the intergenerational trauma of lynchings and the modern form of digital lynchings in their co-authored chapter, "Centering" Yourself Before You Log On: Black Girls and Self-Care in the World of Social Media." Reverend Dr. Danielle Buhuro states that the #BLM was the first ethnographic work on social activism that addressed the dehumanization of Black people in the United States. She and Reverend Dr. Christal Bell argue how the tools of social media have also become tools for oppression and the dehumanization of Black teens. While social media has been helpful for disseminating information, paradoxically, it has also been a tool used for perpetuating harmful messages and images, negating the humanity of people of color. Their co-authored chapter addresses this problem, and they provide resources for self-care.

Part Four: Leadership, Moral Brilliance, and Community Engaged Learning

In their chapter, "Two Leaders Who Are Students of Relationships: A Conversation," Lori and Jonathan Klein articulate their understanding of leadership. Having had important positions of leadership in their respective fields, the siblings reflect about the importance of having mentorships, building relationships, being an advocate, taking calculated risks, and having good friendships. Most importantly, Rabbi Lori Klein knows that being able to self-supervise and being a good judge of her own capabilities is most important. Having deep mutual respect for their employees, leaders are also in the trenches with their team. They know the work that their employees do, because they also take turns doing some of the work. The sibling pair also knows that treating employees like partners and equals is key to sustainability in the role of a leader.

Contrary to what academics may argue, Nadinne Cruz argues that community-engaged learning is no less rigorous or intellectual than sitting in the classroom and reading *about* the theories and case studies. Community-engaged learning helps us create our own case studies—the community itself becomes the platform through which the theories are tested and repositioned. Theories can be developed from the mutual exchange with people in the community. Academia is not the only space or location from which theories are formed, learned, or created. Theory is laden in the spaces and places where people engage in the lived realities of community. Theory and intellectual rigor reside in these spaces. At the same time, it is interesting that many activists or people in the work world disdain the languages of academia as irrelevant to spaces outside of the classroom or outside of the walls of university life.

Community-engaged learning and its participation within the emerging field of public humanities is a new type of grammar—a reinvigorated space for provoking and connecting publicly the humanities with the communities. Public humanities is weaving a new tapestry of epistemologies that speaks to us and brings us into spaces that are neither purely "academic" nor purely "community"—because such spaces induce claustrophobia and narrow-mindedness. We need to be open to the possibilities of how to take the lived realities and creativity in the community and see it as academic, and vice versa, how intellectual rigor and theorizing does not mean we are irrelevant to—and in—the world. The desire of the original Third World Studies (TWS) movement was this desire to connect the community with academia and to explicitly be intimately connected with the other. If this academia-community connection is not made, the movement for TWS would be in vain.

"How Do We Teach Moral Brilliance?" To answer this question, Nathan Reddy has a conversation with Nadinne Cruz, a Filipina American activist who has been a key figure in advancing the service-learning movement in higher education. Service-learning is the philosophy that integrates academic coursework with community engagement. The interview centers around how we can cultivate "moral brilliance" in people, especially youth, through education. Professor Cruz defines moral brilliance as "the capacity to decide what is right to do and to decide to do it." In the spirit of service-learning which strives to ground academic or abstract concepts in the concrete, they focus on one particular (historically significant) instance of moral brilliance: the French rural community of Le Chambon providing refuge for Jews fleeing the Nazis during World War II. This counterstory reveals the power of passing the torch—and the truth that there are many torches out there, up "for grabs"—to do the ongoing work of practicing moral brilliance and service-learning.

One person in particular has definitely been "gifted" with the passing of the torch. Scholar and activist, Akemi Kochiyama, has been continuing the social justice work of her family and shares the story of her grandmother, Yuri Kochiyama, and her activist journey. In her chapter, "Fighting Racism with Solidarity: #knowyourBIPOChistory," Akemi reflects on her activism and the community that helped shape her story. She has been instilled in moral brilliance from birth, as her family has been doing the justice work of building Black-Asian solidarity and antiracism. She shares stories of Yuri, her grandmother, whose friendship with Malcolm X, was life changing. Malcolm X taught her truths and gave her the tools that she would use throughout her life to engage in her civil and human rights work. Akemi underscores the importance of building interracial coalitions and communities and to see our common humanity.

We are honored to have Allegra Lawrence Hardy's chapter, "Speaking Up and Speaking Out: Living at Full Volume," in this anthology. She embodies brilliance in every way. She is an intellectually gifted scholar whose law practice has been recognized to be one of the best in Georgia. She is also a passionate community volunteer, doing everything from Wednesday pizza sales at our children's school, serving as a member on several Boards of Trustees in prominent universities and organizations throughout Atlanta, teaching at her daughter's Sunday school classes, etc.... The list of her moral brilliance—and how she strives to create a beautiful community—is too long. And she does everything with humility, love, and a smile. Like her chapter advises, she knows to speak truth, name things that are problematic, praise the great work of individuals when needed, and connect with everyone as if that person were her best friend. She lifts people up. I hope her practices for success and moral brilliance *can become our practices* for communal success.

In Nathan Reddy's second chapter for this anthology, "*Teh Bà Ta Hkèh Poo*: Sharing Stories," he interviews two Karen community members, Eh Tha Yooi and Hserkaw Ler, about their life journeys thus far. The refugee Karen community are an ethnolinguistic group from Burma who have been persecuted for centuries in their homeland. Eh Tha Yooi Lee and Hserkaw Ler were born in Thai refugee camps and then moved from the camps to Ithaca, New York with their families. Nathan has worked with both of them extensively as an employee of the 4H Urban Outreach Program in Ithaca (Eh Tha Yooi Lee and Hserkaw Ler both participated in the program throughout their youth), and he shares his own reflections about what they taught him regarding his identity development as an Indian American, an aspiring educator, and a human being. This chapter is a conversation of truths that exhibits the best of service-learning and the deep insights and perspectives we gain from community work. People worry that engaging in practices is less "rigorous" than text-based learning, but Nathan demonstrates truths that this is clearly not the case.

In her chapter, "Out Here: Writing with the Unhoused," Christie Towers describes her care work with the Black Seed Writer's Group, a writing group that works with the unhoused community in Boston. She explores the practical, spiritual, social, and human elements of teaching creative nonfiction writing with the unhoused. She acknowledges the challenges presented for all involved in the work of mutual learning. The chapter highlights the simplicity at the heart of such work: all you need to do is show up and be willing to witness, honor, and be changed by the humanity of every person in the community, listen deeply to the stories that are shared, and validate the experiences of everyone in the space. She shares truths and transformations that take place there: revelations of writers discovering that they, too, can write and have a listening audience; the impact of public readings and publishing their own books; folks overcoming fears about literacy; the transformative experience in a person's life of finding a voice and sharing that voice; the power of sharing one's personal story to overcome stereotypes and assumptions about those experiencing homelessness. In this work, she has learned truths about many of her own assumptions about writing, publications, homelessness, and its attendant issues.

Fictions as Truth-Telling

This section explores how fiction itself can be a method for liberative practices of truth-telling. Anthropologist Kamala Visweswaran discusses the myriad ways in which fiction and stories can be ethnographic. This may be especially true for colonized communities or oppressed individuals who may not be able to share their stories, except by fictionalizing their own voice. Ethnographies are methods or attempts of "restoring lost voices."[27] As my daughter and I were working on the book project, we read Bryan Stevenson's—and watched the movie version of—*Just Mercy*.[28] Madeleine was mesmerized by the power of justice and morality and the moral brilliance of Bryan Stevenson. She saw how dedication, courage, and desire for justice could chip away at the foundations of white supremacy and the "scripts of racial difference" that hold up the structures of injustice. We need more people like Bryan Stevenson to serve as a moral guide, a compass, that speaks to liberation from suffering and injustices.

In her chapter, "Walter McMillian: Defeating the Powerful Hands of Death," Madeleine Moon-Chun engages in a literary comparison of Arthur Miller's, *The Crucible*, with the book, *Just Mercy*. She shares what she learned in her eighth-grade classroom about propaganda and the ways in which fictions (or storytelling) help unmask larger truths when society is fearful or cautious about speaking truths. She connects the lies, systemic racism/classism, and the politics of propaganda that work to support structures of white supremacy. She explores the story, *The Crucible*,[29] and how it was a critique of McCarthy era red scare societal propaganda. The Salem witch trials were conducted similarly as the congressional committees of the McCarthy communist hearings. They are also similar—as my daughter learned—to the workings of the criminal justice system. Arthur Miller pointed out, "It is part of the human desire, the same primeval structure of human sacrifice to the furies of fanaticism and paranoia that goes on repeating itself forever as though imbedded in the brain of social man [sic]."[30]

---

27 Visweswaran, *Fictions*, 15.
28 Stevenson, *Just Mercy*.
29 Miller, *The Crucible*.
30 Miller, "Why I Wrote the 'Crucible.'"

Fiction can also provide important avenues of healing and apertures for discussing subjects that might be taboo (or difficult topics) in certain communities or families, as Leenah Safi's fiction story reveals. We might relate to the character[s] in a story more intimately than to have conversations about our own stories of suffering. Safi's story, "Life in a Three-Day Loop," is based on many true stories. This work of flash fiction follows Muslim high school senior Selma Dabaji in the early days of being told about a parent's terminal diagnosis. The reader is invited into Selma's internal world and thought process as she learns to navigate a changed home environment. We, the reader, are asked to consider the ways in which her immediate thinking and planning for life after high school graduation are consequently impacted. Discussion questions are included to invite classrooms to consider together the complexities of decision-making amid life's various transitions. There were so many unknown variables during the COVID-19 pandemic. Did students have time to reflect on how health issues might impact our schoolwork or decisions?

I conclude this section with Madeleine Moon-Chun's flash fiction story, "Dreams That Hold Power." It is a brief, but compelling story of terminal illness that grips the reader with the traumas that impact siblings. The story is a beautiful segue to the afterword that explores the terminal illness and virus of racism in our society that can—*and has*—lead to devastating consequences for humanity.

Afterword

Professor Cécile Accilien writes a most poignant afterword, "Teaching and Learning Through *Konbit*," reminding us of the importance of truth-telling and the necropolitical dangers of propaganda by describing to us her recent trip to Rwanda. Professor Accilien shares how, in the aftermath of the Rwandan genocide, the community is engaging in the work of truth-telling, reconciliation, and instilling "moral brilliance" in their youth. As we read her epilogue, I hope we can be inspired by the repair of their country and to learn that the artificial divides we create among us humans can create fears and objectifications of our neighbors on a massive scale. In quoting Felicien Ntagengwa, "If you knew me and you really knew yourself you would not have killed me,"[31] Professor

---

31 Quote at the Gisozi Genocide Memorial in Kigali, Rwanda.

Accilien highlights the beauty and importance of friendship and deep empathy for one another.

My hope is that we all—the Silent generation, the Boomers, Generation X, the Millennials, the Generation Zs, and Generation Alpha—come together to practice truth-telling, share our stories in our communities, and engage in the justice work needed to have a healthy democratic society. We need to gather and learn from one another and engage in the work of *konbit*—individuals and communities coming together to help one another—intergenerationally, interculturally, and interreligiously. While there are myriad forms of racism, we are one human community, and one of the biggest fictions and forms of propaganda we need to dismantle is the idea of many races. As legal scholar Dorothy Roberts stated, "there is only one race: the human race."[32] We can come together as one race and challenge the lies that the scripts of racial difference have created in terms of hierarchies and hatreds among one another.

Bryan Stevenson's Equal Justice Initiative's (EJI) Legacy Museum is a living testament to the racial violence in our country due to the pernicious myths and "scripts of racial difference." The EJI Legacy Museum should be the site of our national pilgrimage. It is a journey we, Unitedstateseans,[33] all need to make. All proceeds from this book will be donated to the EJI Legacy Museum and the important work of truth-telling being done by Bryan Stevenson.

Hellena Moon
October 2022

---

32 Roberts, *Fatal Invention*.
33 Janet Halley's neologism. See *Split Decisions*.

BIBLIOGRAPHY

Bell, Derrick. *Faces at the Bottom: The Permanence of Racism.* New York: Basic Books, 1992.

Chakrabarty, Dipesh. *Provincializing Europe: Postcolonial Thought and Historical Difference.* Princeton, NJ: Princeton University Press, 2007.

Chang, Robert S. "Toward an Asian American Legal Scholarship: Critical Race Theory, Post-Structuralism, and Narrative Space." *California Legal Review* 81, no. 5 (1993) 1243–1323.

Du Bois, W. E. B. "The Negro and the Warsaw Ghetto," *Jewish Life*, 1952. Reprinted in *The Social Theory of W. E. B. Du Bois,* edited by Phil Zuckerman, 45–46. Thousand Oaks, CA: Pine Forge, 2004.

———. *The Souls of Black Folk.* Reprint ed. Narragansett, RI: Millennium, 2014.

Delgado, Richard, and Jean Stefancic, eds. *Critical Race Theory: An Introduction.* New York: New York University Press, 2017.

Gibson, Lydialyle. "Fugitive Pedagogy: Jarvis Givens Rediscovers the Underground History of Black Schooling." *Harvard Magazine,* April 2022. https://www.harvardmagazine.com/2022/03/features-fugitive-pedagogy-jarvis-givens.

Givens, Jarvis. *Fugitive Pedagogy: Carter G. Woodson and the Art of Black Teaching.* Cambridge, MA: Harvard University Press, 2021.

Halley, Janet. *Split Decisions: How and Why to Take a Break from Feminism.* Princeton, NJ: Princeton University Press, 2006.

hooks, bell. *Belonging: A Culture of Place.* New York: Routledge, 2008.

Huntington, Samuel P. *The Clash of Civilizations and the Remaking of World Order.* New York: Simon & Schuster, 1996.

Losos, Jonathan B. *Improbable Destinies: Fate, Chance, and the Future of Evolution.* 1st ed. New York: Riverhead Books, 2017.

Miller, Arthur. *The Crucible. A Play in Four Acts.* Reprint ed. London: Penguin Books, 1976.

Miller, Arthur. "Why I Wrote the 'Crucible,'" *The New Yorker*, October 13, 1996. https://www.newyorker.com/magazine/1996/10/21/why-i-wrote-the-crucible.

Morris, Simon Conway. *Life's Solution. Inevitable Humans in a Lonely Universe.* Cambridge, UK: Cambridge University Press, 2004.

Palumbo-Liu, David. *Asian/American: Historical Crossings of a Racial Frontier*. Palo Alto, CA: Stanford University Press, 1999.

Plutzer, Eric, et al., "Teaching Evolution in US Public Schools: A Continuing Challenge." *Evolution: Education and Outreach* 13, no. 14 (2020) 1–15.

Robbins, Bruce, ed. *Cosmopolitanisms*. New York: New York University Press, 2017.

Roberts, Dorothy. *Fatal Invention: How Science, Politics, and Big Business Re-create Race in the Twenty-first Century*. New York: The New Press, 2012.

Salomon, Emma. "Dr. Givens's Talk on the Fugitive Life of Black Teaching," *The Mac Weekly*, Februrary 18, 2022. https://themacweekly.com/80717/news/dr-givens-talk-on-the-fugitive-life-of-black-teaching/.

Slobodian, Quinn. *Globalists: The End of Empire and the Birth of Neoliberalism*. Cambridge, MA: Harvard University Press, 2018.

Stevens, Bryan. *Just Mercy: A Story of Justice and Redemption*. Reprint ed. New York: One World, 2015.

Visweswaran, Kamala. *Fictions of Feminist Ethnography*. Minneapolis, MN: University of Minnesota Press, 1994.

Wiegman, Robyn. "Whiteness Studies and the Paradox of Particularity." *Boundary 2* 26, no. 3 (1999) 115–150.

PART ONE:
THEORIES OF LIBERATION

1

Third World Studies: A Conversation[1]

Gary Y. Okihiro

Dear Reader:

Please think about the Third World not as a place but as a condition and cause. When we hear the words, "Third World," we imagine countries led by ruthless dictators, death squads, corruption, poverty, the oppression of women and queers, and above all, disease. The forty-fifth US president called them "shithole countries." When I speak of the Third World in this essay, I am referring to a massive project that changed four hundred years of world history; the cause was to end imperialism, colonialism, and racism. So please read on and join me in this conversation.

Third World Studies:

Third World studies is a conversation about liberation. To converse, we need to speak the same language and hold ideas in common. By language, I refer to the English language in which this essay is written but also to the language of fields of study called disciplines (disciplines are bodies of knowledge with their methods and theories, subject matters, and practices, and organized broadly as the sciences and humanities in the European tradition). A system of ideas comprises ideology. Together, language and ideology constitute discourse or, in my rendering, a conversation.

This discourse on liberation is in dialogue with you, the reader. As a transaction, what I intend to convey might not be the meaning you grasp; despite speaking the same language and sharing ideologies, the speech and its hearing are related but not necessarily corresponding. In addition to that uncertainty, consider this conversation as contingent and never

---

1 This essay was originally published in Moon and Lartey, eds., "Reassessing Third World."

closed or complete; it is in process, open, and accommodates contestation and change.

Our conversation's subject matter, liberation, entails discourses of abolition and emancipation. It is thus dialogical. Third World studies conceives of liberation as sustained struggles, on shifting grounds against oppression and exploitation. Oppression is the curtailment of agency, wherein agency is ability or influence. Exploitation is the expropriation of surplus product. Under capitalism, the surplus product is the profit taken by those who own the means of production. Liberation from oppression and exploitation, accordingly, involves the discourses and material relations of power, which is the ability to move.

So again, Third World studies is a conversation about liberation from the powers that oppress and exploit.

Power resides everywhere. In the physical world, power is expressed as energy. In the social world, power is agency, ability. We, humans, all possess power albeit in differing degrees. Concentrations of power facilitate the ability to name, describe, and rank. Through assignments and enforcements those taxonomies, or classifications produce subjects as individuals and groups.

In concrete terms, the empowered elite specified races, genders, sexualities, and abilities, assigned natures or attributes to those categories, and placed them on hierarchies of merit and worth. Those social constructions created, where none existed before, the four principal races—European, Asian, African, and American (Indian); the two genders—man and woman; the two sexualities—heterosexual and homosexual; and able-bodied and persons with disabilities. Those were not ordered by divine law or natural law, but were inventions by those with the power, the authority to name, describe, and rank. They are social and not scientific truths. They are fictions of the mind.

Although imagined, their creators produce (interpellate) those categories in the lives, the lived experiences of their subjects. Coercion and consent are involved in that production of bodies. Laws and the policing of those laws are examples of coercive actions. For example, racial segregation, when required by law, defined races as well as imposed borders between those so designated. Schools for whites and schools for nonwhites illustrate that classification and divide based upon alleged differences and abilities. Violations might prompt courts and the police to impose fines, corporeal punishments, and imprisonment. But coercion is one method of oppression; consent offers another.

Consent occurs when subjects agree with those powers to name and enforce. We understand that as hegemony. Subjects might choose acquiescence to avoid penalties. Others might comply because they learned, perhaps through the example of role models and schooling, that those categories are real and true. They are self-evident, discernible, and visible; and they are based on reliable evidence and science. Still others might conform without having given it much thought. In those ways, consent can be active and passive.

Resistance against those forces of oppression and exploitation constitutes the struggle for liberation. Coercion and consent fail to exhaust the possibilities of agency. As in the reading of this text, readers can agree but also disagree. Resistance, therefore, is an exercise of agency. We can refuse to accept the named and imposed categories that divide us and pit us against one another. The strategy of divide and rule is not the sole option. And in turn, that resistance can modify the forms and strategies of oppression and exploitation, leading to other, mobile fields of contestation and struggle. That is how liberation is an ongoing, unfolding, and indeterminate process.

> *Power, then, is the ability to influence. Despite its distribution among all, power is not possessed or exercised equally; there are accumulations and more significant exertions of power by the few over the many. Thereby empowered, the elites can oppress and exploit the masses. But the oppressed and exploited, having agency, can resist power, and thereby mobilize and enjoin the struggle for liberation.*

Third World Studies was introduced to US higher education in 1968 at San Francisco State College, where students of the Third World Liberation Front (TWLF) identified and affiliated with the oppressed, the exploited peoples of the Third World. The field emerged from an affiliation with and a commitment to "the people," not "we, the people" of the US Constitution. "The people, united, will never be defeated!" and, as the Black Panthers declared, "All power to the people!" were more than empty slogans for the TWLF. "Serve the people" was their guide, and "for my people" they labored.

In their statement of purpose, the TWLF declared, "As Third World students, as Third World people, as so-called minorities, we are being exploited to the fullest extent in this racist white America and we are therefore preparing ourselves and our people for a prolonged struggle for freedom from this yoke of oppression." Our people, the oppressed, the TWLF understood, extended beyond the borders of the United States. "We adhere to the struggles in Asia, Africa, and Latin America, ideologically, spiritually, and culturally.... We have decided to fuse ourselves with the masses of Third World people, which are a majority of the world's peoples, to create, through struggles, a new humanity, a new humanism, a New World Consciousness, and within the text [sic] collectively control our own destinies."[2]

The TWLF thus demanded of the college the institutionalization of a "Third World curriculum," which they believed would educate them, indeed all students, to the realities of their communities in the United States and their connections with the oppressed and exploited peoples of the Third World. This was not a course of study intended to lead to an appreciation of the nation's diversity as multiculturalism is designed to achieve, nor was it about fostering hatreds and divisions within the US nation-state as caricatured by critics of ethnic studies. Third World studies is not ethnic studies, which began as a national, not a global formation and as ethnic or cultural nationalism for that group's self-determination. From our conversation about liberation thus far we understand the subjects of Third World studies to be the human condition broadly, the locations and workings of power to oppress and exploit, and resistances to the curtailment of agency and expropriation of surplus product.

The Third World contexts of that TWLF strike supply some of the influences at work in that struggle for liberation in US education. Of great significance during the 1950s and 1960s were the Cuban revolution, the related movements for national independence from French colonialism in Algeria and Vietnam, and the liberation movements directed at Portuguese colonialism in Guinea-Bissau, Angola, and Mozambique and against Belgian colonialism in the Congo. Those anticolonial revolutions were allied to freedom struggles in settler nation-states in Palestine,

---

2 "A Non-White Struggle toward New Humanism, Consciousness," *Daily Gater* [San Francisco State College], May 22, 1969.

South Africa, and Bolivia. From those years emerged notable revolutionary figures like Ernesto "Che" Guevara, Patrice Lumumba, Ho Chi Minh, and Nelson Mandela; as well as intellectuals like Frantz Fanon, Amílcar Cabral, and Eduardo Mondlane.

The year 1968, when students organized the TWLF, was remarkable. In January the Vietnamese launched the Tết offensive that led to the war's end, and some 47,000 Japanese antiwar protesters converged on the US navy base at Sasebo, Japan. In March over 10,000 Chicanx high school students in Los Angeles staged a walkout against racism and for a relevant, quality education, while at San Francisco State the TWLF formed. In April, an assassin silenced the incomparable voice of Martin Luther King Jr., and protests engulfed over forty US cities. In China tens of thousands marched, condemning racism against African Americans, and in New York City, a student strike at Columbia University protested that institution's expansion into Harlem and its complicity with the imperial war in Southeast Asia. In May, students and workers erected barricades in Paris, and that summer activists formed the American Indian Movement. In September, the National Organization of Women protested the Miss America beauty pageant in Atlantic City, and students, peasants, and workers demanded an end to government repression in Mexico City. In November, Richard Nixon captured the White House.

Those Third World revolutionary movements against colonialism and settler colonialism—as well as student and worker mass protests against imperialism, wars, racism, sexism, and state violence in Japan, China, France, and Mexico—informed and inspired like resistances in the United States. Students of the TWLF linked their movement for educational transformation with those multiple and interrelated global struggles for liberation.

But 1968 was not the start of Third World studies. Its origins reach back to 1900 when the African American intellectual and activist W. E. B. Du Bois famously declared: "The problem of the twentieth century is the problem of the color line." He delivered that prophetic announcement, appropriately, in London, the seat of the British Empire, on which the sun never set. Imperialism closed the nineteenth century and its counter, the decolonization struggles of Africa and Asia, ushered in the twentieth century. Self-determination and antiracism—the dismantling of the material relations and ideologies that justified and supported colonialism—were the central aspects of those liberation movements, which promised a new dispensation for humanity and, after two global wars and the Cold War's onset, world peace.

The color line, to Du Bois, was the divide between the colonizers and the colonized, what became known during the Cold War as the First (capitalist countries led by the United States), Second (socialist countries led by the Soviet Union), and Third World (the rest). The Third World for Du Bois was the world of color; it was racialized because the colonizers justified their imperial rule based on racism, the inferiority of the colonized. An ideology of oppression thus accompanied and advanced the material relations of exploitation. The solutions to those problems created and installed by Europeans was, therefore, anticolonialism and antiracism. Those causes were central to the field that began as Third World studies.

The problem of the twentieth century was transformative in world history. For over four hundred years, Europeans—through imperialism and colonialism—had dominated the world. They created a world-system of oppression and exploitation in which flowed capital and labor. That structured relationship enriched the core (Europe and the United States) by impoverishing the periphery (the Third World). The core thereby amassed wealth at the expense of the periphery, installing dependencies. It was precisely because the Third World was enormously rich in resources and labor that the core conquered, colonized, and drained it of its capital using its labor. The revolutions against those forces of oppression and exploitation, the problem of the twentieth century, changed four hundred years of world history. Third World studies was a part of that global, anticolonial revolution and movement.

But since 1968 and after the end to formal colonialism, Third World studies in this iteration concerns itself with liberation, broadly conceived, from all forms of oppression and exploitation. At the same time, I believe keeping the name "Third World" studies is an important reminder of its history, origins, and purposes. I realize many of us today recognize the term "Third World" with its associations of bankrupt nation-states, dictatorships, extreme poverty, civil wars, and violence against women, queers, and social outcasts. An answer to those conditions comes from a consideration of imperialism and colonialism and their afterlives, what some have called neocolonialism and the new imperialism.

> *Third World studies emerged from "the problem of the twentieth century." The problem was European imperialism and colonialism that was justified by racism to oppress and exploit the Third World. Since the formal end of colonialism, Third World studies examines all forms of oppression and exploitation for the liberation of all.*

The objective of oppression and exploitation is to rule, that is, to exert controls over and benefit from unruly (resistant) subjects. Modernity justifies its worth on that basis, the imposition of order in an imagined disorderly world. That mission is achieved through science, reason, and evidence, called the "Renaissance" or rebirth, life anew, eclipsing the superstition, faith, and experience of the former, called the "Dark" Ages. That duality of death and birth mirrors the mind and body distinction, rationality versus empiricism, man as opposed to woman. Therein we see values, virtues attached to discourses, history, and bodies and their assigned names, natures, and abilities.

Under modernity, those exertions of power to oppress and exploit work upon the individual (subject) and the social (society). A key instrument in that contest is the discourse and practice of sovereignty. The Treaty or Peace of Westphalia (1648) defined the contours of that relationship between ruler and subject. Westphalia provided for the nation-state comprised of property or bordered space within which sovereigns (the state) ruled over subjects (the nation). Sovereignty, thus, involved private property, the rights (divine or natural) of the state and its subjects (citizens), and self-determination or the ability of nation-states to direct their own destinies without outside intervention.

From Westphalia and its subsequent modifications descend the sovereign nation-state and sovereign subject. Those divisions of the individual and society, premised upon divine and later natural rights, are, of course, the manifestations of power. Rights whether granted by god or nature are appeals to human-assigned authorities, the sureties (positivism) of science notwithstanding, and as such are neither absolute nor eternal. Clearly borders and property include as well as exclude, and private property is a cornerstone of capitalism. Boundedness and ownership can betray the promises of liberation. Individualism can reduce collective identifications and solidarities. Finally, and as we will see, there are compelling reasons to reject the idea of a solitary self and society.

Humanism arises from the Cartesian (named after the 17th-century French mathematician René Descartes) formulation, "I think, therefore,

I am," which is wonderfully optimistic but also woefully negligent. The statement reaffirms the human ability to think, which distinguishes that species from other life forms, and it posits the notion of self-determination. The self, through thought ("I think"), calls forth existence ("I am"). That rebirth arose amidst doctrines of predestination and divine will that determined and directed human, indeed all, life. Humanism, by contrast, expressed a confidence in human abilities to make history.

But as we now know, speciesism or the belief in the primacy of humans is debatable. How is superiority measured, and is human existence separate from and unrelated to other life forms and the environment? Moreover, is cognition a unique human trait or can other species or robots (artificial intelligence) think, plan, and act? The dividing line, if one exists, is certainly thin and porous. Anthropocentrism is a supremacy claimed by its creators and is patently false in that humans relate to, depend upon, and sometimes are subject to their environments, including plants and animals but also the lands, waters, and skies of their planet earth.

In addition, Marx (1818–83) and Freud (1856–1939) cast doubt on the complete autonomy of the human subject. Marx argued that one's class position or location within the relations of production shaped consciousness, while Freud found the unconscious dimension of the self that was inaccessible to thought. Marx pointed to the social context as central to the constitution of the self, while Freud identified the inner workings of the subliminal within the human mind. More basic than thought, the Swiss linguist Ferdinand de Saussure (1857–1913) explained, is language, which is the way humans conceive of themselves and articulate with their worlds. Without language the Cartesian formulation "I think" is impossible; nothing can exist outside of language. In that way, language structures consciousness and the subject.

The French psychoanalyst Jacques Lacan (1901–81), like Saussure, saw language acquisition not as a solitary but as a relational act, a submission of the self to the power and rules of language and its source, the other. For Lacan, language produces the subject in a process he called subjectification or the creation of the subject-self. Besides language, the Italian Marxist Antonio Gramsci (1891–1937) and French philosopher Louis Althusser (1918–90) described how intellectuals produce ideology, which the state uses to interpellate consciousness and subjects. Together, the French philosopher Michel Foucault (1926–84) held that language and ideology (comprising discourse) are what make subjects. In that sense, subjects are variants of discourse, and as such they are social constructs.

> In sum, then, power names, describes, and ranks subjects to rule and exploit. That imposition of order, called modernity, began with the idea and practice of sovereignty and its rights of authority, property, and self-determination. Humanism upheld that sovereign self, which was undermined by subsequent ideas of class-consciousness, the unconscious, and language and ideology (discourse). Even as language acquisition is relational, the subject-self is produced in conversation with society.

The social and civil societies are organized within and ordered by nation-states. They comprise its members or citizens with rights and responsibilities. The nation is a narrative in the making because the official version of a chosen people with a common purpose is at odds with the varying realities of porous borders and diverse peoples. Still race is a foundational feature of the nation-state as we see in the term "nation," which comes from "by birth" or "to be born," indicating kinship of blood, which is a race. That fiction of nation starts with one people, one race, united by blood, sharing a single language and culture, history, and destiny. As John Jay, a founding father of the United States and the first chief justice of the Supreme Court, declared: Americans were "one united people—a people descended from the same ancestors, speaking the same language, professing the same religion, attached to the same principles of government, very similar in their manners and customs."

That nation-state, in addition to race, is implicated in the production and management of gender, sexuality, and ability. As shown in the United States, the state has an interest in distinguishing and therewith instituting prohibitions and rights to men and women, heterosexuals and homosexuals, the abled and disabled. Patriarchal order installed men in the public sphere because of their ability to self-determine and govern and women in the private sphere because of their inabilities and hence "dependency." Men held ownership rights to property, including enslaved people, women, and children, while women had diminished rights to possess because of their alleged incapacities. Those conjured abilities and therewith rights entitled men to occupy the state and rule while women only achieved the vote in 1920, nearly 150 years after the nation's founding.

Compulsory heterosexuality, including sexual behaviors and marriage, is a state prerogative as the guardian of public "morals" while its self-interest requires the reproduction of racialized citizens. The US Naturalization Act (1790) restricted naturalized citizenship to "free white persons." Therewith, freedom, white, and citizen formed correspondences, as opposed to bondage, nonwhite, and alien. Race, freedom, and sexuality also figured in those relations of power. In 1664, colonial Maryland in a single act banned interracial marriage and made slavery a lifetime condition. Also in US law, homosexual and interracial prohibitions often formed equivalences. As "immoral" and "unnatural" acts against god and nature, homosexuality and interracial sex and marriage were denied and punished.

The state—as a locus of power—rules through a strategy of naming, describing, and conferring rights and privileges on the bases of race, gender, sexuality, ability, and nation. Through the apparatuses of language and ideology (discourse), the state produces those subjects as dualities of one set against the other: white v. nonwhite, man v. woman, heterosexual v. homosexual, abled v. disabled, and citizen v. alien. By segregating and pitting one over the other, the state imposes order and rule or hegemony through coercion and consent. Its constitution and laws bestow and deprive powers, and transgressions of those polarities are deviations and threats to the national security. Since the US nation's founding, for example, migrants of color were "aliens" and as such imperiled the homeland.

Even before the US nation-state in settler colonial Virginia we see that term "aliens" used to identify people of color as nonmembers and thus deprived of rights. Anthony Johnson, an enslaved African, arrived in the Colony in 1621, two years after the first Africans landed. He worked on a settler tobacco plantation along the James River, and over twenty years married, Mary, an enslaved African, and together had four children. After gaining their freedom in the 1640s, the Johnson family farmed some 250 acres on the Colony's eastern shore. They kept cattle and had two African servants. In 1669 a settler jury of white men ruled that Anthony Johnson was "a Negroe" and by consequence "an alien" or noncitizen. As such he could not transfer his land to his son, and instead awarded the property to a white settler. Therein we see race, citizenship, and rights of possession conjoined; white, citizen, and owner stood in opposition to black, alien, and dispossessed.

The social, in addition to race, gender, sexuality, ability, and nation, includes the provisioning function to sustain life, societies, and the nation-state. Human labor exerted upon the land (environment) produces goods or value. Food, clothing, and shelter provide for those basic needs. The economy is that process of creating value. Capitalism is but one of several economic systems. We should remember that because in our time capitalism is the dominant world order, and we can easily see its triumph as vindication of its verity and powers. In fact, capitalism emerged in a place and time, and its spread and growth can be attributed in large part to its role in imperialism and colonialism.

Simply, capitalism is an economic system based upon private property, the ownership of the means of production, and upon surpluses or profits derived from the labor of workers. Those constitute classes, those who own and those who work for returns. Whether enslaved, indentured, or free, laborers produce wealth for the owners in exchange for sustenance (food, clothing, shelter) or wages. In that way, accumulations accrue to the owners through the impoverishment of those who create value. The expropriation of surplus product is what we know as exploitation. Super exploitation occurs when profit margins widen from labor systems divided by race (nonwhite), gender (women), or nation (alien) to lower the costs of labor, and from environments such as colonies where resources are more abundant, and labor is plentiful and cheap.

Sovereignty, as ideology and practice, abetted the rise of capitalism. As we saw, property and rights were features of the sovereign state and sovereign subject. Those possessions formed a basis for the ownership of the means of production (resources, factories, and so forth), and ownership of one's own labor. Humanism and individualism, however, were not universally or equally possessed because of assigned abilities and inabilities that merited and denied claims and powers. Accordingly, nonwhites and women were dependent upon white men because of their lack, mainly their mental inabilities to comprehend complexities. Similarly, workers were poor because of their deficiencies, whether of drive and initiative, intelligence, culture, or bad choices. Discourses thus installed and explained social locations and hierarchies.

Imperialism or extraterritorial powers extended sovereignty's reach by advancing the ideas of possessions and rights to places outside the nation-state. Imperialism is both discourse and material relations. Colonialism is an aspect of imperialism as discourse and sites of those extraterritorial powers. Colonies involved military and provisioning bases to defend and facilitate the expansion, and extractive and settler colonies to produce wealth for the imperial power. Gold, silver, tobacco, and sugar flowed from America to Europe while spices, silks, cotton, and porcelain moved from Asia to the core. Enslaved and indentured workers generated that value, and Europe accumulated wealth at the expense of the Third World, drained of its resources and labor. Those imperial processes of conquest, colonization, the exploitation of resources and labor, and capital accumulations comprised and advanced capitalism and "the problem of the twentieth century."

Imperialism and colonialism are thus aspects of nationalism and capitalism. Those features appear in the move from nation-state to imperial or extraterritorial nation-state. In the encounter with Third World peoples, nation-based races, like the German race, the English race, became Europeans or whites. Taxonomies supplied the discursive scaffolding for those essentializing, generalizing human types. Carl Linnaeus (1707-78), Swedish physician and "the father of taxonomy," grouped humans into varieties, later called races, according to the four continents, which were also social, not scientific constructs. Europe was the home of Europeans (whites), Asia, of Asians (brown), Africa, of Africans (blacks), and America, of Americans (red). He later described Asians as yellow in color and assigned natures or traits to each group that descended from the ideal type, the European. White supremacy, realized in the imperial spread, conquest, and colonization of peoples of color, affirmed the (European) discourse of race. And conversely, a justification for imperialism involved the conversion and uplift of pagan, barbarous peoples mired in backward, stagnant cultures—peoples without history or the ability to move.

In 1895, at the height of European imperialism, Kaiser Wilhelm II of Germany commissioned a painting entitled *Yellow Peril*. "On a plateau of rock bathed in light radiating from the Cross—the symbol in which alone Christians win their victories—stand allegorical figures of the civilized nations," read the explanation that accompanied the painting, copies of which the Kaiser sent to several European heads of state and the US president. Led by the archangel Michael, women in martial garb, wearing the names of European nation-states, look with varying degrees of interest and resolve toward an approaching "horror" and "calamity which menaces them." Beneath them stretches "the vast plain of civilized Europe" through which flows "a majestic stream" with cities and churches dotting the peaceful landscape. But "dark pitchy vapors obscure the sky" and "clouds of calamity are rolling up" in the wake of "invaders" with "hellish, distorted faces." Positioned above a burning city are the figures of the Buddha and a Chinese dragon, symbols of the "yellow peril," and inscribed on the painting was the legend: "Nations of Europe, defend your holiest possession."

European civilization and Christianity were the sole possessions of Europe that united the competing and conflicting national interests over empire. To meet the forces of darkness, the invasion of uncivilized, barbarous, and heathen peoples, the civilized nations of Europe must win their victory under the banner of (European) civilization and Christianity. That conflict has a deep history. The Greco-Persian Wars of the fifth century B.C.E. threatened ancient Greece, the font of European civilization, while the eleventh through thirteenth century C.E. Crusades waged "holy" wars in the name of Christianity against paganism (Islam). White and Christian nationalisms and supremacies in the United States grew from those European roots, which some four hundred years of imperialism nourished and strengthened.

Third World studies locates the subject-self within society. Foundational to the constitution of civil society is the nation-state based upon sovereignty. Property rights and the relations between rulers and subjects comprise nation-states, which, to rule, interpellate and police race, gender, sexuality, ability, and nation. Sustaining those state powers is the economy, which, under capitalism, involves the expropriation of surplus product by owners from workers. Rights and privileges accrue from those social hierarchies and relations, even as subjects and workers can resist and thereby alter the forms and outcomes of oppression and exploitation.

Social formation theory purports to explain the subject-self and society as the locations and articulations of power to oppress and exploit, involving the formations of race, gender, sexuality, ability, class, and nation. Those organizations and exertions of power comprise discourses that the material and social relations make real; that is, the discursive enact and shape consciousness, experiences, and lives. Formations are structures, institutions, forms that move; they are in formation, in process. Power (the state and capital) creates and deploys those as single formations, race for example; as multiple, race and gender; and as intersectional, gendered sexualities. In those ways, subjects might be oppressed and exploited singly as nonwhites, multiply as nonwhite and disabled, and intersectionally as the alien, which today might conjure a nonwhite, poor, criminal, sexually deviant threat.

Intended to behave as closed systems, the formations of and relations in society are designed by their creators, those who hold and wield power, to function as a whole to actualize control (rule) and privileges and poverties. But because of human agency and ceaseless contestations, the social formation is not a closed or self-regulating system. Neither is its future and direction predetermined. Rather, the social formation is historical or specific to time and place and is subject to change and transformation.

To visualize the social formation, imagine separate spheres of race, gender, sexuality, ability, class, and nation that converge to overlap and share features and diverge to differentiate; they are elastic, expanding and contracting over space and time. Think in terms of singularities and multiplicities, meetings and departures, stasis and change. In addition, intersecting spheres can result in a third category, neither "a" nor "b" but "c." That is, an intersectional Black woman is oppressed and exploited not as a sum of race ("a") and gender ("b") but as a racialized gender or a gendered race ("c").

The social formation rejects degrees of suffering that measures oppression and exploitation. Quantitative analyses are not only simplifications and misleading; they segregate and rank victims and fail to detect continuities and commonalities that can promote solidarities. Instead of "most oppressed and exploited," the theory posits the qualities of oppression and exploitation. Race, gender, sexuality, ability, class, and nation comprise the varieties that oppress and exploit as single, multiple, and intersectional discourses and material relations. They, then, render subjects susceptible to their powers, accounting for qualitative, not quantitative contrasts.

Moreover, oppression and exploitation differ in contexts of place and time. Colonialism, for instance, served imperialism from the fifteenth through twentieth centuries; it had a beginning and an end. After independence, another form of colonialism called neocolonialism held in bondage Third World nation-states. Former colonial masters and global institutions like the World Bank direct Third World states and economies toward capitalist "development." And following the pattern of European and settler nation-states, Third World versions installed privileged elites to rule over and profit from their oppressed and impoverished masses. If national self-determination was the solution to imperialism, colonialism, and racism, "the problem of the twentieth century;" neocolonialism kept intact the locations of power in the core but also distributed it to the periphery.

Social formation attends to the multiplicity of forces at work in the exercise of power. It demands a complexity in our thinking and politics to ascertain how social categories overlap, interact, conflict with, and interrupt each other. Social formation is not solely the intersections or sum of oppressions; it accounts for those variances and meeting points but also their resistances (and accommodations) and the mutually constituting and shifting relations between discourses and the material conditions. Finally social formation theory supplies a rubric for affiliations among discourses of racial formation, feminist, queer, critical (dis)ability, and critical theories and for solidarities in political insurgencies from oppressed and exploited peoples across the imposed divides of race, gender, sexuality, ability, class, and nation.

In the movement against police profiling and violence as we witnessed in Ferguson, Missouri, and New York City in 2014, thousands marched chanting "Hands up, don't shoot!" and "I can't breathe" across social divides. That cause and movement surged anew in 2020 after the police murders of Breonna Taylor and especially George Floyd. And in the largest single-day protest in US history, the Women's March on January 21, 2017 amassed between three and five million women and men, white and nonwhite, straight and queer, abled and (dis)abled, rich and poor, citizen and alien to affirm that women's rights are human rights. Those mobilizations attest to the single, multiple, and intersectional features and powers of oppression and exploitation and their resistance—the social formation.

> *The social formation examines power as discourses and material relations. It apprehends oppression and exploitation as the*

workings of power to rule and profit from its naming, describing, and ranking race, gender, sexuality, ability, class, and nation. Those taxonomies and their policing impose order through divide and rule even as transgressions erode their borders. Single, multiple, and intersectional formations add complexities to resistances, but they also provide opportunities for mobilizing solidarities for liberation.

Third World studies is a conversation about liberation. As such, it is open, subject to adoption and resistance. It is a work in progress. Liberation suggests necessarily an opposition. It exists in resistance to oppression, exploitation, or the curtailment of agency and expropriation of surplus product. Liberation thus is a form of abolitionism and emancipation from confinement, the prisons of power, discursive and material. Enclosures limit space; isolation prohibits connections across divides of the subject-self and society. That compression, that restriction of boundless possibilities affects us all. Our imaginations must approach the infinite. Third World studies poses to us that challenge.

Synopsis
Third World studies is about liberation.

Liberation involves struggles against oppression and exploitation.

Oppression is the curtailment of agency, wherein agency is the power to move, to influence.

Exploitation is the expropriation of surplus product, wherein surplus product is the profit generated by laborers for owners.

Third World studies is about power or agency, ability.

Everyone has power.

There are concentrations and more influential exercises of power.

Those who possess and flex power comprise the ruling class whose objects include: to rule (oppress) and exploit.

A principal strategy of power is to divide by naming, describing, and ranking, thereby creating separations and hierarchies.

Those divisions include race, gender, sexuality, ability, class, and nation, which are social constructions (created by humans) and are not expressions or mandates of divine law or natural law.

Those locations and articulations of power around race, gender, sexuality, ability, class, and nation constitute society and the social formation.

As social constructions, humans can violate (resist) and abolish them, which is the process of and struggle for liberation.

BIBLIOGRAPHY

Okihiro, Gary Y. "Reassessing Third World Liberation: A Conversation." In *Postcolonial Practices of Care: A Project of Togetherness during COVID-19 and Racial Violence*, edited by Hellena Moon and Emmanuel Y. Lartey, xv–xxix. Eugene, OR: Pickwick Publications, 2022.

2

Listening to Truths:
Democracy & Its Neighbor, Fascism[1]

Hellena Moon

I didn't ask to stand under a crown of spikes
with my book and my torch, forgotten
like the lamp left burning in the corner.

My shoulder aches, my toes are throbbing.

I'd rather bathe in a park fountain
or cast benediction from the shadowy nest
of a cathedral's gilded ribs.

Liberty's pale green maiden, stranded.

Come [and] visit! Ascend to the crown and gaze out
at the nation I've sworn to watch over.
I stand ready to tell you what I have seen.

Who among you is ready to listen?

Epilogue, "A Standing Witness"
Rita Dove[2]

Introduction

I attended a performance called, "A Standing Witness," where mezzo-soprano, Susan Graham, performed a song-cycle, narrating seminal events in the past fifty years of US history. Written by poet Rita Dove, the

---

1 This chapter is a revision of the chapter, "Shepherding as Method & Practice: The Banality of the Shepherding Paradigm," that is part of my monograph. See Moon, *Liberalism and Colonial Violence.*
2 Dove, "A Standing Witness."

twelve testimonies were "bookended by a prologue (about truth) and an epilogue (revealing our witness's identity and her poignant plea that underlies the entire work"."[3] The narrator of the events, witnessing this history, is revealed in the epilogue to be the statue of liberty. "She" narrates "her" version of—and is the "standing witness" to—US history.

Perhaps if we asked a high school student to compose the epilogue and be witness to history as the statue of liberty, today's high school student might ask the important questions, "why is the statue of liberty female?" "Why do Latin words—and the Romance languages—gender all of their words?" It's a statue and at that time, the men who created the statue understood liberté to be feminine, but we don't have gender all our words." One college student shared, "there would be a queering of the statue because true freedom means freedom of gender identity and sexuality, not what we are forcing onto the person." Truth is, "she" is not a "woman" since "she" is a statue and is an allegorical metonym of freedom in a particular historical moment.

The performance, "A Standing Witness," might have been told from an entirely different perspective, depending on whose truths we narrate. These stories constitute what in critical race theory are called counterstories.[4] Counterstorytelling is critical writing that interrogates and deconstructs the validity of accepted premises or myths that dehumanize and criminalize a group of people, especially ones held by the majority, such as yellow peril, "Black criminality," or Muslim terrorism."[5] Through the power of—and the desire to create—images in social media, tweets, etc., we have seen dangerous myths and propaganda that have resulted in killings of innocent people and irreparable injuries to communities. Revisionist critical historiographies, such as the 1619 Project that rewrites the mythic narratives of US history and the #BlackLivesMatter movement that challenge statistical data on police brutality against Black bodies, are important counterstories.

The *counterstories* of the nation's symbol of freedom reveal the layers of oppression and our fixed notions of what *is* freedom. If we heard the statue of liberty narrate stories from the many different voices in our country, we would hear that the statue was never a symbol of freedom

---

3 Danielpour, "Program Notes," 5.
4 Crenshaw, et al., *Critical Race Theory*.
5 Delgado and Stefancic, *Critical Race Theory*, 50.

for all. In his widely read book, *Margins and Mainstreams*, Gary Okihiro notes how Emma Lazarus wrote the poem at the base of the Statue of liberty, "The New Colossus," one year after passage of the Chinese Exclusion Act of 1882.[6] The statue was dedicated on October 28, 1886 by President Grover Cleveland, whose words—'the darkness of ignorance and man's oppression until Liberty enlightens the world'—are so often quoted but not seen in the context of the xenophobia from which they originated.[7] The statue served as an allegorical bulwark against anarchy and alliance with other nations that also stood up for freedom. The meaning of the statue shifted as people interpreted it in their own meaning: welcoming the immigrant. At the same time, history shows that the Asian immigrant was *not* welcomed. Such counterstories of freedom have created ideological divisiveness.

Ideological divisiveness is not a new phenomenon in democracy and has been a part of US history since its origins. We are, however, going through a crucial moment in the survival of our fragile democracy. Our country is being torn in half by ideological divisiveness due to *false* ideologies and the masking of truths. In this chapter, I explore the deeply relevant admonitions of French aristocrat, Alexis de Tocqueville (1805–1859), who observed and critiqued the problems of concentrated political power within American democracy in the late 1800s. In his travelogue, he documented his observations on the biggest problem among white Americans: the unthinking masses. He saw the uncritical masses (the sheep) who were held captive by a demagogue (the shepherd) as part of the problem of democracy. His observations, critiques, and warnings about the precarity of our democracy is deeply relevant to our current society, as well as other democracies. In this chapter, I describe his critiques, his proto-critical race theory as it pertains to the practices of our democracy and treatment of non-white people, and his prescriptive for the flourishing of a democracy.

The recent vitriolic accusations about the dangers of teaching critical race theory (CRT) are confounding, because a white aristocrat like Alexis de Tocqueville (who himself believed in the racial and cultural superiority of white Europeans) had articulated a proto-critical race theory in

---

6 Okihiro, *Margins and Mainstreams*.
7 Okihiro, Margins and Mainstreams, 5.

observing the conditions of race relations, slavery, emancipation, forced migration and colonization of Native American lands, and the prosperity of white Europeans at the expense of infrahumans.[8] Critical race theory (CRT), a collection of legal scholarship, explicates how rule by white supremacy in the United States was systematically created and maintained through the subordination of non-Christians and people of color.[9] Derrick Bell is credited with founding critical race theory, while a student of his, Kimberlé Crenshaw, coined the term. CRT is an academic framework to address racial inequalities and find prescriptives for the flourishing of everyone in society. CRT is a verb and a tool for socio-economic transformation. CRT does not blame individuals; the theory argues that laws and people are a product of society. Since we created the laws, we can help change the laws.

In sharing stories of truths, then, critical race theory discursively outlines and critiques the fundamentals and foundations of US democracy. CRT is opposed to discrimination and desires the flourishing of our humanity by addressing inequalities that can bring about justice for everyone. It is not a zero-sum game. Alexis de Tocqueville also stated what political economist Heather McGhee so eloquently described about interest convergence.[10] That is, he observed how it would benefit nineteenth century white Anglo-Americans to be less racist. They would be more human, less savage, and be more innovative, etc.

In this chapter, I also critique the claim of American uniqueness as a white Christian nation as precariously compatible with tyranny and fascist ideologies. I discuss the coterminous cultural ideological developments of what I term, "the shepherding pastoral paradigm," with the mythical ideology of the palingenesis—the rebirth or re-creation—of the American Adam. Around the time of the born-again American Adam in the nineteenth century, racist scientific theories of polygenesis that buttressed white Christian nationalism were circulating. Such an archetype that foregrounds uniqueness, sacrality, superiority, and hierarchy disavows and defies a healthy democratic and pluralist society that imagines political equality and participatory citizenly practices.

---

8   People who were seen as less than fully human (i.e., white). See Gilroy, "Suffering and Infrahumanity."
9   Crenshaw, et al. *Critical Race Theory*, xiii.
10 McGhee, *The Sum of Us*.

Shepherding as Practice of Soft Tyranny and Despotic Rule

French aristocrat, Alexis de Tocqueville, visited the United States in 1831 to learn more about the country. Many Europeans were curious about "America." Tocqueville was a conservative member of the aristocracy who established relationships with the elite community in America. Here, he had prejudices and biases of the "image of democracy itself"[11] as the leveling of equality. He gauged democracy in America in its implications as a precursor to what would eventually happen—democratization—in his own home country of France. He saw American democracy in its ideal practice to exist in the New England town government.[12] While he saw overall prosperity, he observed a landscape of mediocrity and "complacency" among the white Americans, as he notes later in the book. 1831 was an explosive year, however, as the issue of slavery and abolition were front and center in American politics.

He warned of the dangers stemming from concentrated political power in a democratic nation. He foresaw the problems of soft tyranny that would develop from the state acting like a "national shepherd"—and the people acting like well-fed sheep. There is a clear and sharp demarcation between the shepherd and sheep, i.e., the ones with power to dominate and those who are subordinate to that power. Philosopher Michel Foucault referred to this as "pastoral power." Pastoral power is one of power relations, not one of total control. I refer to this as the shepherding paradigm, which also refers to a patriarch or pastor (i.e., human) "shepherding" or leading his [sic] unthinking sheep (i.e., infrahuman).[13]

Tocqueville thought that soft tyranny would lead to political passivity on the part of the people in their sheep-like docility and oppression.[14] He argued that "soft despotism," a term he coined referring to "a network of small and complicated rules, minute and uniform," which is not obvious to the people, would give people the illusion that they are in control. The people ultimately would have very little influence over their government and *would be* controlled instead. He saw how Christian nations, with similar structures of pastoral power of the church, would be vulnerable

---

11 Becker, "Introduction," *Democracy in America*, xiii.
12 Becker, "Introduction," *Democracy in America*, xxiii.
13 Gilroy https://tannerlectures.utah.edu/_resources/documents/a-to-z/g/Gilroy%20manuscript%20PDF.pdf, 25.
14 Tocqueville, *Democracy in America*, xxxii.

to soft tyranny.[15] He mused, "[t]his led me to think that the nations of Christendom would perhaps eventually undergo some oppression like that which hung over several of the nations of the ancient world."[16] Pastoral power of the sovereign or individual, he argued, is dangerous "without the assistance of intermediate powers." He goes on to say that this form of soft despotism "would be more extensive and more mild; it would degrade men [sic] without tormenting them."[17]

The type of oppression experienced in democratic nations was unprecedented, according to Tocqueville. He stated that he could not find the precise language to articulate the problem he observed. He was concerned for the individualism, complicity, and non-thinking of Americans who are led without knowing how they have relinquished their power and their freedoms. He observed that the American people—in our complacency to be well-fed—superficially cared more about our own material well-being than about true freedom. We did not desire to know our histories, our past, nor our past generations. This following passage is an often-cited, well-known quote of Tocqueville's articulation of the problems of soft tyranny and pastoral power:

> Above this race of men stands an immense and tutelary power, which takes upon itself alone to secure their gratifications and to watch over their fate. That power is absolute, minute, regular, provident, and mild. It would be like the authority of a parent if, like that authority, its object was to prepare men for manhood; but it seeks, on the contrary, to keep them perpetually in childhood.... For their happiness such a government willingly labors, but it chooses to be the sole agent and the only arbiter of that happiness; it provides for their security, foresees and supplies their necessities, facilitates their pleasures, manages their principal concerns, directs their industry, regulates the descent of property... what remains, but to spare them all the care of thinking and the trouble of living?
>
> Thus it everyday renders the exercise of the free agency of man less useful and less frequent; it circumscribes the will within

---

15 While pastoral power may be Foucauldian language, I point out that Tocqueville had these concerns in the 1800s prior to Foucault.
16 Tocqueville, *Democracy in America*, 581.
17 Tocqueville, *Democracy in America*, 582.

a narrower range and gradually robs a man of all the uses of himself....

After having thus successively taken each member of the community in its powerful grasp and fashioned him at will, the supreme power then extends its arm over the whole community.... The will of man is not shattered, but softened, bent, and guided.... Such a power does not destroy, but it prevents existence; it does not tyrannize, but it compresses, enervates, extinguishes, and stupefies a people, till each nation is reduced to nothing better than a flock of timid and industrious animals, of which the government is the shepherd.[18]

When paternalistic state power increases and eclipses self-determining agency and our critical thinking, we become the docile and subservient sheep who are guided and held captive, yet not in cages. Like children, Tocqueville notes, "they want to be led, and they wish to remain free."[19] We live under a cloak of docility and unthinking, veiled in an illusion of our freedom amid such pastoral intimacies of soft tyranny and perpetual childhood. People become dependent on their master, led on a "chain," in a form of "extorted obedience."[20]

Persistence of Racism & Racial Inequalities

Alexis de Tocqueville described our democratic process as a careful paradoxical balance between a simultaneous desire for the centralization of government, yet with a yearning "to remain free" and maintain popular sovereignty. People think their freedoms are protected, when, they unknowingly have relinquished their freedoms to protect their sovereignty. There is tension, he stated, between "administrative despotism" and authority of the people.[21] The paradox of freedom is that we give up our power to have individual liberties, simultaneously while our individual freedom is intertwined with near total disciplinary control. Our freedom from power (individual freedom) is dependent on our obedience to those structures of power. This is the ongoing aporetic tension between care and surveillance.

---

18 Tocqueville, *Democracy in America*, 584–585.
19 Tocqueville, *Democracy in America*, 585.
20 Tocqueville, *Democracy in America*, 585.
21 Tocqueville, *Democracy in America*, 585.

Alexis de Tocqueville described his concerns for the well-fed, unthinking, unfeeling white Americans who were on an invisible leash. Although he noticed that Black and indigenous peoples occupied "an equally inferior position in the country they inhabit," he, too, believed they were inferior to the white Europeans.[22] While Tocqueville concerned himself with the "equality of conditions" in America, his analysis of—and concern for—democracy was provincially focused on the white European man, who he described as "the superior in intelligence, in power, and in enjoyment."[23] In other words, if the non-thinking white sheep (the unthinking masses) were of concern to Tocqueville, the indigenous and Blacks were deplorably oppressed and without any dignity. They were stripped of their customs, traditions, religions, and had none of the privileges given to the white European. They were outside the scope of the herd, as the shepherd had zero regard for the misery perpetrated on people of color. The exploited classes of people by the middle-class white sheep were part of the problem in Tocqueville's analysis of American torpor and complacency caused by economic equality among whites. He saw how liberal democracy and racism in the United States historically and intrinsically fortified—or fed—the other.

Political scientist Jennifer Hochschild has argued that "[r]acism and liberalism are as intertwined in American history as they are antithetical."[24] She counters the argument that slavery and other forms of violence against people of color have been "anomalies," or scars, on an overall healthy liberal democracy. In explicating the ongoing visibility of racism, she states that the persistence of "racism is not simply an excrescence on a fundamentally healthy liberal Democratic body but is part of what shapes and energizes the body."[25] Racism has been symbiotic with US democratic society that is insistent on forgetting its past—or hiding it. "In short," states Hochschild, "the economy of the South, the Revolution, the Constitution, the Western frontier, the Civil War, the labor movement—these facets of American history and others have been molded by the juxtaposition of racism and liberalism."[26] Jennifer Hochschild's symbiosis

---

22 Tocqueville, *Democracy in America*, 200.
23 Tocqueville, *Democracy in America*, 200.
24 Hochschild, *The New American Dilemma*, 1.
25 Hochschild, *The New American Dilemma*, 203.
26 Hochschild, *The New American Dilemma*, 1.

thesis states that liberal democracy and racism in the United States are historically, even inherently, reinforcing.[27]

In reflecting on the "conditions" of people of color (specifically referring to enslaved people of African descent) during his visit to America in 1831, Tocqueville also theorized the permanence of racism in the United States. He described the obvious segregation, elision, and the lack of regard for people of color by the white community. He stated that racism in America grew in proportion to the emancipation of enslaved Blacks. In his chapter on "the three races" and slavery, Tocqueville observed that the "consequences of these evils were different" in antiquity from US slavery, because the enslaved of antiquity were the "same race as his [sic] master and was often the superior of the two in education and intelligence."[28] Even so, he argued that there was a natural prejudice which impacted true equality. In antiquity, such feelings disappeared over time because of the physical similarities between "master" and enslaved. In the United States, however, Tocqueville presciently noted that this racism, as well as a hierarchy of white supremacy and inferiority of people of color, would *always* exist. While Derrick Bell is credited with the idea of the theory of a permanence of racism, Tocqueville's thesis might be its primogeniture. Tocqueville reflected, "[t]his arises from the circumstance that among the moderns the abstract and transient fact of slavery is fatally united with the physical and permanent fact of color.... although the law may abolish slavery, God alone can obliterate the traces of its existence."[29] Tocqueville intimates that when Europeans first enslaved African peoples, they must have believed it would be a permanent condition, because "there is no intermediate state that can be durable between the excessive inequality produced by servitude and the complete equality that originates in independence."[30]

Tocqueville's observations of America in 1831 supported (and pre-dated) what founder of critical race theory Derrick Bell described how "racism is an integral, permanent, and indestructible component of this society."[31] As Blacks have been permanently scarred by the violence

---

27 Hochschild, *The New American Dilemma*.
28 Tocqueville, *Democracy in America*, 221.
29 Tocqueville, *Democracy in America*, 222.
30 Tocqueville, *Democracy in America*, 247.
31 Bell, *Faces at the Bottom*, xxi.

of slavery, other communities of color have been perpetual foreigners and treated with scorn and contempt in this country. We cannot heal from the racism when the narratives and scripts of racial difference continue to uphold ideologies and myths of white supremacy. Racism has been woven into the fabric of our country and, as Bell states,

> Black people are the magical faces at the bottom of society's well. Even the poorest whites, those who must live their lives only a few levels above, gain their self-esteem by gazing down on us. Surely, they must know that their deliverance depends on letting down their ropes. Only by working together is escape possible. Over time, many reach out, but most simply watch, mesmerized into maintaining their unspoken commitment to keeping us where we are, at whatever cost to them or to us.[32]

The prejudice towards Blacks, Tocqueville acknowledged during his sojourn in America, grew stronger in proportion to their freedom, thereby continually sanctioning inequality in the twenty-first century even though it has been eradicated formally in the law.[33]

Tocqueville observed the conditions that created equality for whites, but he also critiqued the deep inequalities between races in US society because ethnic Others were seen as tools for the white settlers to gain and increase their freedoms. Myths and lies were fabricated that people of color have no desires nor needs, except to please their master.[34] Tocqueville noted the contrast of the brutal system of slavery: "the more the utility of slavery is contested, the more firmly is it established in the laws; and while its principle is gradually abolished in the North, that selfsame principle gives rise to more and more rigorous consequences in the South."[35] He was utterly appalled by the legislation of slavery in the South that had "unparalleled atrocities" and saw it as a travesty of humanity.[36]

---

32 Bell, *Faces at the Bottom*, epigraph.
33 Tocqueville, *Democracy in America*, 225.
34 Tocqueville, *Democracy in America*, 203.
35 Tocqueville, *Democracy in America*, 245.
36 Tocqueville, *Democracy in America*, 245.

Grazing and Feeding Our Democracy
Please—
    what becomes of the shepherd
    when the sheep are cannibals?
                  Ocean Vuong, "Prayer for the Newly Damned"[37]

Just as the shepherd needs the sheep, our liberal democracy relies on the infrahuman and racism to thrive. Paul Gilroy describes the words of David Walker (1830) who sought to be recognized as human—to include Blacks within the boundaries of the human family from which they were banished. Gilroy summarizes Walker's sentiments of the "infrahuman beings to which [B]lacks were confined and to identify the bitter quality of their systematic expulsion" from what Walker calls "the human family."[38] This ejection from the human family and reliance on the labor of infrahumans was established early in US history as the 1619 project reveals. Plantation economies of the South flourished due to the work of enslaved Blacks, as well as coerced Asian and Latin/x migrant laborers following emancipation.[39] The dehisced wounds of systemic racial violence in our nation have never been healed, revealing the ongoing tensions of racism and liberalism.

As the Senate was approving the thirteenth Amendment to the Constitution to abolish slavery in 1864, Abraham Lincoln gave his "Address at Sanitary Fair" in Baltimore, Maryland.[40] He reflected on the aporetic double effect of freedom and how it held different meanings for different groups of people. It was this constant see-saw balance of equilibrium which could not be maintained without hindering freedoms for whites. Lincoln states,

> We all declare liberty; but in using the same *word* we do not all mean the same *thing*. With some the word liberty may mean for each man *[sic]* to do as he pleases with himself, and the product of his labor; while with others the same word may mean for some men to do as they please with other men, and the product of other men's labor. Here are two, not only different, but incompatible

---

37 Vuong, *Night Sky*, 56.
38 Gilroy, https://tannerlectures.utah.edu/_resources/documents/a-to-z/g/Gilroy%20manuscript%20PDF.pdf, 25.
39 See Jung, *Coolies and Cane*.
40 Lincoln, "Address at Sanitary Fair," Quoted in Bouie, "What Does 'White Freedom.'"

things, called by the same name—liberty. And it follows that each of the things is, by the respective parties, called by two different and incompatible names—liberty and tyranny.

The shepherd drives the wolf from the sheep's throat, for which the sheep thanks the shepherd as a *liberator*, while the wolf denounces him for the same act as the destroyer of liberty, especially as the sheep was a black one. Plainly the sheep and the wolf are not agreed upon a definition of the word liberty; and precisely the same difference prevails to-day among us human creatures, even in the North, and all professing to love liberty.[41]

Here, Lincoln interpreted freedom cast in the framework of negative and positive rights: freedom *from* domination (sheep), as well as freedom *to* dominate (here, it is the wolf), and those who have the pastoral power to make such decisions (shepherd). In his study of white freedom during the era of Enlightenment, Stovall reminds us of the hierarchy of freedoms that were established on racial terms that privileged whiteness. Such discursive shaping of freedom and racism coincided with the peak of the trans-Atlantic slave trade.[42]

Alexis de Tocqueville clairvoyantly observed the phenomenon of "interest convergence," a term coined by Derrick Bell, in explaining why slavery was abolished in the North (where, he argued, there was more animosity towards Blacks), and why they maintained it in the South (where he observed that the "habits of the people are more tolerant and compassionate").[43] Abolition was not for the benefit of the Black community, Tocqueville states, but for the benefit of whites.[44] Upon reflecting on a century since the founding of the colonies, the areas without enslaved Blacks "increased in population, in wealth, and in prosperity more rapidly than those which contained many of them."[45] He stated that the difference between a state that had slavery versus those that did not was astounding. As an example, he argued that Kentucky (a former enslaving state) and Ohio were worlds apart in its growth and status, productivity of its population, and the overall well-being of the climate. The calculated economic and social benefits of abolition and emancipation—for

---

41 Lincoln, "Address at Sanitary Fair."
42 Stovall, *White Freedom*.
43 Tocqueville, *Democracy in America*, 225.
44 Tocqueville, *Democracy in America*, 225.
45 Tocqueville, *Democracy in America*, 226.

whites—outweighed enslavement. Tocqueville argued that it [abolition] even benefited the character of the white man [sic]: the white inhabitants of Ohio were more bold, entrepreneurial, resourceful, and ambitious. The whites in Kentucky, on the other hand, were described as living in "idle independence," being "combative," and being more "violent."[46] He argued a similar phenomenon to that of Bell's interest convergence: the conduct of whites towards people of color had been that of self-interest.

Racism and the labors of the infrahuman [i.e., racialized capitalism] have fed and fueled our democracy, as well as our capitalist system. While Tocqueville acknowledged that the system of slavery in America was one of the most brutal and inhumane forms of treatment he had ever witnessed, he himself objectified the enslaved and saw them as savages.[47] While he did factor the extreme inequalities between white Europeans and people of color in his analysis of American intellectual indolence and complacency to despotic rule, he was concerned about the savagery in terms of the damage it did to white people. The banality of the shepherding paradigm refers to the unconscionable horrific treatment of people of color—the ethnic Others—who were regarded as inconsequential. They are the tools of the sheep themselves, the grass on which the sheep graze. They simply exist to be the foods from which the sheep grow fat. The grass is stepped on, trampled, grazed upon spread with manure, and while they exist, there is no concern for—or acknowledgement of—their needs, except to benefit the sheep.

The concept of "grazing" in India (*meey* is the verbal root for *meeythal*) is used colloquially to articulate the management of "subordinate human flocks of various sorts."[48] Here, this term is the literal grazing of sheep (the pliable citizens of a democracy) who feed on the grass. *Meeyththal* is to lead birds, beasts, and other creatures in acts of grazing or feeding. It refers to governing, rule over, or policing and shaping of the moral character. Anand Pandian describes the derivative effects of nest damage and increased mortality due to the concomitant consumption of the caterpillars

---

46 Tocqueville, *Democracy in America*, 228–9.
47 He stated that states such as Ohio were better off financially because people were less dependent on the labor and production of enslaved Blacks, he objectifies them. Tocqueville, *Democracy in America*, 203.
48 Pandian, "Pastoral Power," 105.

by the sheep.[49] The non-thinking sheep invariably eat the invertebrate animals on the grass. Grazing management may lead to increased insect mortality, especially for life-stages such as hibernating caterpillars.

Sheep unintentionally destroy and damage hibernating caterpillars, the pupa. The larval and egg stages of the insects have less mobility and are more vulnerable to grazing. They cannot escape from their precarity as easily. Grazing can have a negative impact and cause damage to nests of hibernating caterpillars. The pupa, or hibernating caterpillar, are the entombed souls, "hindered in their natural movement, expression, and development," as W. E. B. Du Bois described early twentieth century Black life in the United States. In a Tocqueville-style analysis of the dangers of democratic demagoguery, the people of color are the invertebrate animals on the grass who are devoured by the sheep. The grazing of sheep is a metonym of Hochschild's and Bell's racial symbiosis thesis, whereby the sheep prey upon the hibernating caterpillars, the entombed souls. They need to be fattened up for the benefit and wealth of the shepherd.

Democracy feeds—grazes and grows—on the banality, the unthinking demos of racist structures that are embedded in its laws, cultures, and institutions. The grass grows in the cracks of the demos. American society is shaped by institutional racism and systemic racial discrimination, transforming, and morphing to privilege the category of whiteness. Derrick Bell argued that racism and religious discrimination are permanent components of our US society and identity formation.[50] Ethnic Others are tools for capitalist consumption.[51] The shepherd needs his [sic] sheep, the sheep that are fed by racism and the devouring of ethnic Others. It is an ongoing cycle of perpetual racism and violence.

We similarly uphold the "anomaly" thesis when desiring healing in our society without doing the ongoing work of disrupting the permanence of racism. Forgiveness is the amnesty—the amnesia of our violent past and ongoing current moment. Proponents of the anomaly thesis argue that racism can be dismantled through forms of political action. Symbiosis theorists disagree, arguing that conventional forms of political action only reinforce racism and that we need radical societal disruption. To dismantle structures, we need to transform the entire "shape and

---

49 Pandian, "Pastoral Power," 105.
50 Bell, *Faces at the Bottom*.
51 Chow, *The Protestant Ethnic*.

ecology of the American landscape."[52] The pastoral grazing by non-thinking sheep needs to be reconceptualized. It is deeply significant, indeed, that a white man like Tocqueville (who himself believed in the racial and cultural superiority of white Europeans) articulated a proto-critical race theory in observing the conditions of race relations, slavery, emancipation, forced migration and colonization of Native American lands, and the prosperity of white Europeans at the expense of infrahumans.

Tocqueville observed the inhumane, barbaric treatment towards Blacks and Native Americans as the necessary racial symbiosis that sustained and contributed to the growth and flourishing of white American equality and democracy. He stated that the physical conditions of the enslaved have been ameliorated to re-position and secure white power to benefit from the oppression. What was most problematic in American democracy, he argued, was the wielding of "their despotism and their violence against the human mind."[53] Even though the ancients kept enslaved people fettered and chained, the enslavers allowed the enslaved to engage in freedom of thought and education. Tocqueville perceived that non-thinking and societal equality that would produce pliant, docile sheep was the problem for the white American community. Equally so, the people of color were "led" by false beliefs because of white prejudices against people of color to uphold white supremacy through various forms of violence, most importantly that of psychic and epistemic violence.[54] The psychic violence is worse, states Tocqueville, than physical captivity.

As Ocean Vuong states,

All freedom is relative—you know too well—and sometimes it's no freedom at all, but simply the cage widening far away from you, the bars abstracted with distance but still there, as when they "free" wild animals into nature preserves only to contain them yet again by larger borders. But I took it anyway, that widening. Because sometimes not seeing the bars is enough.[55]

---

52 Hochschild, *The New American*, 8.
53 Tocqueville, *Democracy in America*, 246.
54 Tocqueville, *Democracy in America*, 245
55 Vuong, *On Earth*, 216.

In America, conditions and laws were maintained to deprive the enslaved from education and knowledge that circumscribed their emancipatory thinking.

Failure to think—and instead be blinded by myth and emotions—has led to forms of genocide and crimes against humanity. The banality of evil denoted the evisceration of true critical thinking to the point that crimes against humanity were occurring more and more. The masses have been manipulated and exploited, and people have become divided to create a binary/border of "us" versus "them." Humanity has become artificially divided by races (socially constructed), classes, cultures, beliefs, and hierarchies—of some being more human than others. The myths conjured by the demagogue/shepherd lead to many sheep participating in the banality—or the unthinking—of evil. The acts and policies that lead to the dehumanization of groups of people result due to pliant obedience and complicity to authority and the failure to think critically, focused solely on individual well-being.

Such lack of thinking—without seeing the consequences of the violence we instantiate towards religious and ethnic Others—also abjures the moral responsibility we have in society. Tender care for the sheep can instantaneously shift to the barbaric slaughter and commodification of people, implicating the ownership, belonging, and property of sheep to their master. The "banality of shepherding" masks the violence and depravity against wo/men,[56] LGBTIQ folk, people of color, religious ethnic Others, as well as people living with disabilities. Alexis de Tocqueville justified the segregation of wo/men and men—maintaining separate spheres of wo/men (in the home) and men (in the public sphere)—claiming that giving equal rights to wo/men and men would dilute and weaken men (i.e., white men) and degrade both sexes of "G*d-given" alleged inherent qualities.[57] Such justification of white male exceptionalism is also the arrogant claim of Samuel Huntington's American pastoral exceptionalism—that

---

56 Scholar of feminist studies in religion, Elisabeth Schüssler Fiorenza, coined the term, "wo/man." "Wo/man" underscores the limits of an essentialized or unitary category, "woman." Wo/men—or those constituted as "women" are a heterogeneous category, fragmented by multiple subject positions of race, class, religion, ethnicity, sexuality, colonialist historiography, national identity, and so on. In using the neologism, I recognize and underscore the constantly shifting positions of subjectivity, agency, and vulnerability in wo/men's lives. See Schüssler Fiorenza, *Sharing Her Word*, 186.
57 Tocqueville, *Democracy in America*, 497.

the dangers of mixing other civilizations with Western civilization would attenuate the unique society of white Christian America.[58] Huntington pointed out that the unique superiority of Western civilization was not meant to be watered down, diluted, or tainted by other cultures.

Shepherding Paradigm as Political Propaganda: Paradoxes of Freedom and Democracy

Democracy's need for racial, sexual, and class inequalities that dehumanize other groups leads me to the topic of flawed ideologies that thrive in democracies. Philosopher Jason Stanley defines a flawed ideology as "a difficult to abandon false belief the presence of which hinders the acquisition of knowledge."[59] Interestingly, democracy sets up the structures to undermine itself and cause its own destruction. The power of democracy, then, paradoxically can be its downfall. The dangers of political passivity and non-thinking in a democracy—as declared and outlined by Tocqueville and later by Hannah Arendt—stem from the lack of critical intellectual activity of the masses, overabundant trust in their leader, and the political rhetoric or propaganda that its leaders use to maintain their power. The very sources of the precarities of power that can arise in a democracy can devolve to fascist rule.

Plato, in book eight of *The Republic*, also argued that the aporias of freedom in a democracy would ultimately lead to its demise.[60] We cannot secure our freedoms unless we rethink notions of autonomy, as well as the lack of accountability or checks on power that would construct a bulwark to demagoguery. Philosopher Jason Stanley argues that the most basic problem for democracy raised by propaganda is the "possibility that the vocabulary of liberal democracy is used to mask an undemocratic reality."[61] Stanley notes how fascists paradoxically employ democracy's freedoms to attack its own liberties. He quotes Nazi propaganda minister Joseph Goebbels who stated, "[t]his will always remain one of the best jokes of democracy, that it gave its deadly enemies the means by which it was destroyed."[62] Nazism itself "performed an assault" against thinking.

---

58 Huntington, *The Clash*.
59 Stanley, *How Propaganda Works*, 199.
60 Plato, *Plato's The Republic*.
61 Stanley, *How Propaganda Works*, 11.
62 Stanley, *How Propaganda Works*.

The aporias of freedom—the myriad puzzles of discursive freedom and its entanglement with our captivity—morph and canalize the patriarchal, Anglo-Christian structures of privilege. As the shepherding metaphor invokes, national socialist ideology involves a hierarchy of race, an elite group, and the dehumanization of other groups. This is what Stanley refers to as a "flawed ideology," allowing for "effective propaganda."[63] In unjust societies, such propaganda exploits people's thinking to cause people to become irrational, see scripts of racial difference (pseudo-speciation), and lose any empathy towards our neighbors. The problem of flawed ideologies is one of the most serious concerns for a democracy.

In James Madison's Federalist Papers #10, he described the problems of factions as those passions or interests that are deleterious to democratic governance and to the interests of community. He was concerned about the rise of false ideologies because of the factions or divisions inherent in human communities. He recognized the problem of factions (the passions and interests) of citizens. He argued that factions are inherent in a democracy if we want freedom of thinking. Factions are essential to political life; they are necessary for our liberty. Differences of opinion—and our ability to manage differences—are key to democracy. The ability to maintain the equilibrium of preserving the right to form factions, at the same time, to secure people from its dangers is the greatest concern for Madison in Federalist Papers #10. The greatest threat to democracy, then, is democracy itself since there is "no cure for the mischiefs of faction."

These are the aporias of freedom and the paradoxes that lead to flawed ideologies. Government tries to protect such differences of opinion. The causes of factions cannot be extricated, but we can *manage* its influence. When a less than majority group embraces factions, it can be contained. Madison argued, "it will be unable to execute and mask its violence under the forms of the Constitution."[64] When a majority embraces such a faction, however, democracies are not equipped to deal with this problem. The majority factions cloak the violence under forms of the Constitution and is the greatest threat to our democracy. We grant power to false ideologies and its problems that are manifest as myths, lies, and non-thinking. Madison recognized that material inequality is a main

---

63 Stanley, *How Propaganda Works*, 3.
64 Hamilton, et. al, *Federalist Papers*, 80.

source of flawed ideologies. Pure democracy is impossible due to flawed ideologies, necessitating a representative democracy that safeguards against illiberal effects of flawed ideologies.

Fascism, Heroism, and the Shepherd as "American Adam"

Alexis de Tocqueville raised the problem of the unthinking, uncritical masses who would give power to political rhetoric. Such an unbridled democracy of nonthinkers ruled by administrative despotism provides the platform for fascist ideologies. In shining a light on the problem of ahistorical exceptionalism, I argue how the language of distinctiveness and difference rhetorically resonates with the language of white Christian nationalist exceptionalism and particularism that dehumanizes religious ethnic Others. Atavism was also employed in fascist ideologies, such as the search for an eternal essence or a pastoral paradise to which we could return. Political scientist and historian Zeev Sternhell notes how our imperfect social order allows us to live a "decent" life with others. At the same time, he argues that "[t]he permanence of Western civilization—the great Christian civilization—could only be ensured if its reality was not touched in its essence."[65]

Political scientist Cedric Robinson stated that the concept of "American exceptionalism" is tied to American capitalist exceptionalism during the 1920s.[66] This idea of American exceptionalism was derogatorily used by Stalin for its stalwart focus on individualism, economic freedom, and capitalism.[67] The essence of Christian superiority is tied to ideals of the exceptionalism of American liberal democracy. There were cultural ideological developments of the shepherding pastoral paradigm and the mythical ideology of the palingenesis—the rebirth or re-creation—of the American Adam, along with racist scientific theories that buttressed white Christian nationalism. This Adam was detached from its origins and was rebirthed here in the United States, where the "white" Adam's genealogy started here in the US pastoral landscape and given

---

65   Sternhell, *The Anti-Enlightenment*, 26.
66   Robinson, *Black Marxism*, 196. Robinson notes that the American Communist Party coined the phrase, "American exceptionalism."
67   McCoy, "How Joseph Stalin.'"

free range to devastate and destroy the lands, peoples, and cultures of its inhabitants.[68]

Scholars have pointed out the dangers of fascist politics and the use of myth in the desire to appeal to people's irrational state in further creating divides, divisions, and artificial "differences." Fascism has an "us-versus-them" mindset that divides us religiously, nationally, ethnically, and racially. Fascist leaders have used divisions to shape ideologies and policies, ultimately solidifying distinctions between people to create hierarchies of superiority. Fascism evokes a mythic past and heroic leader, promotes anti-intellectualism and accentuated differences between peoples, and relies on a propaganda of US exceptionalism.

Hierarchy within the shepherding model instantiates divisions whereby those being "led" are animals and the shepherd is hero-fied. As Ernst Cassirer notes of Thomas Carlyle's theory of hero worship, "The medieval form of hierarchy was changed into the modern form of 'hero-archy.' Carlyle's hero is, indeed, a transformed saint, a secularized saint."[69] Hero worship was one of the best methods of managing social and political order. Fascists stoke a desire to return to a mythic past, a time of purity (either religiously, racially, or culturally) that was tragically destroyed. Such ideas, Jason Stanley writes, were intentionally mythical and were intended to "harness the emotion of nostalgia to the central tenets of fascist ideology—authoritarianism, hierarchy, purity, and struggle."[70] Robert Ellwood notes the primacy of archetypes and myths in creating ideologies and images that support fascism and communism which are ahistorical and atavistic.

The image of the "American Adam" was a mythic national rebirth story of American culture during the 1820s–1860s.[71] It was not a single project by one writer or philosopher. Rather, the transpiring American myth that took shape in literature emerged as a "collective affair." It was an American mythical narrative that detached its story of origins from that of Europe. It was a persistent myth—not much different from the religious studies scholar, Mircea Eliade's primordial myth of the eternal

---

68 Lewis, *The American Adam.*
69 Cassirer, *The Myth of the State*, 192.
70 Stanley, *How Fascism Works*, 5.
71 Lewis, *The American Adam.*

return—as a divergence from a historical process.⁷² The image was that of a new man's (i.e., Adam's) pioneering journey, liberated from history and from the historic "evils" of the past. American Adam was an innocent Adam whose very expedition in this new country helped contour interlocking eschatological and mythical ideas of "the belief in progress toward perfection," coterminus with "a belief in a present primal perfection"—or a "primitive Adamic perfection."⁷³ The metaphor extended beyond just a mythical American Adam—it became an "image of the American as Adam."⁷⁴ The entire country was seen as an innocent, novel, pastoral playground of the white man, disconnected from its sins of the past. While historicism and a march towards the future meant progress, the past could also easily be expunged.

This origins story of the innocent "American Adam" is detached from any critical historicizing of colonial settler destruction, and instead depicts an idealized, romanticized notion of a shepherd who provides tender care for his [sic] flock of animals. The nineteenth century Harvard scientist Louis Agassiz's (1807–1873) racist theory proposed that "people of different races had descended not from a single Adam but rather from different Adams who lived in different parts of the world."⁷⁵ I point out the dangers of an "American Adam" and the racist theory of polygenesis, which stated that races were of distinctly different origins.

Benito Mussolini's ideas were similarly unsettling as was the creation of a mythic American Adam. He believed that the intentional creation of a mythic past of greatness was necessary to help support fascist ideals in the present. In other words, such myths of past glory helped to create hierarchies of subordinate/dominant structures to support and buttress fascists' beliefs in altering present realities. Such "fictions of liberation" bolstered ideas of white supremacy—whites were superior to people of color and non-Christians due to their glorious past.⁷⁶ Since it was their natural birth right, they had the right to maintain positions of superiority. Those fictions of liberation sought to erase—and give clemency to— the past sins of its nations in an obsolescence or extinguishing of any

---

72 Lewis, *The American Adam*, 5.
73 Lewis, *The American Adam*, 5.
74 Lewis, *The American Adam*, 5.
75 Gates, "Foreword," *To Make Their Own Way*, 11.
76 See Moon, "Fictions of Liberation."

wrongdoing or histories that showed otherwise. The amnesty—or amnesia–of its past wrongs was accomplished via a mythologizing of the past, just as the myth of the American Adam sought to do.

Historian of religions Mircea Eliade subscribed to the "American Adam" in his reading of R. W. B. Lewis's book, *The American Adam*.[77] Eliade invoked a similar disavowal of the past and had nostalgia for a "primordial archaic eternal return."[78] Such thinking perhaps had connections to Eliade's own desire to start anew here in the United States and grant self-clemency to the legatees of his own fascist history.[79] Eliade imagined a time of returning to a pristine past and commencing a "*novus ordo seclorum*," (a new order of the ages), and be liberated from history.[80] Thomas Jefferson had similar desires of liberation from America's past history.[81] Consequently, the phrase, *novus ordo seclorum*, was suggested by Charles Thomson in 1782 to be used on the Great Seal of the United States. It reaffirmed "the beginning of the new American Era" with the date of the Declaration of Independence.[82] By inventing such a new beginning, there was a stamp of approval for the disavowal of our country's racial violence—depicted in the 1619 Project—of the enslavement of Africans, the destruction of Native American lands, and violence that undergirded the founding of this country. It signified a new chapter of self-clemency for the violence and of forgiving and forgetting the past.

In eliciting such an image of the innocent white American Adam, a disturbing nostalgia was sought for a non-existent innocent past. The violence of our past was rejected and forgotten; it was America's unique opportunity to start anew—without the stains of original sin—in their history of violence against people of color and the land that was seized from Native Americans. The mask of clement violence was the mythical white American Adam, the shepherd of the non-thinking sheep. The idea of such a myth of eternal repetition entered Christian philosophy. Mircea Eliade argued that while time is real in Christianity, it is linear, not cyclical

---

77 Lewis, *The American Adam*.
78 Ellwood, *The Politics*, 122.
79 Ellwood, *The Politics*, 122.
80 Ellwood, *The Politics*, 123.
81 Ellwood, *The Politics*, 125.
82 The Great Seal, https://www.greatseal.com/mottoes/seclorum.html.

as it is in nature.[83] Eliade, like Henry James's thoughts on the rebirth of the American Adam, asserted the idea of a renewal, of beginning anew, as a repetition of Creation.[84] He argued that while the modern subject is bound to history and progress, there was a rupture from repetition and archetypes because paradise has been found in Christianity.[85] Eliade concludes his book, *The Myth of the Eternal Return*, by asserting, "Christianity incontestably proves to be the religion of 'fallen man.'"[86] He believed in a national, spiritual resurrection that involved a "Christian revolution of the new man."[87] He accepted the conditions of such a vision which involved antisemitism and violence.[88]

Mircea Eliade was not supportive, nor tolerant, of pluralism and saw that it [his intolerance] had to be "camouflaged" through scholarship.[89] Eliade questioned the turn towards tolerance in US academic institutions and critiqued the boundaries of "tolerant pluralism" as political propaganda that destroyed democracy. He longed for a return to a "traditional rural life and its virtues," an ideal pastoral paradise that liberated humanity from history and the past.[90] He believed there was a sacred ahistorical essence in a past time. A search for the sacred was also a tool used by fascists. He saw the United States as a place of pluralistic pragmatism but one that associated with the "primal or eschatological paradise" of which he idealized about America.

Patriarchy is an important structure in fascist political ideology. Fascist leadership needs the same paternalistic model of a father-figure deity/divine pastor leading the nation. Jason Stanley states, "The patriarchal family in fascist politics is embedded in a larger narrative about national traditions."[91] Christianity had an important role in sustaining "nationhood." In other words, bolstering white Christian nationalism supported—and was part of—the fascist agenda. In the United States, such a fascist past mythic glory relies on the very idea of clemency or

---

83   Eliade, *The Myth*, 143.
84   Eliade, *The Myth*, 157.
85   Eliade, *The Myth*, 162.
86   Eliade, *The Myth*, 162.
87   Ellwood, *The Politics of Myth*, 87.
88   Ellwood, *The Politics of Myth*, 88.
89   Ellwood, *The Politics of Myth*, 123.
90   Ellwood, *The Politics of Myth*, 123.
91   Stanley, *How Fascism Works*, 11.

amnesty (a forgetting of the past) and a forging of lies that created the myth of a new, rebirthed American Adam. Such a myth fabricated a new family, a separate genealogy of nationalism that was rooted in Christian individualism, autonomy, and individual rights. It was the androcentric white liberal subject that embodied the American Adam.

Conclusion: Some Thoughts on Neoliberal Fascism and Truth-Telling

W. E. B. Du Bois problematized the ideological myth of US exceptionalism that was constructed by inventing history as propaganda. Propaganda and lies have buttressed racialized ideologies that are not based on "science" but on the myths of ideas that were allegedly *called* science. Du Bois stated, "[b]ut in propaganda against the Negro since emancipation in this land, we face one of the most stupendous efforts the world ever saw to discredit human beings, an effort involving universities, history, science, social life and religion."[92] Soft tyranny and pastoral power as described by Tocqueville, along with the formation of white Christian nationalism, have been instrumental in shaping the neoliberal fascist society into which our US democratic society has precariously devolved.

Like Eliade, comparative religion scholar Joseph Campbell similarly praised individualism, America's past moral virtues, and its traditions.[93] He engaged in a mythification of the past and the construction of Christian heroes. As white Christian nationalism relies on myth; so too, did Campbell rely on an idealized pastoral American landscape. Joseph Campbell prided himself on not being part of the modern world, as he disengaged from current news or television. Religious studies scholar Robert Ellwood notes,

> In Campbell then we see ... an extreme and obviously idealized individualism—the assumption that the knights of capitalism would voluntarily all start equally distant from the prize.... He explained to Toby Johnson that the real danger in modern society was the threat of swamping personal freedom with concern for collective needs, which would lead the government to meddle in people's lives and cater to pressure groups.[94]

---

92 Du Bois, *Black Reconstruction*, 727.
93 Ellwood, *The Politics of Myth*, xiv.
94 Ellwood, *The Politics of Myth*, 151.

A shepherding paradigm, then, aptly describes US political pastoral power and its claim of American Christian exceptionalism.

Historian Niall Ferguson stated that the United States "is a direct descendent of the British Empire," a "dysfunctional descendant."[95] Contrary to political theorist Wendy Brown's assertion that the present-day global, politico-economic climate of neoliberal fascism is a new warped chapter of neo-liberalism from the original vision of its founders, others have argued that fascist ideologies and practices are a continuation of Western modernity.[96] Our country's recent leadership (of the years 2016–2020) of neoliberal fascist modality of governing is part of the genealogy of the British Empire's dysfunctional political empire. The Black radical intellectuals (such as W. E. B. Du Bois, C. L. R. James, Aimé Césaire, Cedric Robinson, and others) have theorized fascism, not as a deviation from the development of Western progress or civilization, but as "a logical development of Western civilization itself." Historian Robin Kelley sums up the Black radical tradition's theories regarding the intimacies of colonialism, fascism, and civilizational progress: "[t]hey viewed fascism as a blood relative of slavery and imperialism, global systems rooted not only in capitalist political economy but in racist ideologies that were already in place at the dawn of modernity."[97] Du Bois keenly observed that the objectives and methods of European colonialism were much the same as that of fascism and Nazi rule. He states,

> There was no Nazi atrocity—concentration camps, wholesale maiming and murder, defilement of women or ghastly blasphemy of childhood—which Christian civilization or Europe had not long been practicing against colored folk in all parts of the world in the name of and for the defense of a Superior Race born to rule the world.[98]

The ideas of establishing hierarchies via scripts of difference are identical strategies in fascism as it is in colonialism. The image of the polished, civilized, white European Christian man was crafted against the backdrop of the devastation wreaked in the two-thirds world via colonial

---

95 Ferguson, "American Democracy," 3.
96 Moon, "Aporia of Freedom."
97 Kelley, *Freedom Dreams*, 56.
98 Du Bois, *The World and Africa*, 23. Quoted in Kelley, *Freedom Dreams*, 56.

pillaging to distinguish against the barbaric "blood-stained bodies" of the infrahuman.[99]

Flawed ideologies continue to *maintain* the racial, sexual, spiritual equilibrium that has sustained the socio-politico-economic hierarchies and inequalities envisioned (and sustained) via liberal and neo-liberal practices and ideologies. The miasma of violence and lies has cloaked the landscape and history of our country. Our democracy and human rights are in danger of a Sisyphean slippage to fascist rule. The politician has woven his [sic] own patriarchal mythic stories of the white American Adam, the shepherd of our US exceptionalism and ahistorical timeless present. We continue to maintain our web of lies and narratives of innocence, uniqueness, and exceptionalism.

My hope is that all of us across generations—the Silent generation, the Boomers, Generation X, the Millennials, the Generation Zs, and Generation Alpha—can come together to practice truth-telling, share our stories in our communities, and weave a new cloak of justice for a healthy democratic society.

---

99 Kelley, *Freedom Dreams*, 56.

BIBLIOGRAPHY

Bell, Derrick. *Faces at the Bottom: The Permanence of Racism.* New York: Basic Books, 1992.

Bender, Thomas. "Introduction," In *Democracy in America*, Alexis de Tocqueville. Abridged and edited by Thomas Bender. New York: The Modern Library, 1981.

Butler, Judith. "Hannah Arendt's Challenge to Adolf Eichmann," August 29, 2011. https://www.theguardian.com/commentisfree/2011/aug/29/hannah-arendt-adolf-eichmann-banality-of-evil.

Cassirer, Ernst. *The Myth of the State.* New Haven, CT: Yale University Press, 1946.

Cassuto, Leonard. *The Inhuman Race: The Racial Grotesque in American Literature and Culture.* New York: Columbia University Press, 1997.

Chow, Rey. *The Protestant Ethnic & the Spirit of Capitalism.* New York: Columbia University Press, 2002.

Crensaw, Kimberlé, Neil Gotanda, Gary Peller, Kendall Thomas, eds. *Critical Race Theory: The Key Writings That Formed the Movement.* New York: The New Press, 1995.

Danielpour, Richard. "Program Notes," in "A Standing Witness," performed by Susan Graham. Executive director, Richard Danielpour, Friends of Copland House. Schwartz Center for the Performing Arts, Emory University, September 23, 2022.

Delgado, Richard, and Jean Stefancic. Critical Race Theory: An Introduction. 3rd edition. New York: New York University Press, 2017.

Du Bois, W. E. B. *Black Reconstruction in America: 1860–1880.* 3rd ed. New York: The Free Press, 1998.

———. *The World and Africa: An Inquiry into the Part Which Africa Has Played in World History.* Reprint. New York: International, 2015.

Dove, Rita. "Epilogue," in "A Standing Witness," performed by Susan Graham. Executive director, Richard Danielpour, Friends of Copland House. Schwartz Center for the Performing Arts, Emory University, September 23, 2022.

Eliade, Mircea. *The Myth of the Eternal Return: Cosmos and History.* 2nd ed. Princeton, NJ: Princeton University Press, 2005.

Ellwood, Robert. *The Politics of Myth: A Study of C.G. Jung, Mircea Eliade, and Joseph Campbell.* Albany, NY: SUNY Press, 1999.

Ferguson, Niall. "American Democracy: The Perils of Imperialism?" In *America at Risk: Threats to a Liberal Self-Government in an Age of Uncertainty*. Edited by Robert Faulkner and Susan Shell, 29–56. Ann Arbor, MI: The University of Michigan Press, 2009.

Foucault, Michel. *Security, Territory, Population: Lectures at the College de France, 1977–1978*. Edited by Michel Senellart. Translated by Graham Burchell. New York: Palgrave, 2007.

Gates, Henry Louis, Jr. "Foreword: Who Are These People?" In *To Make Their Own Way in the World: The Enduring Legacy of the Zealy Daguerreotypes*, edited by Ilisa Barbash, Molly Rogers, and Deborah Willis, 9–13. Cambridge, MA: Peabody Museum, 2020.

Gilroy, Paul. *Suffering and Infrahumanity: The Tanner Lectures on Human Values*. https://tannerlectures.utah.edu/_resources/documents/a-to-z/g/Gilroy%20manuscript%20PDF.pdf.

Hamilton, Alexander, James Madison, and John Jay. *The Federalist Papers*. Edited by Clinton Rossiter. New York: Penguin Books, 1961.

Hochschild, Jennifer L. *The New American Dilemma: Liberal Democracy and School Segregation*. New Haven, CT: Yale University Press, 1984.

Huntington, Samuel P. *The Clash of Civilizations and the Remaking of World Order*. New York: Simon & Schuster, 1996.

Jung, Moon-Ho. *Coolies and Cane: Race, Labor, and Sugar in the Age of Emancipation*. Baltimore, MD: Johns Hopkins University Press, 2006.

Kelley, Robin D. G. *Freedom Dreams: The Black Radical Imagination*. Boston, MA: Beacon Press, 2003.

Lewis, R. W. B. *The American Adam: Innocence, Tragedy, and Tradition in the Nineteenth Century*. Chicago: The University of Chicago Press, 1959.

Lincoln, Abraham. "Address at Sanitary Fair, Baltimore, MD. April 18, 1864." *Collected Works of Abraham Lincoln*. https://quod.lib.umich.edu/l/lincoln/lincoln7/1:665?rgn=div1;singlegenre=All;sort=occur;subview=detail;type=simple;view=fulltext;q1=april+18+1864. Quoted in Jamelle Bouie, "What Does 'White Freedom,' Really Mean?" December 17, 2021. https://www.nytimes.com/2021/12/17/opinion/freedom-liberty-racial-hierarchies.html.

McCoy, Terrence M. "How Joseph Stalin Invented 'American Exceptionalism.'" March 15, 2012. https://www.theatlantic.com/politics/archive/2012/03/how-joseph-stalin-invented-american-exceptionalism/254534/.

McGhee, Heather. *The Sum of Us: What Racism Costs Everyone and How We Can Prosper Together*. New York: One World, 2021.

Moon, Hellena. "Aporias of Freedom and the Immured Spirit," In *Postcolonial Images of Spiritual Care: Challenges of Care in a Neoliberal Age*, edited by Emmanuel Y. Lartey and Hellena Moon, 169–89. Eugene, OR: Pickwick, 2020.

———. "Fictions of Liberation: A Paradoxical 'Palimpsest of Colonial Identity' of *Chŏng (Jeong)*." *Journal of Pastoral Theology* 28, no. 3 (2018) 160–174.

———. *Liberalism and Colonial Violence: Charting a New Genealogy of Spiritual Care*. Eugene, OR: Wipf & Stock Publishers, December 2022.

Okihiro, Gary. *Margins and Mainstreams: Asians in American History and Culture*. Seattle: University of Washington Press, 1994.

Pandian, Anand. "Pastoral Power in the Postcolony: On the Biopolitics of the Criminal Animal in South India," *Cultural Anthropology* 23, no. 1 (2008) 85–117.

Plato, *Plato's The Republic*. New York: Vintage Books, 1961.

Robinson, Cedric J. *Black Marxism: The Making of the Black Radical Tradition*. 2nd ed. Chapel Hill, NC: University of North Carolina Press, 2000.

———. *The Terms of Order: Political Science and the Myth of Leadership*. Albany, NY: SUNY Press, 1980.

Schüssler Fiorenza, Elisabeth. *Sharing Her Word: Feminist Biblical Interpretation in Context*. Boston: Beacon Press, 1999.

Stanley, Jason. *How Fascism Works: The Politics of Us and Them*. New York: Random House, 2018.

Sternhell, Zeev. *The Anti-Enlightenment Tradition*. New Haven, CT: Yale University Press, 2009.

Stovall, Tyler. *White Freedom: The Racial History of an Idea*. Princeton, NJ: Princeton University Press, 2021.

Tocqueville, Alexis de. *Democracy In America*. Abridged and edited by Thomas Bender. New York: The Modern Library, 1981.

Vuong, Ocean. *Night Sky with Exit Wounds*. Port Townsend, WA: Copper Canyon, 2016.

3

Are Queers Dangerous?
What I wish I Had Known about the Intersections of Race, Gender, Class, and Sexuality in High School

Sig/Sara Giordano

When I was twenty years old, I took a women's studies course in college as an elective. I was a physics and math major and later went on to earn a PhD in Neuroscience. My mind and body were changed in that class forever. The night after we read Adrienne Rich's "Compulsory Heterosexuality and Lesbian Existence,"[1] I kissed a woman for the first time. I had spent time—like many of us did around the turn of the twenty-first century—trying to figure out the "truth" about my sexuality. Popular lore, along with basic biology lessons, told us that sexuality was an innate feature in animals. Politically you could fall on two sides both stemming from this same base assumption—on one side you could believe that all animals were meant to be "straight," and that "homosexuality" was unnatural. This perspective aligned with an idea of nature where God (Christian) determined what was natural or not. On the other side, you could believe that sexuality was diverse, and it was natural to have hetero and homosexual types of animals within each species. The latter was the so-called progressive viewpoint at that time. However, what Rich's article and that class gave me was the beginning of a third way of thinking about sexuality. This third way began from the premise that ***sexuality is a socially constructed category***. With this new approach, I could abandon the search for my innate biological truth. Over the next decade, my understanding of what this meant went beyond Rich's article—challenging its assumptions about the universality of sex/gender that missed the role of racism and coloniality, unintentionally furthering ideas of "natural" types even as it dispelled the idea of the naturalness of heterosexuality.

---

1 Rich, "Compulsory Heterosexuality."

In this chapter, I write about sexuality from a feminist science studies perspective. I interweave my personal story of understanding sexuality with critical histories of sexuality through the work of feminist, Black, decolonial, and queer studies scholars. I trace relationships between sex/gender and sexuality and how they developed through colonial sciences together with concepts of race and ability. Understanding sexuality as a socially constructed category that organizes our capitalist society together with race, gender, and ability had a big impact on not only my day-to-day life and how I structure my relationships/community, but also on my activist commitments. I am not alone in coming into my own queer identity through political education. Queer activism, queer identities, and lived experiences have intersected for decades.

This chapter also focuses on how our understandings of queerness as a challenge to white, capitalist, heteronormative structures have helped to build activist communities where critical biology lessons are shared and developed. It was in activist communities that I first learned that gender and sex were not "naturally" binary categories. It was also in activist community where I learned about how important eugenic science was (and is) to how inequalities are justified based on ideas of better and worse genetic traits and types of people. Therefore, some of the most important biology lessons I learned happened beyond Biology classrooms—in women's (women's, gender, sexuality) studies classrooms and in activist workshops and informal relationships where books and knowledges were shared among comrades. I wish I and others knew what I know now about sexuality when I was in high school. I see what worlds queers are building within this one, and I can only imagine what beautiful queer experiments could proliferate if we taught these lessons in high school biology classes.

Learning about Compulsory Heterosexuality at the Turn of the Twenty-First Century

I went through high school at a time (mid–1990s) when being gay was beginning to be an acceptable identity in the US mainstream. This does not mean there were not gay cultures and politics in the United States before this—there definitely were;[2] nor does it mean homophobia and

---

2 Mattson, "Stonewall Riots."

heterosexism were about to end. Gay activism in the United States against medical treatment in the 1970s[3] and around HIV in the 1980s and early 1990s[4] brought gay identity out in new ways. My world, however, was pretty straight growing up. There was an older "cousin" who came alone to holiday dinners. Questions about his sexuality were not so subtly whispered about so that at an early age I inferred that there was something potentially deviant about him. While it was clear, in my straight world, that the matter was to be kept quiet, I was less sure whether I should fear him or feel bad for him. As a pre-teen, I once again heard whispers around the house about a group of men who had just moved to the neighborhood. Gay men in a group were more of a threat than one family member who kept his sexuality appropriately quiet. But more so, these men were white and wealthier than many neighbors thereby representing my first look at gentrifiers. This enmeshed gay identity with the racist, classist phenomenon of gentrification that I could righteously abhor. Despite my family's upward class mobility and whiteness, I considered myself politically allied closely with my neighborhood's identity which population-wise was poor/working class, the majority of whom were people of color. I also learned over time that the inclusion into whiteness and class mobility for my family were strongly linked. While this meant that it was easier for me to "escape" the neighborhood, I was able to understand that my neighborhood was subject to environmental injustice, over-policing, and other forms of violence because of racism.

So what evidence do I have that out gay identities were entering the mainstream in the United States in a new way in the mid-nineties? Well, in 1997 Ellen DeGeneres made history by coming out on her television sitcom and then in real life at the same time. While there had been other gay and lesbian characters on television and in movies, as well as other celebrities coming out in the 1990s (e.g., Elton John, Melissa Etheridge, k.d. lang, George Michael), this particular "coming out" has been used as a marker of the larger shift in cultural politics.[5] It was shocking—perhaps only to me and other straight people who were fully invested in the norms of the day. The next week, I stopped watching her sitcom, *Ellen*, to allay suspicions that I, myself, might be a lesbian. This fear was not

---

3 Lewis, "'We Are Certain.'"
4 Epstein, *Impure Science*.
5 Dow, "Ellen;" Skerski, "From Prime-Time;" Reed, "The Three Phases."

imagined; my brother chased me around the house calling me a lesbian directly linking his accusation to my loving the show *Ellen* and wearing pants instead of a dress or skirt to a formal event. I was invested in my straightness and did not want to leave any evidence to the contrary. I was not the only one uncomfortable with *Ellen* post-coming out. The show only lasted one more season before being canceled. However, Ellen went on to become the most visibly identifiable lesbian and her career took off in the aftermath of the original show cancellation.[6]

This was the backdrop to entering college in 1997. A few of my friends began to identify as bisexual or gay. However, practically no one was out at the rather conservative majority white liberal arts college I attended. By the turn of the twenty-first century, I had a college boyfriend and was enrolled in my first women's studies class to fulfill a general education requirement. This is when I first came across the concept of compulsory heterosexuality.

But how can reading an article change one's sexuality?

I write this chapter in the midst of right-wing attacks on critical and social justice teaching in K–16 classrooms.[7] While some might argue that the conservative premise that teaching about queer sexualities are safe because they cannot "make" someone gay, I take a different approach here. What I think conservatives have correct is that the kind of knowledge we pass on to our children and each other matters a lot for who we are and can become.

What I mean is this: if we start to learn about systems of race, gender, nation, sexuality, ability, etc. as socially and historically constructed, we may begin to ask more questions about why and how these categories gained importance and remain so important in our society. We may ask why these categories are so highly regulated. Why are we told we are naturally one or the other? Why do we have to choose a binary gender? Why are we assigned a binary sex at birth? We may further interrogate *how the regulation of sex/gender leads to the production of heterosexuality and what that regulation has to do with other systems of power.* After asking the "why" and "how" about these categories of difference, we may start *imagining and dreaming together about what else could be possible.*

---

6 Dow, "Ellen;" Skerski, "From Prime-Time;" Reed, "The Three Phases."
7 Friedman and Tager, "Educational Gag Orders."

When I read Rich's "Compulsory Heterosexuality and Lesbian Existence," I identified as a feminist. If asked, I think I would have without consternation identified as a heterosexual woman. Part of the power of her essay is that she spoke directly to heterosexual women. She states,

> To take the step of questioning heterosexuality as a "preference" or "choice" for women—and to do the intellectual and emotional work that follows—will call for a special quality of courage in heterosexually identified feminists but I think the rewards will be great: a freeing-up of thinking, the exploring of new paths, the shattering of another great silence, new clarity in personal relationships.[8]

With great rewards promised, why wouldn't I be moved to give it a shot? I say this only partially in jest. The promise of feeling freer, feeling more connected to women, and having more (sexual) fun was a part of my excitement about the article. As a feminist, the idea of doing liberatory work for myself and all women was also quite compelling. Here she was flipping the script, instead of asking whether 'homosexuality' was natural and why some people were gay, she asked what made women heterosexual? Was it really a preferred choice? Was it natural and inevitable? Rich's main points are the following:

1. the assumption that heterosexuality is a natural preference for most women is false,
2. that to maintain this "lie" great violence and coercion has been used against women to force marriage to men as a societal norm,
3. the existence of resistance and joy among women has always existed,
4. the denial of this existence which she calls the "lesbian continuum" is part of how heterosexuality's dominance is maintained.

Rich calls on all feminists to interrogate the assumption that "in [any] context ... women would choose heterosexual coupling and marriage."[9] After all, she asks, if heterosexuality were so natural, **why has**

---
8 Rich, "Compulsory Heterosexuality," 648.
9 Rich, "Compulsory Heterosexuality," 633.

such violence been necessary to enforce it? She points to "constraints and sanctions" such as witch-hunts and killings, economic dependence of women based on gendered divisions of labor, religious and political laws, and the science of gender/sex/sexuality.

While, as a nineteen- or twenty-year-old, I may have been preoccupied by challenging the physical connection that I now felt had been denied to me, the point of the article is more significant than suggesting that women having sex with other women will bring liberation. The lesbian continuum, she describes, includes relationships between women from mother–daughter to friendships to shared political activism to sexual and/or romantic. This definition has power to thus challenge the structures that keep women in a subservient role to men by working together, enjoying time alone and together to find new ways to get our needs and desires met. With this new approach to sexuality, I was able to both enjoy my body and others in new ways AND to "recognize and stud[y]" heterosexuality as "a political institution."[10]

How do we change our orientation to sexuality to study it as a political institution instead of a biological fact? I suggest here that we use feminist science studies to understand that Biology itself is a political institution. I use a capital B for Biology here to distinguish the institution of Biology which has claimed itself as the most legitimate way to know our bodies and environments from other ways of knowing. This Biology is based on the idea that its knowledge is universal and ahistorical. Biology, however, was only institutionalized over the last two hundred years. I will use lowercase biology or biologies to acknowledge that there have always been competing (often marginalized) knowledges challenging Biology's absolute truths and to leave open possibilities for multiple, context-specific ways of knowing ourselves and worlds.

Does **Wearing Pants to a Formal Make Me a Lesbian???**

Over time, I understood that a key piece of Rich's and other lesbian feminists' insights was premised on the idea that gender and sexuality were intertwined. It seems obvious to me now; our terms/definitions of various sexualities continue to be based on what we understand as possible genders/sexes. Sexologists in the nineteenth century could not

---

10   Rich, "Compulsory Heterosexuality," 637.

have developed the idea of homosexuality without the idea of two sexes. Homosexuality meaning same-sex attraction and heterosexuality meaning opposite sex attraction. Bisexuality developed within this binary gender system as well, and newer definitions such as pansexuality still rely on gender/sex even if the latter sees gender/sex as multiplicitous.

In 2022, US legislators proposed and sometimes succeeded in passing state legislation limiting public accessibility and participation for trans kids and adults (e.g., bathroom and sports teams bans).[11] This political backlash against trans and nonbinary genders must be understood as deeply connected to the fear that the heterosexuality/homosexuality binary will be rendered unintelligible. The connection between these has been described as the heterosexual matrix[12] where your assigned sex (female/male) is supposed to determine your gender (girl, woman/boy, man) and in turn determines your sexual attraction to the opposite sex/gender pairing. If the naturalness and stability of the pairings at the heart of the matrix are disturbed, we can see how (hope that) the whole matrix may fall apart. Sex is assigned at birth by the attending physician based on looking at a newborn's genitals. There is an assumption that there are two sexes—female or male—despite longstanding medical evidence that a spectrum of bodily differences fits our variation better than a binary. The assumption continues that one's genitals will match so-called sex chromosomes and secondary sex characteristics (e.g., hair patterns on one's body and breast size). When either someone's genitals do not fit neatly in one or the other box or a lack of correspondence between genitals, chromosomes, and hormones is revealed, the person is considered to be intersex. While intersex activists have fought for bodily autonomy,[13] intersex people, in the US as well as in many other nations, are subjected to surgeries and medical interventions.[14]

While Rich insightfully challenged the naturalness of heterosexuality, her work left the category of female/women itself mostly intact and self-evident. Therefore, there was a universalism that assumed all women across race, class, ability, etc. experienced and participated in heterosexuality in the same ways and that this category of sex/gender was itself

---

11 Lopez, "Anti-Transgender;" Burns, "Massive Republican."
12 Butler, *Gender Trouble*.
13 Chase, "Hermaphradites with Attitude."
14 Wall, "Standing at the Intersections," 117–19.

natural. To better understand the construction of sexuality, we must interrogate the idea of binary sex/gender[15] itself.

The idea of sexual dimorphism—that female and male bodies represent two distinct, complementary types of people—became "fact" through the field of Biology in the nineteenth century. The sciences of sexual difference were entangled with the creation of other biological-social categories of difference such as race, sexuality, class, and ability. Two somewhat competing ideas about sex existed as Biology developed into an alleged objective field of study. One was that all beings were on a hierarchical system, with white men at the top, and white women were thought to be less evolved/lower beings sometimes analogous to or slightly above non-white men with non-white women below (if acknowledged at all).[16] This followed from the pre-scientific, Christian idea of the Great Chain of Being where all matter was thought to be organized in a hierarchical order. White men were closest to God within the category of human, and so-called lower races linked humans to the next category of animals. However, the idea of sexual dimorphism which became dominant in Biology, placed white men and white women as complementary beings, thereby also setting up the idea of heterosexuality as normative.

---

15 I am conflating sex/gender here on purpose. The distinction between sex and gender was introduced by psychologists in the mid-20th century setting the stage for some feminists to take it up in the following decades (Rubin, "An Unnamed Blank," 883-908). The idea was to split the social produced aspects and the "real" physical/biological aspects of sex/gender. However, critical scholars and activists quickly challenged the usefulness and accuracy of the sex/gender distinction (Rubin, "An Unnamed Blank," 883-908). Splitting sex/gender into a supposedly natural or biological part (sex) and a social dimension (gender) obscures the way that both are socially constructed, thereby leaving out how Biological and Medical truths are also politically and historically contingent. The illogic of splitting the two quickly becomes clear when we try to separate out what exactly are biological/physical parts and which are social/political? For example, when someone trains for a sport and begins to produce more testosterone, is that a biological or social change? Choosing to exercise seems to be a social choice, however testosterone levels are considered biological. Or when a doctor examines a newborn's genitals and assigns them to either female or male, is that a biological characteristic or a social characteristic? What if the newborn's genitals do not clearly fit in the two options given and the physician performs surgery to make the baby's body fit in to the socially prescribed binary? What about when someone practices speaking with a more typically characteristic male or female voice or walking with a different swagger, are those social or biological changes? Have they changed their sex or gender?

16 Markowitz, "Pelvic Politics;" Stepan, "Race and Gender."

Evolutionary ideas about racial differences were proven in part (cyclically) through the demonstration that so-called lower races exhibited no (or less) sexual dimorphism within their race.[17] That is, the idea of complementary gender was based on white body norms. European scientists and explorers/colonialists worked together to claim that non-white bodies did not show distinct sexed bodies and therefore "proved" that these people as a group were less evolved. Of course, the very idea of splitting people into two distinct sexed kinds of bodies had been created by Europeans only recently and reinforced scientifically and culturally. One way to reinforce these new norms about sex and sexuality was through the threat of comparison to non-white races. Therefore, we have to understand the categories of female/woman vs. male/men as always raced.[18] This point has been made over and over throughout the last several decades by women of color and specifically Black feminists, most well-known through the concept of intersectionality.[19] However, conversations about intersectionality in the mainstream often do not fully interrogate how categories of difference were co-created historically and importantly through biological thought.[20] The idea that the truth of our differences can be found in biology continues to be a powerful belief. Here I argue that it is indeed true that our differences are based in Biology, but not in the sense of our differences being natural and unchanging, instead in the understanding that our differences were *produced through* the field of Biology, which was and is a historical, social, economic, and political production. How would we understand our differences differently if we learned about this history of Biology in our Biology classes?

The Rise of Biology: Locating Sexuality in Our Bodies

I first learned about Biology as a historically and politically situated institution through lessons shared by activists, in a public teach-in. The now defunct Committee on Women, Population, and the Environment (CWPE) was presenting. They defined themselves as "a multi-racial

---

17 Markowitz, "Pelvic Politics."
18 Hammonds, "Black (W)holes;" Higginbotham, "Metalanguage of Race;" Bailey and Stallings, "Metalanguage of Sexuality;" Lugones, "Heterosexualism."
19 Crenshaw, "Demarginalizing the Intersection;" Cho, Crenshaw, and McCall, "Intersectionality Studies."
20 Hamilton, Subramaniam, and Willey, "What Indians Can Teach."

alliance of "feminist community organizers, scholarly activists, and health practitioners committed to promoting the social and economic empowerment of women in a context of global peace and justice; and to eliminating poverty."[21] Through their praxis, they brought together issues of environmental, reproductive, and economic justice showing how these spheres were already interrelated and arguing that therefore, they must be challenged together. The teach-in was open to everyone—free education is possible! Through the specific workshop I attended, CWPE broke down the science of eugenics explaining the intersections of race, sex/gender, and sexuality with Biology.

I may have heard the term eugenics before, but I had not really understood its premises. After all, I should have known something about eugenics since my maternal grandparents were survivors of the Nazi Holocaust in which the rest of their immediate family members were killed for being Jewish. However, as German Jewish (and Italian immigrants), my family's racial categorization changed in the United States so that by the time I was born, we were considered white without question.[22] Some of the important lessons I learned—or began to learn—that day were that eugenics was not created by the Nazis. There was much intersection between US, British, and German scientists and policies in the late nineteenth and early twentieth centuries.[23] Eugenics was a respected science at that time in Europe and the United States. The basis of eugenics was the following: 1) there were different natural types of people, 2) there was something in our bodies that made us (these kinds of people) called "genes," and 3) we passed on genes through reproduction.

Following from this foundation of eugenics was that a society could control more and less desirable population level traits by controlling who reproduced. This led to both positive and negative eugenics—with positive eugenics meaning encouragement for "desirable" women and men to partner and reproduce more, and negative eugenics in which

---

21 See the website, https://www.sourcewatch.org/index.php/Committee_on_Women,_Population,_and_the_Environment.
22 My grandparents and their families were immigrants. See Brodkin, *How Jews Became White*; Roediger, *Working Toward Whiteness* for historical contextualization of how the racial categorization of the groups my family identifies with changed over time.
23 Kuhl, *The Nazi Connection*.

"undesirable" women and men were discouraged or forcibly stopped from reproducing.[24] Of course, we can see in retrospect how ideas of what kind of people were deemed to be desirable or undesirable were racist, classist, and ableist—all clearly politically determined. What I began to understand from this political education was that our dominant ideas about differences today is a legacy of these past ideas. And importantly, that today our dominant scientific ideas are also biased based on socio-cultural-political ideas. It may be challenging for us to see how historically and culturally specific our scientific ideas are today because we are so immersed in dominant cultural ideas. Our challenge, therefore, is to analyze our current knowledge systems to see what kind of cultural values are embedded.

Eugenics is one clear example of how sexuality is always raced by being tied up in ideas of racial "purity" in the interest of protecting the Nation.[25] Besides directly controlling people's ability to reproduce, these ideas impacted—and were impacted by—marriage laws in terms of who could marry or not. The prohibition on interracial marriage had previously been bolstered by various biological theories; for example, some scientists had previously argued that people of different races represented wholly different species and were unable to reproduce together.[26] Eugenics represented another biological argument for stopping interracial marriages. Eugenics further entrenched the idea of racialized heterosexuality as natural. Single mothers were deemed to be unfit to reproduce and raise children, while the optimal family structure was reinforced as white property-owning men and women living with a gendered division of productive/reproductive labor. Homosexuality, therefore, was also a trait

---

24 Control over reproduction did not always mean limiting non-white reproduction. For example, as I come back to later, during US slavery maintaining an enslaved population to work relied in part on forcing currently enslaved people to reproduce and increasing the size of the working classes has often been important to maintain enough workers that capitalists have surplus labor. Therefore, while eugenics represents one way reproduction was controlled, at different times and under different contexts the same groups of people may have been encouraged or forced to reproduce. The balance between creating the needed number of laborers and the fear of being overtaken by oppressed people who outnumber the elite is one that is often being managed. An example of this control today can be seen in Western immigration policies that act to maintain a vulnerable workforce.
25 Ordover, *American Eugenics.*
26 McWhorter, "Enemy of the Species."

to be eradicated as it challenged the desired racialized, gendered relations (heteronormative family structure). This means that homosexuality became located in one's body, and therefore *became* (biological) "truth."[27] Proper heterosexual pairing, made up of the proper sexually dimorphic couple (read: white, monied), was also thought to be an evolutionarily more advanced way of structuring relationships. The late twentieth century is also when the idea of "love" as biological capacity emerged as a European bourgeois marker of the proper heterosexual relationship.[28]

Today in the twenty-first century, how do you determine your sexuality? In modern terms we think of sexuality as a kind of attraction that we have. We often imagine this attraction to be biological, as in "located in our bodies (and therefore natural)," as in "unchangeable and something with which we are born." We also hear that everyone should have the right to "love" whomever you want. These ideas are often thought of as a progressive view and justification for gay rights.

After my brief review here of how European scientists, politicians, and other elite members of society came to understand proper and improper kinds of sexuality by locating sexual desire in one's body and as part of the matrices of racial and gendered belonging, we might want to reconsider the assumptions behind sexuality today. Many have critiqued liberal impulses to find a so-called "gay gene" which happened at the turn of the century and the claim that queers are "born this way" as justification for deserving rights, as well as physical and emotional safety. The concern is that while some queer people may begin to be included as "acceptable" members of society, other people (of all sexualities) will continue to be excluded because the criteria itself has not been challenged. But why is it so important for differences to be created and reinforced? Some have answered this by relying once again on the recent advent of Biology to claim that seeing difference and being in opposition to those who are "different" than you are natural and have always happened. What we have seen here, however, is that some very specific differences were produced—regarding sex, race, sexuality, ability—in the last few hundred years. Once we understand Biology itself as a rather new social invention and as historically located, we may be implored to ask more questions

---

27 Foucault, "Sexuality, Volume 1."
28 Markowitz, "Pelvic Politics."

about why the production of supposedly natural biological differences was and perhaps is so important? Going back to Rich's article on compulsory heterosexuality, I suggest we delve further into understanding the creation and maintenance of heterosexuality as a political institution.

Before, I delve further into this question, I go back to Ellen DeGeneres's public coming out as an example of how race and sexuality continue to be interrelated. As part of the lead-up to Ellen DeGeneres's TV character's confessional coming out, she was interviewed by various news outlets and talk show hosts. In one notable interview in 1996 with comedian and talk show host Rosie O'Donnell (who herself came out "officially" in 2002), they both jokingly talked about their coming out and their own sexualities without ever saying the words lesbian or gay.[29] DeGeneres responds to O'Donnell's question about rumors of a big reveal on the *Ellen* show,

> We do find out that the character is Lebanese... There have been clues. I mean, you've seen her eating baba ghanoush, if you've watched the show at all, and hummus, and [she's] a big, big fan of Casey Kasem.[30]

In response, O'Donnell says,

> "Hey, wait a minute. I'm a big fan of Casey Kasem ... Maybe I'm Lebanese!"

DeGeneres acts as a witness to the presentation of evidence, confirming that she has suspected that O'Donnell might be Lebanese as well. Here I go back to this important moment in my own and arguably US gay politics,[31] to ask why this play on words worked so well. On the surface, the idea of just finding out that one is a particular nationality or ethnicity, might be funny for its ridiculousness because one should know their cultural background and it should be evident to others.

By understanding the history of biology as I have laid it out here, we see that there are some long lasting intersections between the idea of natural categories of race/ethnicity and sexuality. The rise of biological ideas of both race and sexuality set the stage for the "truth" of each to be something that can be discovered and that may be located in one's body. The signs may be there without you even realizing at first, as the two

---

29 Sieczkowski, "Rosie O'Donnell Reveals."
30 Degeneres, "The Ellen Degeneres Show."
31 Dow, "Ellen, Television."

comedians jest with one another. We often hear "evidence" of someone's gayness after (or before) someone comes out. For example, parents might say something like, 'I always knew' because my boy did not like cars or some other reference to a failure at proper gendered performance. I suggest that this joke works well because of the tension between both the similarities and differences between race/nationality and sexuality.

The comparison in part is made to establish that being gay is just as natural and self-evident as one's nationality. But it also is notable that the nationality in question, Lebanese, has been racialized as "Other." Orientalism as a part of white supremacy has set up Arab people as both exotic and dangerous.[32] At that time in the 1990s through this decade (2020s), the United States has used the idea of Arab people as "terrorists" to wage war on the region. Therefore, DeGeneres also contrasts her kind of gayness as appropriate (read: white) with racialized otherness.[33] Ellen DeGeneres in her coming out, established over and over that gayness was safe and acceptable.[34] A key way that she brought certain kinds of gay identity into the mainstream was by distancing from political queers[35] and asserting her inclusion in consumer culture as an upstanding US citizen of financial means.[36] Her whiteness and her class position became deeply connected, essentially making her sexuality non-deviant. Next, I go back to the question of why justifying differences as natural has been so important in European history and specifically look at the economic structuring of society.

What Does Capitalism Have to Do with Who I love?

Marriage, which is clearly a political institution because its rules are determined by the State, has been a central place where heated debates over sexuality have taken place in the last few decades. In supposedly progressive, liberal terms, marriage is argued to be a personal choice about love. If marriage is primarily about this, would it matter whether there was legal confirmation of one's relationship or not? In the United States, arguments for state-sanctioned marriage for all have often revolved

---

32 Said, *Orientalism*; Smith, "Heteropatriarchy."
33 Bociurkiw, "It's Not About the Sex."
34 Bociurkiw, "It's Not About the Sex."
35 Dow, "Ellen, Television."
36 Bociurkiw, "It's Not About the Sex."

around the financial benefits that one can legally claim if married (e.g., health insurance and retirement benefits). Such benefits are important of course since it impacts our ability to live and thrive. Importantly, these are tied to employment. Queer critics of the push for extending marriage benefits to gay couples have asked, "what about people who are not in a romantic relationship?" Or "what about people who are in romantic relationships but neither have a job that offers these benefits?" Instead, many queer activists have called for fighting for healthcare and social support for all throughout our lifespans.[37]

While one might choose to get married today in the name of love, the institution of marriage has not been—as I argued above—primarily about love, nor about sexual pleasure. Besides health insurance and other legal economic possibilities that open up for married people, coupling even without marriage (or even monogamy)[38] in modern society has a lot to do with our economic system. When one couples, it often means an eventual sharing of resources. This may begin with one person paying for the other's dinners, it may lead to sharing an apartment, buying a home, a car, and other shared property. In the United States in 2020, less than half of households consisted of married couples with this figure steadily declining over the last few decades,[39] and a growing number of people are not living in romantic relationships at all.[40] The idea of heterosexual pairing, therefore, is more of an ideal than a normal practice. Whether married, coupled, or single, over one third of people living in the United States still do not own their own home with continuing racial disparities favoring white home ownership.[41] A majority struggle to pay medical bills causing many to cut back on other basic necessities, go into bankruptcy, and/or make other sacrifices.[42] The idea of economic stability, therefore, is also an ideal that most will not be able to reach in the US. As one of the

---

37 Conrad, *Against Equality*; Bernstein, *That's Revolting!*
38 Willey, *Undoing Monogamy*.
39 Chamie, "The End of Marriage in America?"
40 Fry and Parker, "Rising Share."
41 Fry, "Amid a Pandemic," reports an increase in home ownership with continuing racial disparities during the pandemic. It is unlikely that increased homeownership will continue with widening wealth inequalities during the pandemic (Weller, "Wealth Inequality"). Also, the homeownership gap between white and Black Americans has widened in the last decades (Ray et al., "Homeownership").
42 Palosky and Singh, "New Kaiser/New York Times Survey."

wealthiest countries in the world, the global prospects are not promising. How then is it possible that we continue to believe this ideal is possible or even desirable?

To better understand the staying power of an ideal that is unattainable to the vast majority, we must ask where this modern system that ties economic benefits, childbearing and rearing, and sex/gender together through sexuality originates. The specific system I have described was imposed in Europe over centuries and much struggle during the transition from feudalism to capitalism.[43] The modern gender system relied on the production of another side to contrast against this system—I refer to the way gender was developed (or not) through colonization:

> Colonialism did not impose precolonial, European gender arrangements on the colonized. It imposed a new gender system that created very different arrangements for colonized males and females than for white bourgeois colonizers. Thus, it introduced many genders and gender itself as a colonial concept and mode of organization of relations of production, property relations, of cosmologies and ways of knowing.[44]

The modern gender system was forced on European women through laws (e.g., only allowing men to own property), witch-hunts, killings of women (who lived alone or in community with other women), and theft of land (closing in of formerly commonly accessible land).[45] These methods together enclosed what was in some places, and now more broadly, called "the Commons." This took away most people's ability to grow or gather one's own food or build safe shelter across Europe. The theft of this land created a more clearly stratified society that was dependent on the hierarchical relationship of capitalists/workers. Workers had to labor for wages to then buy basic necessities from capitalists who had taken control over the raw materials necessary for the production of food, shelter, etc. Women and men had prescribed relationships within this structure so that the productive labor (wage-labor) was men's responsibility and reproductive labor (caring for men and children, in addition to oneself) was women's responsibility. Physical reproduction was extra

---

43 Federici, *Caliban and the Witch*.
44 Lugones, "Heterosexualism," 186.
45 Federici, *Caliban and the Witch*.

important to maintain a workforce during this time because of the many deaths caused by the "Black Plague."

The colonial side of the gender system was both different than—and necessary for—the creation and maintenance of the larger globalized system of capitalism.[46] The concept of racial capitalism may be useful here in understanding that, "[c]apital can only be capital when it is accumulating, and it can only accumulate by producing and moving through relations of severe inequality among human groups."[47] Naturalizing inequalities through the category of race was and is critical for the production and maintenance of the capitalist system. Remember that colonized people were determined to be lacking both biological sexual dimorphism and appropriate heterosexual cultural norms such as the affective capability to fall in love.[48] This cast colonized people as primitive or behind the progress of Europeans. Racialized colonial difference, therefore, provided justification for the violence of Europeans against colonized people. This included genocide, land theft, and enslavement. Sometimes the violence could be justified through the logics that colonized people were not human and therefore not granted liberal humanist protections and autonomy. At the same time, there was the paternalistic, seemingly benevolent, position which acted to "teach" colonized people how to be modern subjects. Through the assumption that European culture was the most advanced and progressive, various diverse kinds of gender/sexuality were eliminated around the globe.

The idea that European bourgeois systems of gender/sexuality were the most advanced has often been challenged although new waves of belief in the supremacy of Western gender/sexuality continue today. Despite the erasure of many histories and cultural systems through colonization, ample evidence has been gathered to show that gender/sex as we know it today was not a universal distinction. There are examples of many societies that were not organized around gender/sex divisions at all and that did not even have ideas of binary sex/gender based on anatomy.[49] Therefore, the research conducted by scholars that Lugones cites

---

46 Lugones, "Heterosexualism."
47 Melamed, "Racial Capitalism," 77.
48 Markowitz, "Pelvic Politics."
49 Lugones, "Heterosexualism."

(e.g., Oyěwùmí and Allen)[50] impel us to question not only the idea about the naturalness of the modern categories of women/men but the claim that the modern European system was most progressive.

What does it mean if colonization forcibly disrupted systems where there was not gender oppression to create a hierarchical heteropatriarchal system in its place? This history should cause us pause when we hear the claims today that supposedly progressive nations such as the United States need to wage war or send charity programs and development programs to so-called "underdeveloped" countries in the name of saving women or teaching those nations about gender equality. This is not to say that the globalized system of gender has not harmed many women around the world. Instead, it is to ask whether the governments and corporations that benefit and helped to create gender inequality are truly the best to intervene and correct these problems. In terms of queer communities in the West today, activists and scholars have suggested we rethink our collusion with imperial powers, including challenging our desires to join in wars against so-called "less" progressive nations, directly (as in wanting to join the military) or more indirectly (by rhetorically supporting the wars). The incorporation of queer people into nationalistic, imperial politics has been called homonationalism to call attention to how a category once Othered has now been included in the service of global imperialism/racism.[51]

While white bourgeois women were forced into (often unequal) partnerships and assigned all domestic responsibilities to maintain their class benefits, colonized, enslaved, working class, and poor women were assigned different gendered relationships to property-owning men. The gendered ideals of passivity and purity were reserved for the elite, by contrasting these with the supposed aggressiveness and sexual deviance of colonized, poor, and working-class women. Thereby, controlling elite women by offering the class benefits of behaving properly under the threat of being cast into the category of the Other. At the same time these ideas allowed for rape, violence, and harsh working conditions for colonized, poor, enslaved, and working-class women.

---

50 Oyěwùmí, *The Invention of Women*; Allen, *The Sacred Hoop*.
51 Puar, *Terrorist Assemblages*.

Men were also controlled through this system, with non-white, poor, and non–heterosexual men being cast out of the category of "proper Man" which was reserved for white, property-owning men. As we might try today for the ideals of normative coupling and economic success that are beyond most of our grasps, those goals were set in place hundreds of years ago. While unattainable to most, the justification for entire groups of people never reaching those goals was often blamed circularly on their inability to gain such stature. This might keep groups trying to get as close as possible to prescribed norms to gain a chance at being included in the elite.

Going back to my own personal story, learning about the history of the creation of an intersecting hierarchy of gender, race, and class helped me to make sense of the place white gay men gentrifying my neighborhood played in my story and the larger socio-economic landscape. I have since learned that it has been common for groups of white gay men and young queer folks to be a first stage of gentrification for neighborhoods.[52] The typical way this works is that these groups have on average less access to wealth and may be considered undesirable neighbors when trying to move into wealthier neighborhoods. These groups can afford and be accepted into poorer, neighborhoods of color. Over time, their whiteness is a sign for more normative (wealthier and heterosexual or gay) people to feel "comfortable" moving in and completing gentrification. Homophobia may serve to create distance between the initial wave of gentrifiers and original residences —as was the situation in my story. This served to ignore the larger (mostly heterosexual) economic structures and blame queer people—as if it were their sexuality and not economic privilege that is the problem. At the same time the simplification of white gay men as the stand in for "normal" or all gay people, erases the experience of queer people of color and poor queer people. Instead of creating a solidarity among marginalized people, we see fighting amongst us. I can now see how these complicated—yet obvious once you learn history—dynamics played out in my own life.

While these ideas did not begin as biological in nature when European colonization began (around 1492), by the nineteenth century,

---

52 See Bryant and Poitras, *Flag Wars* for one such story of a specific neighborhood; See Schulman, *The Gentrification of the Mind* for a complicated history of queers relationship to gentrification in New York City.

Biology was developing and reinforcing ideas that had roots in other Enlightenment ideas such as the splitting of thought and emotion with rationality thought to be superior.[53] The binaries developed through colonial philosophy became enshrined in our bodies through Biology leading to our current understandings today. These understandings link rights and autonomy to biological evidence of what types of people we are.

One main point I have aimed to make in this essay is that we are often stuck in binary thinking. When we are given two choices, we often use a rejection of one to prove the other must be correct. However, almost always, the two choices themselves are part of the same system and looking for third ways or ways to understand the root assumptions may be more necessary for truly challenging systemic injustices. Chela Sandoval argues that we might all learn from those in oppressed positions who have developed methods that allow us the flexibility to move between strategies as we try to dislodge longstanding but ever adapting systemic oppression.[54] So in the case of sexuality, how might we think and act ourselves out of the colonial/modern binaries developed over the last 500 years? As Willey asks, "[t]o what, apart from (or perhaps above or alongside) coupling and child rearing, might our deepest desires be oriented? What might we become?"[55] Rich[56] and Willey[57] each suggest ways to disrupt and think beyond our modern ideas of sexuality with the lesbian continuum and erotic bio-possibilities, respectively. They each point us to Audre Lorde's, "Uses of the Erotic: The Erotic as Power,"[58] as a way to think more broadly about what desire, joy, and bodily pleasure might mean. Lorde argues that the *erotic* has been controlled and wrongly defined as pornography "by men and used against women."[59] She instead defines as follows:

> The erotic is a measure between the beginnings of our sense of self and the chaos of our strongest feelings. It is an internal sense of satisfaction to which, once we have experienced it, we know

---

53 Anzaldúa, *Borderlands*.
54 Sandoval, *Methodology of the Oppressed*.
55 Willey, "Biopossibility."
56 Rich, "Compulsory Heterosexuality."
57 Willey, "Biopossibility."
58 Lorde, "Uses of the Erotic."
59 Lorde, "Uses of the Erotic," 54.

we can aspire. For having experienced the fullness of this depth of feeling and recognizing its power, in honor and self-respect we can require no less of ourselves... Once we know the extent to which we are capable of feeling that sense of satisfaction and completion, we can then observe which of our various life endeavors bring us closest to that fullness.[60]

Lorde suggests that by learning to be in touch with our erotic desires, we begin to change the way we live and what/how we choose to spend our time and energy. Relationships and sharing of erotic power are key to this understanding. She expands the definition from the sexual to also include activities that bring her joy such as painting, writing poems, and creating activist connections with other women. The claiming of this power, she argues, will give us an opportunity to fight against interlocking oppressions, as she says, "women so empowered are dangerous."[61] What does it mean to reevaluate our very understanding of sexuality in this way and together with others?

Fulfilling Our Queer Potential: Homosexuals are Dangerous!

While Lorde[62] and Rich[63] each focus their time on the power of women organizing together; many, Lorde concluded, have pointed to the ways that the desire for solidarity across women—while perhaps desirable—is not possible without acknowledging the deep differences that have been created. By the 1990s, the emergence of queer theory and a growing radical political movement was met with both excitement and hesitation by Black feminists who wondered whether Black people's experiences would be erased/ignored;[64] and colorblind analyses might miss how interrelated control over sexuality and race were ultimately causing further erasure and harm to more marginalized people across a range of sexualities.[65] Queer politics and theory offered an opportunity to go beyond the hetero/homo binary of sexuality and ask deeper questions about how society was structured. Would this queering work to disrupt these intersections? Would it be a third way to oppose homophobia, or would it end

---

60 Lorde, "Uses of the Erotic," 54–55.
61 Lorde, "Uses of the Erotic," 55.
62 Lorde, "Uses of the Erotic."
63 Rich, "Compulsory Heterosexuality."
64 Hammonds, "Black (W)holes."
65 Cohen, "Punks."

up simply becoming a synonym for homosexuality or an umbrella term for non-heterosexual identities?

It was several years after reading Rich's article that I found my way from the bisexuality that I claimed that evening after class to a queer identity. Queer identification for me came through a political journey that took a sharp turn after September 11, 2001. While I often say it is 9/11 that radicalized me, it is probably more accurate to say that it was the US response to 9/11 that did it. It seems impossible to disentangle the two at this point but just as it it important to understand capitalism or sexuality or anything else as developing in a specific moment, it is important to name that the aftermath was not the only possible result.[66] The politicization from that time took me through initial anti-war organizing eventually to finding a home in queer political community. This was the place where all the parts came together for me.

Queer politics offered me the potential to understand and challenge the links between capitalism and sexuality in a way that felt powerful and fun—from dropping a banner over a highway overpass that read, "Make Queer Love, Not Straight War," to queer burlesque and drag performances as fundraisers for political prisoners being charged with terrorism, to restructuring my relationships to revalue feminist friendships. This orientation to queer identity is sometimes hard to explain. A long-term lover had this problem trying to explain to a therapist who understood LGBTQ "issues" but was having trouble understanding what queer could mean beyond a sexual desire/practice. Finally, she used an example from one of our dates, saying 'changing plans to have sex to go to protest Trump's Muslim Ban[67] instead is my sexuality.' Without having time to provide a long history lesson on Biology, Colonization, and the production of Difference, this definition by way of example may open up enough

---

66 E.g. Butler, *Precarious Life,* analyzes how the categories of "us" vs "them" were produced after 9/11 and might be reimagined, leading to questions to consider alternative responses.

67 See ACLU, "Timeline of the Muslim Ban," for the legal and political battle over four years beginning with US President Trump's Executive Order on January 27, 2017 banning entry for visitors and immigrants from seven predominantly Muslim countries for ninety days, halting refugee entry for 120 days, and indefinitely banning Syrian refugees. Protests erupted at airports and in the streets (e.g., Knefel, "Huge JFK Airport Protest"). See Price, "Queering Reproductive Justice;" Shah, "Body on the Line," for reflection and theorizing about queer coalitional politics around immigration.

questions to get to the coalitional possibilities and radical potential of queerness.

It was around 2005 that I began to embrace this orientation. At that time, as queer identified people who saw the intersections between political issues and forms of oppression, a clear target for intervention was with the growing mainstream LGBT communities of which we often felt both a part—and feared its co-optation. As LGBT people became "included" in malestream society, we understood that it might mean more protection for some and potentially more exclusion for all those still deemed outside of it.[68]

Several of us in a local queer organization decided to follow the lead of other queer radicals[69] and make our politics visible by disrupting the Atlanta Pride event that year. We did not have the coordination or numbers to pull something off like larger groups that have caused major disruptions to Pride celebrations (e.g., in San Francisco), but we could still do what we could while corporate floats rolled by and threw rainbow condoms at us. Taking turns standing on an upside-down milk crate (our soapbox), we used a bullhorn to read from our flyer titled, "Homosexuals are Dangerous!"—enumerating ten reasons we were dangerous[70] to the status quo, including taking down capitalism, racism, and all other isms! At the same time, we fanned out dispersing flyers to the crowds who were watching the parade and not sure initially what to make of a bunch of queer-looking folks yelling about how dangerous homosexuality was. By the way, we used the term homosexual tongue-in-cheek because none of us preferred that term due to its medical-biological roots.

About a decade later, young folks who I was helping to raise, stood on the sidelines of Pride with me in glitter and rainbow flags enjoying the annual parade. I guess I had become more complacent (do they still say you can't trust anyone over 30?). I watched as I took the condoms off the other goodies thrown to them since my underage charges only needed so many to blow up and make water balloons. And then a group of police officers came marching down as part of the parade, and no one doubted

---

68 Rubin, "Thinking Sex;" Spade and Willse, "Marriage Will Never;" See Hong, "Neoliberalism;" Duggan, *The Twilight of Equality?*
69 For example, *Gay Shame;* see Winn-Lenetsky, "Common Ground."
70 Perhaps someone had intentionally used the term dangerous in reference to Lorde's claim that I mentioned earlier. If so, I did not realize it at the time.

that I still held on to the belief that homosexuals could be dangerous as I shouted that Police had no place in a Pride event! After all, Pride commemorates the Stonewall Rebellion where a group led by trans women of color fought back against police harassment.[71]

In 2022, I am not sure what the queer potential still is or has led to. As Cohen lamented more than twenty years prior, the possibility for radical change from "antiassimilationist activists committed to challenging the very way people understand and respond to sexuality," were narrowing already at that time because the binary between heterosexuality and queer had been reinforced instead of disrupted.[72] While her call at the time has definitely influenced much activism and scholarship, it has not been taken up in the more widespread ways necessary to meet its full radical potential.[73] Her call for a new politics is as needed today as twenty years ago,

> I envision a politics where one's relation to power, and not some homogenized identity, is privileged in determining one's political comrades. I'm talking about a politics where the *nonnormative* and *marginal* position of punks, bulldaggers, and welfare queens, for example, is the basis for progressive radical transformative coalition work. Thus, if there is any truly radical potential to be found in the idea of queerness and the practice of queer politics, it would seem to be located in its ability to create a space in opposition to dominant norms.[74]

With the legislative attacks on educators teaching or discussing "gay" topics and gender policing of bathrooms and sports team membership, it

---

71 Nevius, "The First Pride Was a Riot." In the last several years, protestors have successfully disrupted Pride parades to call attention to problems with its corporate ties and police. In 2017, several cities had huge protests against police and corporations in Pride (e.g., Hart, "Happening Now;" Michelson, "Pride Organizers."). Uniformed officers were banned from marching in San Francisco's parade, but after the mayor and other groups planned a boycott in response, the Pride organizers changed their mind (Phillips, "S.F. Pride's Police Uniform Ban;" Solis, "San Francisco Pride Parade Will Allow").
72 Cohen, "Punks."
73 For example, see *GLQ* Forum with multiple reflections on *The Radical Potential of Queer* twenty years after Cohen's original essay, "Punks." Including Cohen, "Twenty Years Later"; Hanhardt, "Queer Political History"; Ramos, "Twenty Years of Punks"; Reddy, "Neoliberalism Then and Now."
74 Cohen, "Punks," 438.

seems that the right wing may be the ones most likely to believe in Cohen and others' belief that challenging homonormativity might be dangerous! I hope their fears are correct. I hope this essay helps to lead more queer youth to live fully and see how all our struggle and liberation is connected.

BIBLIOGRAPHY

ACLU of Washington. "Timeline of the Muslim Ban," May 23, 2017. https://www.aclu-wa.org/pages/timeline-muslim-ban.

Allen, Paula Gunn. *The Sacred Hoop: Recovering the Feminine in American Indian Traditions.* Boston, MA: Beacon Press, 1992.

Anzaldúa, Gloria. *Borderlands/ La Frontera: The New Mestiza.* San Francisco: CA. Aunt Lute Books, 1987.

Bailey, Marlon M., and L. H. Stallings. "Antiblack Racism and the Metalanguage of Sexuality." *Signs: Journal of Women in Culture and Society* 42, no. 3 (2017) 614–21.

Bernstein, Mattilda. *That's Revolting!: Queer Strategies for Resisting Assimilation.* New York: Soft Skull Press, 2008.

Bociurkiw, Marusya. "It's Not About the Sex: Racialization and Queerness in *Ellen* and *The Ellen De Generis Show.*" *Canadian Woman Studies* 24, 2/3 (2005) 176–181.

Brodkin, Karen. *How Jews Became White Folks and What That Says about Race in America.* New Brunswick, NJ: Rutgers University Press, 1998.

Bryant, Linda Goode, and Laura Poitras, directors. *Flag Wars.* PBS POV, 2003. 60 min. http://archive.pov.org/flagwars/.

Burns, Katelyn. "The Massive Republican Push to Ban Trans Athletes, Explained." *Vox*, March 24, 2021. https://www.vox.com/identities/22334014/trans-athletes-bills-explained.

Butler, Judith. *Gender Trouble: Feminism and the Subversion of Identity.* New York: Routledge, 1999.

———. *Precarious Life: The Powers of Mourning and Violence.* New York: Verso, 2006.

Chamie, Joseph. "The End of Marriage in America?" *The Hill*, August 10, 2021. https://thehill.com/opinion/finance/567107-the-end-of-marriage-in-america/.

Chase, Cheryl. "Hermaphrodites with Attitude: Mapping the Emergence of Intersex Political Activism," *A Journal of Lesbian and Gay Studies* 4, no. 2 (1998) 189–211.

Cho, Sumi, Kimberlé Williams Crenshaw, and Leslie McCall. "Toward a Field of Intersectionality Studies: Theory, Applications, and Praxis." *Signs: Journal of Women in Culture and Society* 38, no. 4 (June 2013): 785–810. https://doi.org/10.1086/669608.

Cohen, Cathy. "The Radical Potential of Queer? Twenty Years Later." *GLQ: A Journal of Lesbian and Gay Studies* 25, no. 1 (2019): 140–44.

Cohen, Cathy J. "Punks, Bulldaggers, and Welfare Queens: The Radical Potential of Queer Politics." *GLQ: A Journal of Lesbian & Gay Studies* 3 (1997) 437–65.

Conrad, Ryan, ed. *Against Equality: Queer Revolution, Not Mere Inclusion.* Chico, CA: AK Press, 2014.

Crenshaw, Kimberlé. "Demarginalizing the Intersection of Race and Sex: A Black Feminist Critique of Antidiscrimination Doctrine, Feminist Theory and Antiracist Politics." In *University of Chicago Legal Forum* 1, no. 8 (1989) 139–167.

Dow, Bonnie. "Ellen, Television, and the Politics of Gay and Lesbian Visibility." *Critical Studies in Media Communication* 18, no. 2 (2001) 123–40.

Duggan, Lisa. *The Twilight of Equality?: Neoliberalism, Cultural Politics, and the Attack on Democracy.* Boston, MA: Beacon Press, 2004.

Epstein, Steven. *Impure Science: AIDS, Activism, and the Politics of Knowledge.* Oakland, CA: University of California Press, 1996.

Federici, Silvia. *Caliban and the Witch: Women, the Body and Primitive Accumulation.* Brooklyn, NY: Autonomedia, 2004.

Foucault, Michel. *The History of Sexuality: An Introduction.* Volume 1. New York: Vintage, 1978.

Young, Jeremy C. and Jonathan Friedman, "Educational Gag Orders: Legislative Restrictions on the Freedom to Read, Learn, and Teach," *Pen America*, November 8, 2021. https://pen.org/report/educational-gag-orders/.

Fry, Richard. "Amid a Pandemic and a Recession, Americans Go on a near-Record Homebuying Spree." *Pew Research Center*, March 8, 2021. https://www.pewresearch.org/fact-tank/2021/03/08/amid-a-pandemic-and-a-recession-americans-go-on-a-near-record-home-buying-spree/.

———, and Kim Parker. "Rising Share of US Adults Are Living Without a Spouse or Partner." Pew Research Center, October 5, 2021. https://www.pewresearch.org/social-trends/2021/10/05/rising-share-of-u-s-adults-are-living-without-a-spouse-or-partner/.

Hamilton, Jennifer A., Banu Subramaniam, and Angela Willey. "What Indians and Indians Can Teach Us about Colonization: Feminist

Science and Technology Studies, Epistemological Imperialism, and the Politics of Difference." *Feminist Studies* 43, no. 3 (2017) 612–23. https://doi.org/10.1353/fem.2017.0032.

Hammonds, Evelynn. "Black (W)holes and the Geometry of Black Female Sexuality." *More Gender Trouble: Feminism Meets Queer Theory* 6, 2–3 (1997) 126–145.

Hanhardt, Christina B. "The Radical Potential of Queer Political History?" *GLQ: A Journal of Lesbian and Gay Studies* 25, no. 1 (2019) 145–50.

Hart, Benji. "Happening Now: Trans-Led Coalition Shuts Down Chicago Pride Parade." *Radical Faggot* (blog), June 25, 2017. https://radfag.com/2017/06/25/happening-now-trans-led-coalition-shuts-down-chicago-pride-parade/.

Higginbotham, Evelyn Brooks. "African-American Women's History and the Metalanguage of Race." *Signs: Journal of Women in Culture and Society* 17, no. 2 (1992) 251–74.

Hong, Grace Kyungwon. "Neoliberalism." *Critical Ethnic Studies* 1, no. 1 (2015): 56–67. https://doi.org/10.5749/jcritethnstud.1.1.0056.

Jones, Dustin, and Jonathan Franklin. "Not Just Florida. More than a Dozen States Propose So-Called 'Don't Say Gay' Bills." *NPR*, April 10, 2022. https://www.npr.org/2022/04/10/1091543359/15-states-dont-say-gay-anti-transgender-bills.

Knefel, John. "Inside the Huge JFK Airport Protest Over Trump's Muslim Ban." *Rolling Stone*, January 29, 2017. https://www.rollingstone.com/politics/politics-features/inside-the-huge-jfk-airport-protest-over-trumps-muslim-ban-124190/.

Kuhl, Stefan. *The Nazi Connection: Eugenics, American Racism, and German National Socialism*. New York: Oxford University Press, 2002.

Lewis, Abram J. "'We Are Certain of Our Own Insanity': Antipsychiatry and the Gay Liberation Movement, 1968–1980." *Journal of the History of Sexuality*, December 18, 2015. https://doi.org/10.7560/JHS25104.

Lopez, German. "Anti-Transgender Bathroom Hysteria, Explained." *Vox*, May 5, 2016. https://www.vox.com/2016/5/5/11592908/transgender-bathroom-laws-rights.

Lorde, Audre. "Uses of the Erotic: The Erotic as Power," In *Sister Outsider*, 53–59. Freedom, CA: Crossing, 1984.

Lugones, María. "Heterosexualism and the Colonial/Modern Gender System." *Hypatia* 22, no. 1 (2007) 186–219.

Markowitz, Sally. "Pelvic Politics: Sexual Dimorphism and Racial Difference." *Signs: Journal of Women in Culture and Society* 26, no. 2 (2001) 389–414.

Mattson, Greggor. "The Stonewall Riots Didn't Start the Gay Rights Movement." *JSTOR Daily*, June 12, 2019. https://daily.jstor.org/the-stonewall-riots-didnt-start-the-gay-rights-movement/.

McWhorter, Ladelle. "Enemy of the Species." In *Queer Ecologies: Sex, Nature, Politics, Desire*, edited by Catriona Mortimer-Sandilands and Bruce Erickson, 73–101. Bloomington, IN: 2010.

Melamed, Jodi. "Racial Capitalism." *Critical Ethnic Studies* 1, no. 1 (2015) 76–85. https://doi.org/10.5749/jcritethnstud.1.1.0076.

Michelson, Noah. "Protesters Disrupt D.C. Pride Parade, Hit Organizers with List of Demands For 'Justice.'" *HuffPost*, June 11, 2017. https://www.huffpost.com/entry/no-pride-no-justice-capital-pride-protest_n_593d35f8e4b0c5a35ca047c9.

Nevius, Molly. "The First Pride Was a Riot: How Queer Activism Has Partnered with Police to Hurt the Community's Most Vulnerable." *Hastings Women's Law Journal* 29, no. 1 (2018) 125–46.

Ordover, Nancy. *American Eugenics: Race, Queer Anatomy, and the Science of Nationalism*. Minneapolis, MN: University of Minnesota Press, 2003.

Oyèwùmí, Oyèrónkẹ́. *The Invention of Women: Making an African Sense of Western Gender Discourses*. Minneapolis, MN: University of Minnesota Press, 1997.

Palosky, Craig, and Rakesh Singh. "New Kaiser/New York Times Survey Finds One in Five Working-Age Americans with Health Insurance Report Problems Paying Medical Bills." *Kaiser Family Foundation*, January 5, 2016. https://www.kff.org/health-costs/press-release/new-kaisernew-york-times-survey-finds-one-in-five-working-age-americans-with-health-insurance-report-problems-paying-medical-bills/.

Phillips, Justin. "S.F. Pride's Police Uniform Ban Was Years in the Making. The Backlash to It Is Troubling." *San Francisco Chronicle*, May 29, 2022. https://www.sfchronicle.com/bayarea/justinphillips/article/Pride-police-uniform-ban-17204447.php.

Price, Kimala. "Queering Reproductive Justice in the Trump Era: A Note on Political Intersectionality." *Politics & Gender* 14, no. 4 (2018) 581–601. https://doi.org/10.1017/S1743923X18000776.

Puar, Jasbir K. *Terrorist Assemblages*. Durham, NC: Duke University Press, 2018.

Ramos, Nic John. "GLQ Forum /Twenty Years of Punks: Introduction." *GLQ: A Journal of Lesbian and Gay Studies* 25, no. 1 (2019) 137–39.

Ray, Rashawn, Andre Perry, David Harshbarger, Samantha Elizondo, and Alexandra Gibbons. "Homeownership, Racial Segregation, and Policy Solutions to Racial Wealth Equity." *Brookings Institute,* September 1, 2021. https://www.brookings.edu/essay/homeownership-racial-segregation-and-policies-for-racial-wealth-equity/.

Reddy, Chandan. "Neoliberalism Then and Now: Race, Sexuality, and the Black Radical Tradition." *GLQ: A Journal of Lesbian and Gay Studies* 25, no. 1 (2019) 150–55.

Reed, Jennifer. "The Three Phases of Ellen: From Queer to Gay to Postgay." In *Queer Popular Culture: Literature, Media, Film, and Television*, edited by Thomas Peele, 9–26. New York: Palgrave Macmillan, 2007.

Rich, Adrienne. "Compulsory Heterosexuality and Lesbian Existence." *Signs: Journal of Women in Culture and Society* 5, no. 4 (1980) 631–60.

Roediger, David R. *Working Toward Whiteness: How America's Immigrants Became White: The Strange Journey from Ellis Island to the Suburbs*. New York: Basic Books, 2006.

Rubin, David A. "'An Unnamed Blank That Craved a Name': A Genealogy of Intersex as Gender." *Signs* 37, no. 4 (2012) 883–908. https://doi.org/10.1086/664471.

Rubin, Gayle. "Thinking Sex: Notes for a Radical Theory of the Politics of Sexuality." In *Social Perspectives in Lesbian and Gay Studies: A Reader*, edited by Peter M. Nardi and Beth Schneider, 100–133. New York: Routledge, 1998.

Said, Edward W. *Orientalism*. New York: Vintage Books, 1979.

Sandoval, Chela. *Methodology of the Oppressed*. Minneapolis, MN: University of Minnesota Press, 2000.

Schulman, Sarah. *The Gentrification of the Mind: Witness to a Lost Imagination*. Berkeley, CA: University of California Press, 2012.

Shah, Nayan. "Putting One's Body on the Line." *GLQ: A Journal of Lesbian and Gay Studies* 25, no. 1 (2019) 183–87.

Sieczkowski, Cavan. "Rosie O'Donnell Reveals Who Stopped Her from Coming Out in 1992." *HuffPost*, February 15, 2014. https://www.huffpost.com/entry/rosie-odonnell-cosmopolitan-coming-out_n_4794250.\.

Skerski, Jamie. "From Prime-Time to Daytime: The Domestication of Ellen DeGeneres." *Communication&Critical/CulturalStudies* 4, no. 4 (December 2007) 363–81. https://doi.org/10.1080/14791420701632964.

Smith, Andrea. "Heteropatriarchy and the Three Pillars of White Supremacy." In *Color of Violence: The INCITE! anthology*, edited by INCITE! Women of Color Against Violence, 66–73. Durham, NC: Duke University Press, 2016.

Solis, Nathan. "San Francisco Pride Parade Will Allow Some Uniformed Police to March, Easing a Ban." *Los Angeles Times*, June 3, 2022. https://www.latimes.com/california/story/2022-06-02/san-francisco-pride-parade-allow-some-uniformed-police.

Spade, Dean, and Craig Willse. "Marriage Will Never Set Us Free." *Organizing Upgrade*, September 2013.

Stepan, Nancy Leys. "Race and Gender: The Role of Analogy in Science." *Isis* 77, no. 2 (1986) 261–77. https://doi.org/10.1086/354130.

Wall, Sean Saifa. "Standing at the Intersections: Navigating Life as a Black Intersex Man." *Narrative Inquiry in Bioethics* 5, no. 2 (2015) 117–19. https://doi.org/10.1353/nib.2015.0046.

Weller, Christian. "Wealth Inequality on The Rise During Pandemic." *Forbes*, December 22, 2021. https://www.forbes.com/sites/christianweller/2021/12/22/wealth-rises-at-all-income-levels-but-faster-at-the-top/.

Willey, Angela. "Biopossibility: A Queer Feminist Materialist Science Studies Manifesto, with Special Reference to the Question of Monogamous Behavior." *Signs: Journal of Women in Culture and Society* 41, no. 3 (2016) 553–77.

———. *Undoing Monogamy: The Politics of Science and the Possibilities of Biology*. Durham, NC: Duke University Press, 2016.

Winn-Lenetsky, Jonah Ari. "Common Ground: Performing Gay Shame, Solidarity and Social Change." Dissertation, University of Minnesota, 2015.

4

A Politics of Our Time: Reworking Afro-Asian Solidarity in the Wake of George Floyd's Killing[1]

Yuichiro Onishi

Introduction

I live in south Minneapolis, not too far from the Third Precinct station that burned down on May 28, 2020. Four officers involved in the killing of George Floyd, now convicted and sentenced, worked at this station. At the time of writing this essay, the *Minneapolis Star Tribune* reported systemic problems and revealed truths about the south Minneapolis precinct, which had a "reputation for being home to police officers who played by their own rules."[2] Libor Jany, now a staff writer for the *Los Angeles Times*, described in appalling detail, the unhinged character of state-sanctioned violence, especially its gender dynamics and sexual violations, baked into this precinct. He wrote,

> One officer kicked a handcuffed suspect in the face, leaving his jaw in pieces. Officers beat and pistol-whipped a suspect in a parking lot on suspicion of low-level drug charges. Others harassed residents of a south Minneapolis housing project as they headed to work and allowed prostitution suspects to touch their genitals for several minutes before arresting them in vice stings.[3]

---

1 The essay was first published online in mid-June 2020, amid fury over the killing of George Floyd. It appeared in *Unmargin* (Unmargin.org), an Asian American platform for critical thought. I am grateful to Bao Phi, Vidhya Shanker, and Stevie Peace for feedback, and I have utmost respect for the members of the *Unmargin* collective for shaping a dynamic Asian American movement space. The power of self-activity is palpable. For this publication, I did not alter the text, except for making formatting changes and small edits, adding citations, and writing the new opening paragraphs to set the context.
2 See *LA Times*, "Libor Jany Joins *The Times*;" Cobb, "Derek Chauvin's Trial."
3 Jany, "Minneapolis' Third Precinct."

The culture of state violence specific to this station was an outgrowth of the shuffling of officers—transfers of 'old timers' and 'young Vietnam vets,'—in the Minneapolis Police Department (MPD) in the 1980s.[4]

The combination of recklessness and the infusion of mores and habits connected to warfare overseas, namely the US war in Vietnam, ossified this culture throughout the 1990s, further animated by the advent of an anti-gang task force known as the Metro Gang Strike Force in the early 2000s.[5] This task force's gangsterism (irony highlighted on purpose) soon came under investigation for criminal conduct.[6] Its officers committed all kinds of crimes and civil rights violations: stealing money and cars, as well as other evidence seized from suspects and those wrongfully perceived as such, so often without search warrants, and assaulting them on a regular basis. Not surprisingly, people of color and immigrants of color were hyper-profiled and specifically targeted. Tim Nelson of MPR News discovered—based on the 2008 Metro Gang Strike Force annual report that he obtained—that two agents from the Immigration and Customs Enforcements were embedded in the task force to round up the undocumented. They contributed to the creation of a huge database of "gang members," totaling nearly 17,000, which was considered one of the task force's primary objectives.[7] After the investigation conducted by a former federal prosecutor and a former FBI agent documented its widespread criminality in the report published in 2009, the task force was disbanded, and the victims of police violence reached a settlement in a federal class action lawsuit a year later. The state was made to pay more than $3.6 million to its victims.[8]

Yet there has not been closure or healing after all of this. As the moment-defining MPD 150 Report that elevated Minneapolis as the vector of abolitionism emphasizes, "none of the officers involved, many of whom worked for MPD, were held accountable for their crimes."[9] Not at all sur-

---

4 Jany, "Minneapolis' Third Precinct."
5 Jany, "Minneapolis' Third Precinct."
6 "On the connection between state violence and gangsterism, see Kelley, "Thug Nation."
7 Nelson, "Behind the Scenes;" Jany, "Minneapolis' Third Precinct."
8 Nelson, "Investigator Says Gang Strike Force;" Jany, "Minneapolis' Third Precinct."
9 MPD 150 is a collective that has been engaging in the critique of police and policing in Minneapolis, long before the murder of Floyd. It originally published the report titled, *Enough Is Enough*, in 2017 for the occasion of the 150th anniversary of the Minneapolis Police Department (MPD)'s founding in 1867. The notion, MPD

prising—to return to Libor Jany's superb reporting—is that "some task force officers ended up in the Third Precinct." The south Minneapolis station was one of the anchors of task force's thuggery, a microcosm of broader concerns about police, policing, and state violence raised by activists and organizers throughout the Clinton years, during which they engaged in concerted activity to lay bare the interconnectedness of carceral, criminalization, and deportation regimes. The MPD's Third Precinct was the very product and, in fact, clear-cut embodiment of statecraft rooted in endless wars on the minoritized and the racialized.[10]

These snippets about the Third Precinct help affirm the main thrust of this essay, which is *to start seeing the warfare state that catalyzes the renewal of a highly militarized and punitive society within the United States. Such state-sanctioned violence cannot be separated from histories of US imperial adventures and colonial conquests abroad, the hallmark of this country's past and race-making in it.* The warfare state constantly recalls and revives what critical ethnic studies scholar Dylan Rodriguez calls "the white supremacist state's terms of engagement" in the present. Such is the nature of "dangerous alignments of the inner and outer wars," to borrow the historian Nikhil Pal Singh's formulation.[11] The activation of antiracism that anchors Afro-Asian solidarity demands an optic that apprehends militarization and its reach, here and abroad, as well as the coordinated exercise of war power. Such a critique can help inform what "peace in the struggle" can become, both in our imaginations and in action. We will do well, perhaps, to salvage the towering scholar-activist W.

150, refers to this conjuncture, as well as decades-long freedom struggles involving multiple communities and organizations to call into question, "the narrative that police exist to protect and serve." The expanded version, published in the wake of George Floyd's killing, is available online. It is called *Enough Is Enough: A 150 Year Performance Review of the Minneapolis Police Department.* Its vision of abolitionism reads: "MPD 150 is a participatory, horizontally organized effort by local organizers, researchers, artists, and activists to shift the discussion around police and policing in Minneapolis from one of procedural reforms to one of meaningful structural change. It is not the project of any organization. We stand on the shoulders of the work that many organizations have been doing for years and welcome the support of everyone who agrees with our approach. We approach the process we are developing will help organizers in other cities establish practical abolitionist strategies."

10 Jany, "Minneapolis' Third Precinct;" Rodriguez, "Warfare and the Terms of Engagement;" Camp and Heatherton, *Policing the Planet.*

11 Singh, *Race and America's Long War*, 26. Rodriguez, "Warfare and the Terms of Engagement," 95.

E. B. Du Bois's thoughts of war and peace. He argues that the deliverance of a truly lasting peace would require ending poverty, racism, and colonialism, all causes of war.[12] The articulation of antiwar politics is essential, and it is our language of struggle, the center-lane of Asian American movement-building.

Witnessing State Violence

On May 25, 2020, the whole world witnessed the horrific killing of George Floyd on thirty-eighth and Chicago in South Minneapolis when the video taken by a bystander went viral. The two officers caught on camera were white and Asian American: Derek Chauvin and Tou Thao. Thao is a Hmong American. Later, we learned that two more officers—J. Alexander Kueng and Thomas Lane—were involved. While Chauvin pinned a handcuffed George Floyd on the ground, face down, and kneeled on his neck to kill him, the other three did nothing to stop him. Chauvin is now in custody, charged with murder. The other three who aided and abetted have been charged as well. Increasingly, we have all become spectators of such scenes of state-sanctioned killings in recent times where unarmed Black men and women have been shot with impunity by the police.[13]

Asian Americans are aware of Asian American involvement in the killing of Floyd. Like many, we are outraged. Many of us have taken to the streets, day in and day out, to join the multitude in demanding justice for Floyd. Coming on the heels of the surge in anti-Asian hate crimes and xenophobic outbursts caused by the nefarious characterization of the coronavirus as the "Chinese virus," political activism of Asian Americans has been more visible.[14] In Minnesota, Asian Americans are showing great strength and taking actions in solidarity and support for Black lives. Yet, Breonna Taylor, Ahmaud Arbery, and now George Floyd's names presents a different order of challenge.

---

12 Du Bois, "The African Roots of War."
13 Jelani Cobb's essays published in *The New Yorker* are essential. See, for instance, Cobb, "An American Spring."
14 See the six-part series called "The Asian American Voices from the Pandemic," in *Unmargin* (unmargin.org).

In Flames: Los Angeles, 1992

The 1992 Los Angeles Uprising brought the complexity of Asian Americans' relationship to state violence into sharp relief. It is considered one of the key moments in US urban history. The genesis was the viral footage of the severe police beating of Rodney King, which occurred on March 3, 1991. The bystander, with a camcorder, captured King on the ground, being clubbed, kicked, and tasered by four Los Angeles police officers. These officers were indicted in a grand jury, charged with excessive use of force. The trial followed. After the verdicts were rendered to acquit the officers on April 29, 1992, the city went up in flames. The uprising that started in South Central spread northward. Koreatown was hit especially hard; the police were nowhere to be found as businesses and buildings were targeted and destroyed. As a result, Korean Americans fended for themselves, including some taking arms. The media coverage took hold of Black-Korean conflicts and looped readily available stereotypes about Asian Americans, as well as Black and brown people. Asian Americans were cast as the "good minority" unfairly targeted as scapegoats in a city under siege by "rioters" and "looters." Racial hierarchy often produces a good-and-bad morality play, and Asian Americans were, as Claire Jean Kim has argued, triangulated within this system of white over Black as neither of the two, unprotected by the law and placed outside the body politic as forever foreigners.[15]

---

15 See Gooding-Williams, ed., *Reading Rodney King/Reading Urban Uprising*, a key text of the 1992 uprisings in Los Angeles. contains essays written by leading activist-scholars, all of whom deftly responded to the moment of critical emergence in the wake of the 1992 uprising in Los Angeles. It is a key text: Gooding-Williams, ed., *Reading Rodney King/Reading Urban Uprising*. Elaine H. Kim, one of the foremost Asian American Studies scholars, contributed to the essay titled "Home Is Where the Han Is: A Korean American Perspective on the Los Angeles Upheavals." Most recently, Lynn Mie Itagaki has made important conceptual and analytical interventions into existing scholarly work on the 1992 Los Angeles urban uprising. She posits the responses of artists, writers, and creative people of color to the urban crisis as a wellspring for shaping critical theory and practice against structural racism. The work she examines lays bare the problem of insistence on "civility" to reverse racism, which cropped up in the wake of the 1992 uprising. She argues that such stance-taking, which is referred to as civil racism, is constitutive of the entrenched structural reality of racial inequality. Itagaki, *Civil Racism*. On the theory of racial triangulation, see Kim, "The Racial Triangulation of Asian Americans." This article is undeniably paradigm-setting.

Still, this triangulation has a way of denying all the uneasiness and irresolution surrounding everyday human experiences with violence, suffering, and grief from being made known. The antagonisms between Black people and Korean Americans, to be clear, intensified in Los Angeles at a particular juncture. The city was in the throes of a convergence of mass criminalization, the fast-eroding welfare state, and the reorganization of the global political economy toward deregulation, privatization, and financialization that affected those who were minoritized and racially aggrieved unevenly. Hyper-segregation, by the early 1990s, had become the norm for urban life. Ascendant at the same time was the rhetoric of individual choice, freedom, and responsibility that buttressed white flight to the suburbs and the widening of the racial wealth gap. Not surprisingly, immigration from Asia and Latin America and refugee resettlement from Southeast Asia, rising steadily throughout the 1980s, became, in the quotidian, a cauldron of racial dramas in cities under an emergent austerity order.[16]

The Messiness of Race

Still the above contextualization of the 1992 LA Uprising is not entirely sufficient. To add another dimension, specificity matters. We need to know why group identifications among Black Americans and Korean Americans stiffened dramatically *when it did* in Los Angeles. The killing of a fifteen-year-old Black girl Latasha Harlins by Soon Ja Du, a Korean woman liquor store owner, was pivotal. On March 16, 1991, Du shot Harlins in the back of her head in the store, killing her instantly. This killing coincided with the beating of Rodney King, both of which were captured on videos that went viral. These two events were inseparable and certainly informed how the media shaped the story about Korean-Black conflicts. Du, in the end, walked away without serving any jail time. The presiding judge Joyce A. Karlin's sentencing was a major blow: five years of probation, four hundred hours of community service, and a $500 fine. This judgment came a week before the acquittal of four officers in the Rodney King case. Meanwhile, in the aftermath of the uprising, Korean Americans

---

16 Davis, *City of Quartz*; Davis, "LA: The Fire This Time." On the connection between hyper-segregation, precarity, and policing in the wake of welfare reform from the perspective of refugees, see Tang, *Unsettled*.

took to the streets to denounce the police and denial of their right to protection as citizens. They recalled the historical tradition of Black struggles to demand reparations. Justice in the United States almost always appears through racial fault lines.[17]

Another deeply confounding and contested instance of the messiness of race is a more recent one. The murder of Akai Gurley on November 24, 2014 by Chinese American officer Peter Liang was a high-profile case of police violence in Brooklyn, New York. Liang was prosecuted and convicted of manslaughter, which was later reduced to criminally negligent homicide.[18] In response, Chinese Americans in large cities rallied behind Liang in 2015-16. They saw him, again, as a scapegoat. In all the cases of police killings before, they argued, the white officers were exonerated. Their stance was that of equality with whites; Liang should not be treated any differently. Asian Americans who stood in solidarity to demand justice for Gurley clashed with Liang's supporters.[19]

Here, too, racial hierarchy matters; this division makes clear the two predominant modes of the Asian American racial experience. There are those who subscribe to colorblind meritocracy and celebrate material success. In other words, they believe in the "American" dream. Then, there are those who struggle against structural and institutional racism. They recognize that the perception of Asian Americans as a "model minority" has a crippling effect, for it becomes a way of condemning, disciplining, and policing the racialized poor as a "misbehaving minority." It also hides hard realities of Asian American poverty and educational gaps, as well as persistent anti-Asian discrimination and criminalization experienced

---

[17] Ishle Yi Park's poetry and prose strike a tragic tone with deep introspection on matters of violence and race experienced by Korean Americans in the urban setting. Park, *The Temperature of This Water*. The 36-minute documentary titled *Sa-I-Gu*, released in 1993 and distributed by the Center for Asian American Media, was directed and produced by three Korean American women: Christine Choy, Dai Sil Kim-Gibson, and Elaine H. Kim. It is at once powerful and conversation changing. "Sa-I-Gu" refers to the date, April 29, in Korean, on which the uprising erupted in the wake of the verdict of the Rodney King trial. On Latasha Harlin, see Jennings, "How the Killing of Latasha Harlins."

[18] Wagner, "Former NYPD Officer."

[19] Phi, "Unprotected by Assimilation: Lessons from the Case of Duy Ngo"; Wang, "'Awoke' by N.Y. Cop Shooting, Asian American Activists Chart Way Forward."

among Asian Americans in the everyday.[20] Asian Americans' relationship to state violence that disproportionately affects Black men and women is entangled within the existing relations of hierarchy and exploitation in complex ways. Given this reality, we would do well to hone a politics of our own time.

"Asian American": Not Merely an Identity

As always, the past is our guide. At the height of the US war in Vietnam in 1968, Asian American activists thoroughly understood this imperative of fashioning a new politics. Their approach was to pivot around opposition to US imperialism and militarism. Coining a movement-building nomenclature, "Asian American," in and of itself was politics. They made a conscious choice to fundamentally rebuke the racist appellation, "Oriental," through political organizing, action, and education; this shift was paradigmatic.[21]

Because of their involvement in Black struggles for liberation, Yuri Kochiyama and Grace Lee Boggs, two iconic figures of Asian American movement history and Black-Asian solidarity, moved closer to identifying with "Asian American," not because of their interest in identity or heritage. Far from it. By entering movement-building spaces created by such organizations as Asian Americans for Action (for Kochiyama in New York City) and Asian Political Alliance (for Boggs in Detroit), they learned to articulate a distinctly Asian American conception of politics derived from the currents of resistance that were anti-imperialist and anti-war.[22]

Politics, for them, was antagonistic and contingent. It was hardly static, and it would flare up in dynamic ways in times of crisis. The birth of "Asian American" as a political category of struggle is a great case study

---

20 Jung, "The Racial Justice Movement Needs a Model Minority Mutiny"; Park, "Continuing Significance of the Model Minority Myth: The Second Generation"; Jin, "6 Charts That Dismantle the Trope of Asian Americans as a Model Minority"; Pew Research Center, July 2018.

21 Maeda, *Chains of Babylon*; Maeda, *Rethinking the Asian American Movement*; Ishizuka, *Serve the People*; Fujino and Rodriguez, *Contemporary Asian American Activism*.

22 Fujino, "Yuri Kochiyama;" Fujino, "Grassroots Leadership and Afro-Asian Solidarities;" Fujino, *Heartbeat of Struggle*; Boggs, *Living for Revolution*; Boggs and Kurashige, *The Next American Revolution*; Kurashige, "Responding to Trump;" Fu, "On Contradiction;" Ishizuka, "Flying in the Face." Two notable documentaries are *Yuri Kochiyama: Passion for Justice*, and *American Revolutionary*.

of how politics works. What could our politics look like in the context of the current policing crisis that gave form to Black Lives Matter? When a wave of protests spread throughout the country in 2014–15 in the wake of the shooting death of Mike Brown in Ferguson, thousands of Asian Americans linked up with Black Lives Matter. We called out anti-Black racism within our own communities and families to highlight complicity with the police and carceral state. We also revolted against the model minority discourse. Some of these efforts were clumsy at best, especially "Letters for Black Lives," a multilingual open letter campaign addressed to "Mom, Dad, Uncle, Auntie, Grandfather, Grandmother, Family." It appeared woefully unschooled in Asian American studies, especially the movement culture that created this field in the first place. The very notion of "Asian American" remained impaled within the existing racial hierarchy.[23]

Largely overlooked is a *political* stance of Asian American activists who have been engaging in the work of resisting state-sanctioned violence long before "Hands Up, Don't Shoot" and "I Can't Breathe" became the touchstone for contemporary struggles against the police state. These activists have always operated with understanding that (1) policing is part and parcel of punishing and terrorizing state power that is deployed routinely at those marked as threats and enemies and (2) critical interventions would require exposing militarization as a central problem. Such is the point of departure for a politics of our time.[24]

Going Deep into Race-Making

At a deeper philosophical level, police power produces what Charles W. Mills calls "a partitioned social ontology," which entails bifurcating human life based on worthiness and drawing a sharp line between personhood and sub-personhood. The subjugated are denied a bundle of inalienable rights, an essential requirement to be human. Policing is race-making *par excellence*. Historically speaking, this power has been perfected through Indigenous dispossession, enslavement, Jim Crow racial order, the exploitation and deportation of Mexican and Asian labor, and countless imperial wars within the continental United States

---

23 Chan, "How a Group."
24 Phi, "Untitled;" Phi, "War Before Memory;" Combs, "Miss Saigon Protest;" Camp and Heatherton, *Policing the Planet*; Hong, *A Violent Peace*; Singh, "Enough Toxic Militarism;" Camp, *Incarcerating the Crisis*.

and overseas with the purpose of protecting property: stolen lands and wealth derived from racist violence. This is what Nikhil Pal Singh means by the "whiteness of police." Whiteness, as he explains, "emerges from the governance of property and its relationship to those who have no property and thus no calculable interests, and who are therefore imagined to harbor a potentially criminal disregard for propertied order."[25]

The word "gook," for one, is lodged inside the "whiteness of police." While it is commonly associated with the carnage of the U.S. war in Vietnam, its usage and meaning as a synonym for an enemy are tightly interwoven with the U.S. history of race-making, imperial hubris, and militarism in the first half of the twentieth century, as David Roediger shows. Wherever the United States carried out warfare and plunder and established military presence, be it in the Philippines, Haiti, Central America, Hawai'i, and Korea, to rule and police the vast areas of the globe and its markets, resources, territories, and the people, this repulsive and soul-killing word cropped up.[26]

The ongoing War on Terror has also emboldened the exercise of police power globally. The torture and indefinite detention of enemy combatants took the center stage, and aerial warfare, especially drone strikes, expanded. Myriad domestic counterterrorism programs took root in the United States and across the Global North to institutionalize profiling and surveillance. An outcome has been that the clouds of suspicion around Muslims, Sikhs, Arabs, and South Asians have normalized the mainstream perception that "Islam is a threat" and "Muslims are terrorists." With it, xenophobia has helped to create an incredibly hostile environment in politics and social life.[27]

The Culture of Justice for Fong Lee

This history of racist violence, along with ongoing militarization, was not lost on Asian American movement activists when they came together in 2006–2009 to respond to the killing of an unarmed nineteen-year-old Hmong American Fong Lee on the North Side of Minneapolis by officer Jason Andersen. It was uppermost in their political consciousness. Truth is, in the last forty years, policing has become ever more lethal.

---

25 Charles W. Mills, *The Racial Contract*, 16; Singh, "The Whiteness of Police."
26 Roediger, "Gook."
27 Bayoumi, "How the War."

The connection between domestic policing and low-intensity warfare and pacification tactics deployed abroad in places such as Vietnam, for instance, is well-documented. In *City of Quartz*, Mike Davis discusses the emergence of the Los Angeles Police Department's militarized culture that was triumphantly shaped by city officials and some of the senior officers who were veterans themselves. He draws connections between "Vietnam here" and abroad to make it explicit how the experience of mass murder and terror—the US imperial war in Southeast Asia—found a new articulation in a war against gangs throughout the 1980s.[28]

Bao Phi's poem, "8(9)," written in memory of Fong Lee and for the Lee family and the Justice for Fong Lee committee, powerfully captures American policing born out of the history of race-making, militarism, state violence, and subjection. The title refers to nine bullets that Minneapolis police officer Anderson fired, eight bullets penetrating Fong Lee's body, who was marked as a "gang member," and one bullet missing the target.[29] The eighth section of the poem that denotes the final bullet that struck him appears to recall Hmong people's history of fleeing persecution and being entangled in many wars. Their participation in U.S. Central Intelligence Agency-led covert military action during the U.S. war in Vietnam, for instance, made them enemies in the eyes of Vietnamese and Lao soldiers. And in the aftermath of the U.S. defeat in April 1975, the Pathet Lao forces swiftly began an elimination campaign against Hmong people, in essence, ethnic cleansing. The refrain, "men with guns," underscores the reach of militarization in their lives, both before and after they resettled in the United States, many of them in Minnesota, as refugees. By framing the poem in this way, Bao Phi renders the ethos of Justice for Fong Lee movement building that pivoted around demilitarization. This movement culture, in many ways, prefigured the cutting-edge of contemporary Asian American radicalism.[30]

Ways of Reworking

In the wake of George Floyd's killing, Minneapolis is now the pacesetter for the movement to dismantle the police. Afro-Asian solidarity has a

---

28 Williams, "Fong Lee's Family;" Phi, "Fong Lee;" Davis, *City of Quartz*, 267.
29 Phi, "8 (9)," 93–95. The poem is available online on the writer's website: http://baophi.com/8-9/.
30 Vang, "Dreaming of Home;" Vang, "Unlawful or Not."

place in it. It is vital and urgent as before. But this political project cannot be the same as in the past, nor begin and end on a critique of anti-Blackness. To recast an optic on Asian American identification with the Black struggle against the racist warfare state, we need to retrieve our own experiences and memories of living through wars, aggressive militarism, invasion, and occupation in Asia and Southeast Asia, US-led or otherwise. We need to think about exclusion, detention, and interrogation at the borders, here and elsewhere around the world. We have to think about the consequences of forced mass removal and displacement, deportation, surveillance, and incarceration, then and now.[31]

Afro-Asian solidarity will be made anew, no doubt. Speaking at the Justice for George Floyd rally at the Minnesota State Capitol in St. Paul, Fong Lee's mother, Youa Vang, has shown us how to say Fong's name. "Here's what I saw with Fong," she told the crowd in Hmong, recalling the days of fighting for justice in the wake of state-sanctioned killing that took Fong Lee's life. "Black people were with us the whole time, morning or night," she said. "Whenever we needed something, they were there. Whether it was day or night, even up until one in the morning." This is a description of Afro-Asian organizing for a defense campaign, beyond that of solidarity.[32]

Her statement speaks of people's commitment to do all that they can to defend the life and human rights of martyrs and, by extension, perhaps, prisoners and all those who are suffering under the carceral state and militarized culture. It also speaks of collective popular urgency to fight for martyrs' lives and their human rights as though they are our own as we contend the force of violence, "for if they take you in the morning, they will be coming for us that night," as James Baldwin famously wrote in the closing sentence of "An Open Letter to My Sister, Miss Angela Davis."[33] This is about banding and struggling together against the predatory state for the cause of a collective defense of all those who are condemned by this force.

---

31 MPD 150, *Enough Is Enough*; Gilmore, *Abolition Geography*; Camp and Heatherton, *Policing the Planet*; and Taylor, "The Emerging Movement for Police and Prison Abolition."
32 Youa Vang's words, along with the footage of her rally speech appear in the MPR News report. See Yang, "'We Need to Help Them.'"
33 Baldwin, "An Open Letter."

The reworking of Afro-Asian solidarity in the service of demilitarization is a politics of our time. It has critical purchase in manifold struggles for peace, justice, and genuine security embedded within fortified cities and the U.S. military's "empire of bases" in Asia and the Pacific. Thinking through justice for George Floyd is to take such detours in the struggles of the past and present.[34]

---

34 Making connections with policing, militarism, and US empire is critically important to help expand our imagination and action in service of demilitarization and de-occupation. Places like Okinawa, Puerto Rico, Hawai'i, Guam, and elsewhere offer ways of reworking Afro-Asian solidarity. See Camp and Heatherton, *Policing the Planet*; Shigematsu and Camacho, *Militarized Currents*; Saranillio, *Unsustainable Empire*; Johnson, "Empire of Bases;" and finally the Black Lives Matter solidarity statement coming out of occupied Okinawa, which was issued by the collective, "Project Disagree."

BIBLIOGRAPHY

Baldwin, James. "An Open Letter to My Sister, Miss Angela Davis." *The New York Review*, January 1971. https://www.nybooks.com/articles/1971/01/07/an-open-letter-to-my-sister-miss-angela-davis/.

Bayoumi, Moustafa. "How the War on Terror Created the "Muslim American"." *The Nation*, September 2021. https://www.thenation.com/article/society/muslim-american-race/.

Boggs, Grace Lee. *Living for Revolution: An Autobiography*. Foreword by Robin D. G. Kelley. Minneapolis: University of Minnesota Press, 2016.

———, and Scott Kurashige. *The Next American Revolution: Sustainable Activism for the Twenty-First Century*. Berkeley: University of California Press, 2012.

Camp, Jordan T. *Incarcerating the Crisis: Freedom Struggles and the Rise of the Neoliberal State*. Berkeley: University of California Press, 2016.

———, and Christina Heatherton, eds. *Policing the Planet: Why the Policing Crisis Led to Black Lives Matter*. New York: Verso, 2016.

Chan, Rosalie. "How a Group of Asian Americans Is Spreading Support for Black Lives Matter." *Times*, July 14, 2016. https://time.com/4404229/black-lives-matter-letter-alton-sterling-philando-castile/.

Cobb, Jelani. "An American Spring of Reckoning." *The New Yorker*, June 22, 2020. https://www.newyorker.com/magazine/2020/06/22/an-american-spring-of-reckoning.

———. "Derek Chauvin's Trial and George Floyd's City." *The New Yorker*, July 5, 2021. https://www.newyorker.com/magazine/2021/07/12/derek-chauvins-trial-and-george-floyds-city.

Combs, Marianne. "Miss Saigon Protest Draws Hundreds." *MPR News*, October 9, 2013. https://www.mprnews.org/story/2013/10/09/miss-saigon-protest-draws-hundreds.

Davis, Mike. *City of Quartz: Excavating the Future in Los Angeles*. New York: Vintage Books, 1992.

———. "LA: The Fire This Time." *Covert Action Information Bulletin*, no. 41 (1992) 12–21.

Du Bois, W. E. B. "The African Roots of War." In *W. E. B. Du Bois: A Reader*, edited by David Levering Lewis, 642–651. New York: Henry Holt and Company, 1995.

Fu, May C. "On Contradiction: Theory and Transformation in Detroit's Asian Political Alliance." *Amerasia Journal* 35, no. 2 (2009) 1-23.

Fujino Diane C., and Robyn Magalit Rodriguez, eds. *Contemporary Asian American Activism: Building Movements for Liberation*. Seattle: University of Washington Press, 2022.

———, "Yuri Kochiyama." *Densho Encyclopedia*. June 3, 2014. https://encyclopedia.densho.org/Yuri_Kochiyama/.

———. *Heartbeat of Struggle: The Revolutionary Life of Yuri Kochiyama*. Minneapolis: University of Minnesota Press, 2005.

———. "Grassroots Leadership and Afro-Asian Solidarities: Yuri Kochiyama's Humanizing Radicalism." In *Want to Start a Revolution? Radical Women in the Black Freedom Struggle*, edited by Dayo F. Gore, Jeanne Theoharis, and Komozi Woodard, 294-316. New York: NYU Press, 2009.

Gooding-Williams, Robert, ed. *Reading Rodney King/Reading Urban Uprising*. New York: Routledge, 1993.

Hong, Christine. *A Violent Peace: Race, U.S. Militarism, and Cultures of Democratization in Cold War Asia and the Pacific*. Stanford, CA: Stanford University Press, 2020.

Ishizuka, Karen L. "Flying in the Face of Race, Gender, Class, and Age: A Story About Kazu Iijima, One of the Mothers of the Asian American Movement on the First Year Anniversary of Her Death." *Amerasia Journal* 35, no. 2 (2009) 24-48.

———. *Serve the People: Making Asian America in the Long Sixties*. New York: Verso, 2018.

Itagaki, Lynn Mie. *Civil Racism: The 1992 Los Angeles Rebellion and the Crisis of Racial Burnout*. Minneapolis: University of Minnesota Press, 2016.

Jany, Libor. "Minneapolis' Third Precinct Served as a Playground' for Renegade Cops." *Star Tribune*, June 7, 2020. https://www.startribune.com/minneapolis-third-precinct-served-as-playground-for-renegade-cops/571076562/.

Jennings. Angel. "How the Killing of Latasha Harlins Changed South L.A. Long Before Black Lives Matter." *Los Angeles Times*, March 18, 2016. https://www.latimes.com/local/california/la-me-0318-latasha-harlins-20160318-story.html.

Jin, Connie Hanzhang. "6 Charts That Dismantle the Trope of Asian Americans as a Model Minority." *NPR*, May 25, 2021. https://www.npr.org/2021/05/25/999874296/6-charts-that-dismantle-the-trope-of-asian-americans-as-a-model-minority.

Johnson, Chalmers. "Empire of Bases." *New York Times*, July 13, 2009. https://www.nytimes.com/2009/07/14/opinion/14iht-edjohnson.html.

Jung, Soya. "The Racial Justice Movement Needs a Model Minority Mutiny." *Race Files*, October 13, 2014. https://www.racefiles.com/2014/10/13/model-minority-mutiny/.

Kelley, Robin D. G. "Thug Nation: On State Violence and Disposability." In *Policing the Planet: Why the Policing Crisis Led to Black Lives Matter*, edited by Jordan T. Camp and Christina Heatherton, 15–33. New York: Verso, 2016.

Kim, Claire Jean. "The Racial Triangulation of Asian Americans." *Politics & Society* 27:1 (1999) 105–138.

Kim, Elaine H. "Home Is Where the *Han* Is: A Korean American Perspective on the Los Angeles Upheavals." In *Reading Rodney King/Reading Urban Uprising*, edited by Robert Gooding Williams, 215–235. New York: Routledge, 1993.

Kurashige, Scott. "Responding to Trump: Lessons from Grace Lee Boggs." *Unmargin*. https://www.unmargin.org/glbscottkirashige.

Lee, Grace, director. *American Revolutionary: The Evolution of Grace Lee Boggs*. LeeLee Films, 2013.

Los Angeles Times. "Libor Jany Joins *The Times* as Law Enforcement and Justice Issues Reporter." *Los Angeles Times*, March 7, 2022. https://www.latimes.com/about/pressreleases/story/2022-03-07/libor-jany-joins-the-times-as-law-enforcement-and-justice-issues-reporter.

Maeda, Daryl J. *Chains of Babylon: The Rise of Asian America*. Minneapolis: University of Minnesota Press, 2009.

———. *Rethinking the Asian American Movement*. New York: Routledge, 2012.

Mills, Charles W. *The Racial Contract*. Ithaca: Cornell University Press, 1997.

MPD 150. *Enough Is Enough: A 150 Year Performance Review of the Minneapolis Police Department*. Expanded Edition, 2020. https://

www.mpd150.com/wpcontent/uploads/reports/report_2_compressed.pdf.

Nelson, Tim. "Behind the Scenes with the Gang Strike Force." *MPR News*, August 5, 2009. https://www.mprnews.org/story/2009/08/05/gangstrikeforce-report.

———. "Investigator Says Gang Strike Force Actions were 'Criminal'." *MPR News*. August 20, 2009. https://www.mprnews.org/story/2009/08/20/strikeforce-report.

Park, Ishle Yi. *The Temperature of This Water*. Los Angeles: Kaya Press, 2004.

Park, Lisa Sun-Hee. "Continuing Significance of the Model Minority Myth: The Second Generation." *Social Justice* 35, no. 2 (2008) 134–144.

Pew Research Center. "Income Inequality in the U.S. Is Rising Most Rapidly Among Asians." July 2018.

Phi, Bao. "War Before Memory: A Vietnamese American Protest Organizer's History Against 'Miss Saigon'." *Hyphen*, September 24, 2013. https://hyphenmagazine.com/blog/ 2013/9/24/war-memory-vietnamese-american-protest-organizers-history-against-miss-saigon.

———. "Fong Lee: The Human Cost and the Strength of His Family." *Star Tribune*, September 28, 2010. https://www.startribune.com/fong-lee-the-human-cost-and-the-strength-of-his-family/103979934/.

———. "8 (9)," *Sông I Sing*. Minneapolis: Coffee House Press, 2011.

———. "Unprotected by Assimilation: Lessons from the Case of Duy Ngo." *Reappropriate: Asian American Feminism, Politics, and Pop Culture*, May 5, 2015. http://reappropriate.com/2015/05/unprotected-by-assimilation-lessons-from-the-case-of-duy-ngo/#more-8610.

———. "Untitled: A Reflection from a Vietnamese American in Minneapolis." *DiaCRITICS*, June 2, 2020. https://dvan.org/2020/06/reflection-from-minneapolis/.

Project Disagree. "A Statement of Solidarity with Black Lives Matter." June 15, 2020. http://www.projectdisagree.org/2020/06/a-statement-of-solidarity-with-black.html.

Rodriguez, Dylan. "'Warfare and the Terms of Engagement'." In *Abolition Now! Ten Years of Strategy and Struggle against the Prison Industrial Complex*, edited by The CR 10 Publications Collective, 91–102. Oakland: AK Press, 2008.

Roediger, David. "Gook: The Short History of an Americanism." In *Towards the Abolition of Whiteness: Essays on Race, Politics, Working-Class History*, 117–120. New York: Verso, 1994.

Kim-Gibson, Dai Sil, director. *Sa-I-Gu: From Korean Women's Perspectives*, DVD. Co-Produced by Christine Choy and Elaine H. Kim. San Francisco: Center for Asian American Media, 1983.

Saranillio, Dean Itsuji. *Unsustainable Empire: Alternative Histories of Hawai'i Statehood*. Durham, NC: Duke University Press, 2018.

Shigematsu, Setsu, and Keith L. Camacho, eds. *Militarized Currents: Toward a Decolonized Future in Asia and the Pacific*. Minneapolis: University of Minnesota Press, 2010.

Singh, Nikhil Pal. "The Whiteness of Police." *American Quarterly* 6, no. 4 (2014) 1091–1099.

———. *Race and America's Long War*. Berkeley: University of California Press, 2017.

———. "Enough Toxic Militarism." *Quincy Brief*, No. 2 (2019) 1–7.

Tajiri, Rea, director. *Yuri Kochiyama: Passion for Justice*. New York: Women Make Movies, 1993.

Tang, Eric. *Unsettled: Cambodian Refugees in the NYC Hyperghetto*. Philadelphia: Temple University Press, 2015.

Taylor, Keeanga-Yamahtta. "The Emerging Movement for Police and Prison Abolition," *The New Yorker*, May 7, 2021. https://www.newyorker.com/news/our-columnists/the-emerging-movement-for-police-and-prison-abolition.

Vang, Her. "Dreaming of Home, Dreaming of Land: Displacements and Hmong Transnational Politics, 1975-2010." Ph.D. diss., University of Minnesota, 2010.

Vang, Nengher N. "Unlawful or Not: Reassessing the Value and Impact of Hmong American Transnational Politics." *Amerasia Journal* 44, no. 2 (2018) 43–64.

Wagner, Laura. "Former NYPD Officer Peter Liang Gets Probation for Fatal Shooting," *National Public Radio*, April 19, 2016. https://www.npr.org/sections/thetwo-way/2016/04/19/474846986/former-nypd-officer-peter-liang-gets-house-arrest-probation-for-fatal-shooting.

Wang, Hansi Lo. "'Awoke' by N.Y. Cop Shooting, Asian American Activists Chart Way Forward." *NPR Code Switch*, April 23, 2016. https://www.npr.org/sections/codeswitch/2016/04/23/475369524/

awoken-by-n-y-cop-shooting-asian-american-activists-chart-way-forward.

Williams, Brandt. "Fong Lee's Family Angered by Verdict." *MPR News*, May 28, 2009. https://www.mprnews.org/story/2009/05/28/fong-lees-family-angered-by-verdict.

Yang, Hannah. "'We Need to Help Them': Asian Americans Demand Justice for Floyd." *MPR News*, June 11, 2020. https://www.mprnews.org/story/2020/06/09/we-need-to-help-them-asian-americans-demand-justice-for-george-floyd.

PART TWO:
PRACTICING & SHARING STORIES OF LIBERATION

5

can't stop, won't stop: The Tradition of Black Education as the Practice of Freedom

Anthony Downer II

I sat staring at the page in front of me, feeling myself warming up and uncomfortable, emotions stirring in mind and soul. I was embarrassed and ashamed, not for myself, but for my white fourth grade teacher lecturing to her classroom of predominantly unassuming scholars. As Ms. Crawford presented on the history of American slavery, my eyes wouldn't leave the image on my page: a group of enslaved Africans chained at the necks, wrists, and ankles. We hadn't discussed Black people until this day; our history was reduced to this image and this historical event. *She's not telling the entire story.* I thought. *Why isn't she telling the truth?* She talked about the desperate need for labor, used the word "slave," and stopped short of details about the violent system. As a teacher now, I wonder what it was like for Ms. Crawford to introduce most of her students, many of them descendants of enslaved Africans, to such a topic. What did she know? What didn't she know? How did she prepare? How did it make her feel? I now realize the full extent of my embarrassment and shame at eight or nine years of age. The US education system had failed Ms. Crawford; it had failed all of us. It excluded my people and their history from the curriculum, creating a chasm between teacher and students, leaving stranded a white educator charged with the education of Black and brown learners.

Even then, I felt the tension between the textbooks and standards in the brick-and-mortar and the holistic learning my ancestors and family afforded me. When I thought, *why isn't she telling the truth?* I really meant, *why isn't she telling the truth that I know?* You see, my mom committed herself to an age-old Black proverb: each one, teach one. She passed along to me what her family gave her: our history. Before hearing my teacher's version of slavery in the fourth grade, my mom introduced me to the institution years before. I was born to a young, married couple in 1994. My mom was a junior at Spelman College, my dad a Navy veteran. She carried me to her classes and by two years old, she had disciplined me enough to read and write. Through books, obituaries, reunion programs, and photos; she showed my brothers and me our family history interwoven into the Pan-African story, the history of our people across time and space.

I learned what I should have learned in fourth grade and every grade—that my people were not just enslaved. Around 1883, two, former slaves settled in what would become Fairview, Texas. They were David Crockett, my great-great-great grandfather who descended from Africans and Seminole native people, and Charlie Westbrooks, my great-great-great-great grandfather, a product of rape. New generations were born, with marriages sometimes resulting in seventeen children. In the 1930s, my great-grandparents, J.B. Westbrooks and Vidalia Adams married and in 1939, their families joined a movement of Blacks fleeing the terror and oppression of the South. They landed in Oakland, California. J.B. became a longshoreman and made sure he left a mark on the world, intertwining his family in US history. The Westbrooks in Oakland championed equal rights and justice by refusing to unload ships that came from South Africa to protest apartheid. They pushed the city to hire more Blacks on the waterfront. My great-uncle, Aaron, founded and sold what became skycapping at airports. J.B.'s daughter, Connie, became the first female truck driver of any race in Oakland and his daughter, Carol, my grandmother, organized with the Black Panthers and later served as chapter president and national recording secretary of the National Council of Negro Women. My ancestors' activism, education, entrepreneurship, and resilience made me. I discovered this outside of the classroom.

An authentically Black-centric classroom has criticality, identity development, intellectualism, and joy. These are the pillars in learning environments I cultivate today based on the scholarship of Drs. Adam Green, Zaretta Hammond, Bettina Love, Gholdy Muhammad, and others. Most of the classrooms I've entered have lacked these essential ingredients to nurturing a Black boy's brilliance. As I explored complex personal inquiries, "Who am I? Where did I come from? Why am I here," I was largely left to my own academic and scholarly devices. As my imagination flowed and brain developed, I navigated a disconcerting dilemma. As I demonstrated superior performance in gifted classes and on standardized assessments, I had to code-switch in an environment that conflicted with and rejected my culture and identity. I did, however, have advocates in the classroom who resisted the Eurocentric status quo. Mrs. Williams, my fifth grade and first Black teacher, directed me from the *Harry Potter* series to books about civil rights and with Black protagonists. By the eighth grade, my peers secretly called me a Black supremacist because of my public curiosity about—and vocal passion for—Black history. Each year, I advocated for Black History month celebrations, submitted assignments about unsung Black figures, and followed Barack Obama's campaigns and presidency. I resisted my culturally white homogenous education every chance I could.

By high school, the race to college was on. I knew my charge and the expectation for me. I excelled in my Advanced Placement classes that were void of African-centric lessons and literature. But still I rose. To counteract the white fictional characters in books such as *A Series of Unfortunate Events*, *A to Z Mysteries*, and *Magic Tree House*; I dug deep into works by Black artists that inspired my own poems and short stories.

In college at the University of Chicago, I began adopting the Black radical tradition, shedding the respectability politics my suburban school district impressed upon me. I read Fred Hampton and Assata Shakur and explored Black political ideologies and movements. During my second year, Dr. Dwight Hopkins facilitated a comparative analysis between the Reverend Dr. King and Malcolm X. I was in awe at reading and observing their remarks and writings in a new light, arriving at a refreshed interpretation of their legacies. A course led by the illustrious Dr. Cathy Cohen followed. The founder of the Black Youth Project ensured we studied not just past events and topics but contemporary Black political moments, from Cory Booker's first mayoral race to the historical figures who made Obama's rise possible to the lessons on policing and mass incarceration learned from the Ferguson report.

I took a course with my second Black male educator, Dr. Adam Green, in the last semester of my senior year, while Dr. Michael Dawson served as my BA advisor. Dr. Green brought his impassioned intellectual pursuit and critical historical lens to the classroom. I was profoundly impacted. I recall his intentionally challenging presentations of the Black Christian tradition on the Southside of Chicago, the Chicago race massacre of 1919, and the Chicago Public Schools student boycotts of the 1960s. Interestingly, he never mentioned his famous father, Ernest Green, the oldest and first to graduate of the Little Rock Nine. I forgive him for this grave academic violation. At the time, I did not know that these sociocultural spaces were molding my future pedagogy, the foundation of my teaching philosophy and approach to teaching history and social studies.

Drs. Hopkins, Cohen, Green, and Dawson brought our history to life with their primary sources, soulful cadences, and incisive feedback. In turn, they brought the scholar in me to life. I wrote my bachelor's degree thesis, my first serious scholarship, on the ebb and flow of Black conservatism during Obama's presidency. Without my intellectual guides, I could not grasp the specific battles between Black conservatives and progressives across time. By the time I graduated college, I understood that I was not entirely alone in the classroom.

In the early twentieth century, educator and historian Carter G. Woodson, the father of Black history and my fellow University of Chicago alum, argued, "What we need is not a history of selected races or nations but the history of the world void of national bias, race hate, and religious prejudice."[1] A hundred years later, we still have not achieved historically accurate and inclusive curricula. We exclude Black and brown students and their history and culture. For instance, the Georgia state standards for US history have just two Black people, ethnic studies is usually an elective, and Black and other racial/Ethnic Studies courses are absent! And it's not just the curriculum; schools have consistently made their anti-Blackness and Eurocentrism clear in all areas, from gifted program enrollment to the various disciplines. Our scholars of color and their education are under attack.

In order to rebuild an inclusive, representative school system, we need culturally responsive teaching, which is "a pedagogy that empowers students intellectually, socially, emotionally, and politically by using cultural referents to impart knowledge, skills, and attitudes."[2] Culturally responsive and relevant classrooms allow students to sharpen their critical consciousness in a learning environment that is welcoming and affirming with high expectations and access to a rigorous and multicultural curriculum. Georgia State University's Dr. Gholdy Muhammad goes further. She states,

---

1 Woodson, "The Celebration of Negro History."
2 Ladson-Billings, *The Dreamkeepers,*" 17.

Intellectually invigorating and deeply humanizing education is urgently needed, especially for our students of color, to overcome decades of oppression and lost opportunity. We must interrogate and reframe our learning standards, curriculum, state assessments, and teacher evaluations to be aligned with *historically responsive education*. All children should experience the power and joy of self-discovery, and the expansion of the mind and heart to become their most excellent and brilliant selves. The lessons of our ancestors provide a perfect place to start.[3]

Let's be clear, we cannot meet this standard of equity and inclusion, of justice and liberation in education with the white supremacist capitalist heteronormative patriarchal model. We will achieve our collective vision with revolutionary education that builds on, rather than denies, the cultural knowledge in our communities and throughout history.

If I had Drs. Cohen or Green earlier in my education, I would have had a more thorough analysis and deep knowledge of our world. As a civics and history educator, I'm committed to bringing concepts, events, and figures in history to my scholars that were absent or brushed over in my education. They will learn their history, laws and state curriculum be damned. It is my honor to share these gaps in our education here.

My Own Fugitive Pedagogy

During the early decades of the twentieth century, Carter G. Woodson supported a network of Black teachers who acted as 'double agents' throughout the Jim Crow South and elsewhere in the United States. These 'fugitive pedagogists' kept constant the "heritage of black education: a lived tension between antiblack persecution in 'the American School'... and the intellectual and embodied acts of subversion black people deployed to navigate those constraints."[4] According to Dr. Jarvis Givens of Harvard University, Woodson's coordinated and often covert campaigns in education challenged the control of Black bodies and minds. Indeed, "[f]ugitive pedagogy names the educational acts of escape constituting the precondition of black freedom implied by the very notion of 'education as freedom.'"[5] Nearly a century later, Black academics, educators, and

---

3 Muhammad, "Historical Black Excellence."
4 Givens, *Fugitive Pedagogy*, 5–6.
5 Givens, *Fugitive Pedagogy*, 13.

intellectuals continue this tradition by resisting and subverting white supremacist curriculum, instruction, policies, and practices.

Frederick Douglass, the namesake of my most recent school where I taught, vehemently fought the status quo and oppression of his era. We're not quite sure of Douglass's exact birth date. He was born Frederick Augustus Washington Bailey around 1817–1818 in Talbot County, Maryland to a Native American mother and Black/European father. The wife of one of his enslavers taught him the alphabet, and he taught himself to read and write. He taught other enslaved Africans using the Bible, risking brutal beatings. In 1838, after several failed attempts, he escaped slavery by train to New York. He sent for a girl he loved, named Anna Murray. They married in September 1838, relocated to Massachusetts, and had five children. Douglass did not just escape and end his mission. He began traveling across the country and world, meeting with allies and advocating for the abolition of slavery. He carried the power of the word through the social media of his time, a newspaper he founded called *The North Star*. In 1877, Douglass met with Thomas Auld, the man who once "owned" him, and the two reportedly reconciled. In 1882, Douglass' wife, Anna died. In 1884, he married white activist Helen Pitts. In 1888, he became the first African American to receive a vote for President of the United States during the Republican National Convention. In 1895, Douglass died from a heart attack on his way home from a meeting of the National Council of Women, a women's rights group. Douglass was the most photographed Black man in history. His story reminds us of the struggle for liberation led by Black people, that the white-centric approach to teaching slavery does not include a few Black, special abolitionists but a movement of Black *espirit de corps* and courage that depended on strategic allies.

In fact, the alliances built proved complex and destructive at times. Frederick Douglass and Susan B. Anthony, the New England activist for abolition and women's rights, became friends in Rochester, New York around 1849. Douglass had attended the Women's Rights Convention in Seneca Falls the previous year. As a result, Anthony knew him as a staunch supporter of women's rights, especially the right to vote. And Douglass, primarily through her family, knew Anthony as a committed ally of Black rights. But by the late 1860s, following the Civil War, disagreements ensued. As Congress debated the fifteenth Amendment, which would grant

Black men the right to vote, white suffragists were enraged. Anthony and other activists such as Frances Willard traveled across the country, even to Southern spaces, to express their sentiments. They appealed to white supremacists for their support for women's right to vote and manipulated members of their race by playing to their inhumane views of Black people. They argued that uneducated, poor Black men should not vote before white women, the nation's moral protectors. This betrayal infuriated Ida B. Wells, a former enslaved-turned-journalist from Mississippi. She was also active in the women's right movement before the turn of the century. And as Black women do today, she decried this betrayal as well as the general silence of liberal white women on issues of race. In 1893, she traveled to Great Britain to gain support for her anti-lynching campaign. The following year, she was scheduled to speak at an event with Willard, a popular figure in London. In her brief time, Wells read the words of Willard from an interview in which she stated that "the colored race multiplies like the locusts of Egypt" and that the local tavern "is the Negro's center of power."[6]

Clearly, Willard, known as an ally to Black Americans, revealed her racist ideology as she pursued Southern support for suffrage and prohibition. Wells believed her to be a prime example of a false ally who in truth did not believe Black lives mattered. Allies of Willard's attempted to seek revenge against Wells. One even wrote to Douglass requesting a public reprimand. Although he refused, he failed to stand in solidarity with and condemn the attacks against Wells, she later revealed. Anthony and Douglass eventually reconciled, with the latter fervently recommitting to women's rights following the passage of the 15th Amendment. They were together at the National Council of Women meeting hours before Douglass died in 1895. Such complicated narratives are important as our scholars learn about intersectionality and white supremacy.

During Black August, the annual but largely unknown recognition of Black abolitionists, political prisoners, and revolutionaries, my students learn about revolutionaries like Angela Davis. Angela Davis, like the Black Panther and Communist Parties she joined in the late twentieth century, is continuously misrepresented and vilified. Our scholars deserve the truth. Angela Davis was born on January 26, 1944, in Birmingham, Alabama.

---

6 *The Voice*, "The Race Problem."

Davis is a global citizen who has fought oppression on all fronts, everywhere. Her studies at Brandeis University, the University of Frankfurt, University of California, San Diego, and the Humboldt University of Berlin radicalized her and expanded the scope of her work. During second-wave feminism, the movement against the Vietnam War, and the waning Civil Rights Movement, Davis became a vocal agent for change. In 1969, she became a professor of philosophy at the University of California, Los Angeles. Ronald Regan, then governor of California, orchestrated her firing by the Board of Regents because of her Communist ties. They were forced to rehire her after a court ruled her firing was unconstitutional. However, they fired her again, citing inappropriate and inflammatory language.

During fellow Black Panther Party member George Jackson's trial in August 1970, the Soledad brothers attempted to free Jackson and killed several people in the courthouse. They used guns registered to Davis, who was subsequently charged with murder. Davis went on the lam and was placed on the FBI's most wanted list. Eventually, she spent over a year in jail, which led to the "Free Angela Davis" campaign and the Angela Davis Legal Defense Committee, complete with shirts and songs. In 1972, she was acquitted of all charges. A free woman, she used her newfound fame to center police and prison abolition and anti-imperialism abroad.

In a 1997 interview for *Out* magazine, Davis came out as a lesbian. Across decades of global change, Davis has remained steadfast in her activism against intersectional oppression, from the United States to Palestine. She currently is a professor at the University of California, Santa Cruz, where she teaches courses on critical race studies and the history of consciousness. Davis is founder of Critical Resistance and the author of several books including *Women, Race, and Class* (1983) and *Are Prisons Obsolete?* (2003). I am an academic and personal fan of hers; her work has assisted in the development of my own abolitionist ideology. In fact, I placed a large tapestry of her younger self with her signature Afro in my classroom and office, bearing her quote, "I am no longer accepting the things I cannot change. I am changing the things I cannot accept"—a mantra that guides my work.[7]

---

7 Brownworth, "LGBT HISTORY MONTH."

The absence of Marsha P. Johnson—and LGBTQ+ history and narratives in general—from our curriculum sends out a clear message to all scholars, but especially to those who would benefit from the representation of her story. Marsha 'Pay It No Mind' Johnson was born Malcolm Michaels, Jr. in 1945 in Elizabeth, New Jersey. After enduring the bigotry of her family and community, she moved to New York to freely live her life as a gender non-conforming person. She entered the world of drag and sex work and began shining a light on the experience of people living on the margins of society. Her struggles with mental health issues made her a complicated figure in the budding gay rights movement of the late 1960s and 1970s. She was, nevertheless, central to the work. She was one of the first drag queens to begin frequenting the Mafia-owned Stonewall Inn, a popular gay bar in the Greenwich Village neighborhood of New York City. On June 28, 1969, as the night turned to morning, one of the regular police raids of the bar went terribly wrong. As police made arrests, resistance rose. Someone threw a glass or brick. Reports on this, however, vary. Patrons and bystanders fought back, furious at the discrimination, harassment, and targeting. Although Johnson is often credited as one of the people who initiated the riots, she acknowledged that she arrived at the bar after the riots began. Still, a new movement had been born and Johnson was at the front. She joined the Gay Liberation Front and on June 28, 1970, to commemorate the one-year anniversary of the Stonewall riots, marched in the Christopher Street Liberation Day parade, the first organized Gay Pride rally.

From marches and protests to sit-ins and political participation, Johnson used the Black and queer organizing tradition to advance public discourse and change. I often teach Johnson's story to emphasize intersectional coalition-building, noting Johnson's partnership with fellow queer activist, Sylvia Rivera. Together, they founded the Street Transvestite Action Revolutionaries (STAR) and STAR House, a shelter for homeless LGBTQ+ individuals. In 1973, when drag queens were banned from the Gay Pride parade in New York City, they raised their voices and powered ahead. By the 1980s, Johnson was committed to caring for others during the AIDS epidemic. She was HIV-positive and directly experienced the policy failures and loss of life. Despite her sincere and faith-inspired contributions, Johnson struggled financially and mentally. In 1992, her body was found in the Hudson River, the result of a mysterious and unsolved attack. Johnson's unapologetic and bold approach to her activism and care stands as a model for our own resistance today.

Bayard Rustin is an unsung hero, more of a composer than drum major for justice as he was relegated to the background of the Civil Rights Movement. Rustin was born in 1912 in West Chester, Pennsylvania. He revealed his gay identity to his family early on, notably receiving support from his grandmother. He also adopted an ideology founded in non-violence and racial justice. In 1937, he attended the City College of New York. He became a member of the Young Communist League but left when World War II began in 1939. In 1944, he went to jail for the first time for refusing to participate in the war draft. In 1941, his arrests continued after he joined the Fellowship of Reconciliation (FOR), which centered labor rights but excluded homosexuals from their work.

In 1953, Rustin was arrested and charged with "sex perversion" in Pasadena, California when he was found having consensual sex in a car with another man. This arrest led to his firing from FOR. He maintained a key relationship with A. Phillip Randolph, a fellow labor rights organizer. Together, they planned a March on Washington for Black workers, specifically in the defense industry. In 1956, Randolph invited Rustin to meet a young Dr. Martin Luther King, Jr. during the Montgomery Bus Boycott. The two became allies and Rustin was a pivotal member of Dr. King's inner circle. In fact, Rustin is credited with convincing Dr. King to fully adopt peaceful, nonviolent resistance as the cornerstone of the movement. In 1960, however, Congressman Adam Powell threatened to publicly accuse Dr. King and Rustin of having an affair. The threat came in response to Dr. King's planned protest at the 1960 Democratic National Convention over the exclusion of a stronger position on civil rights from the party platform. Rustin resigned from the Southern Christian Leadership Conference. The protest, nevertheless, continued as planned. Still, Rustin remained engaged if not deeply involved. He continued to advocate for a March on Washington, though others made sure he was not the face of the march. While Randolph chaired the organizing efforts, Rustin was key to its success. He faced homophobia at every turn—from Black leaders to racist politicians. He realized the movement's work was grander, more impactful than any individual. His activism for Black and gay rights continued until his death in 1987.

One of my favorite figures to teach in world history is Mansa Musa, the world's richest man to ever live. At its peak, his net worth was an estimated $400 billion, outpacing today's top billionaires. The son of Sundiata, the Lion King of the Mali Empire, he was born sometime in the last decade of the thirteenth century CE. When he took the throne around 1312, he set his eyes on expanding the rich, Muslim empire of his father. He expanded the borders and military. While it is unclear his exact wealth, he likely benefited greatly from the gold-salt trade route and possibly the slave trade. In 1324, he went on hajj to Mecca, stopping along African and Arabic cities along the way. His fame rose as he passed out gold nuggets and other gifts. His voyage deeply impressed him. Upon his return home, he strengthened the connection between the Mali Empire and the rest of the Muslim world. He brought with him scholars from diverse backgrounds, who helped him build mosques and a university, especially in the city of Timbuktu. Trade and cultural exchanges flourished. Between 1332 and 1337, Mansa Musa died, passing the throne to his son briefly and leaving a generous legacy and sprawling empire in West Africa. I recently had a student who used her time in class to work on her apparel business. I was inspired to provide her support and share Musa's story when she declared on the first day of class, "I'm going to be the world's first trillionaire."

In a 2018 interview, rapper Kanye West remarked, "When you hear about slavery for four hundred years...For four hundred years? That sounds like a choice."[8] He suggested then and later the following lies: 1) our enslaved ancestors fully accepted their positions, and 2) they never resisted or rebelled. At the time, I dismissed his comments. No one could agree with such ignorance, right? Wrong. By the next year, I had heard more than a few students ask a question founded in similar ignorance: "Why didn't the enslaved fight back?" The truth is they did. Despite the multitude of differences among them, Africans and their descendants struggled against European invasion, colonization, enslavement, and imperialism. They won some battles and lost others. But each generation of agitators and disruptors inspired the next. Today, Black people like me continue the storied tradition.

---

8 Charlemagne, "Kanye West."

Queen Nanny was born in the late seventeenth century in Ghana and kidnapped into slavery as a child. She was taken to Jamaica, then a British colony. Eventually, she joined her brothers and others and escaped the plantations, fleeing to the mountains and jungles of Jamaica. They became the Windward Maroons, one of several groups of Jamaican escapees. In 1720, the British attacked the Maroons but were met with strategic resistance. Queen Nanny led scores of successful battles and freed around eight hundred enslaved Africans. In 1733, however, Queen Nanny was killed in battle and her town destroyed. Still, the war ended in 1739 and the British recognized the freedom of the Maroons in 1740. In 1775, Jamaica recognized Queen Nanny as a National Heroine and endowed her with the title, 'Right Excellent.' Her face adorns the $500 bill.

Anacaona, another fierce fighter for her people, was born in 1474 in the chiefdom of Jaragua in Hispaniola. She was destined to rule. She was the sister of the Jaragua chief, and wife of the Maguana one, making her one of the most powerful Taíno caciques. In 1496, on one of the voyages Columbus made to Hispaniola, Anacaona and her brother, Bohechio, greeted the voyager. The Spaniards sought their usual arrangement: fake civility, kill some of the leaders, then demand tribute in exchange for relative peace. The Spaniards proceeded to pillage the island through massacres and slavery. Anacaona eventually became chief, having lost her brothers and husband to execution following suspicions of an impending attack on the Spanish. She decided that fighting the Spaniards in small rebellions was nonsensical and only made everything worse. In 1502, Spain named a new governor of Hispaniola, Nicolás de Ovando. For Ovando, the most dangerous local was Anacaona. He used a peace treaty meeting to kill many of Anacaona's leaders and turn others against her. She was captured, charged with treason, and sentenced to death by hanging. According to one legend, she was offered clemency if she became a concubine to a Spanish official. Whatever happened officially, Anacaona resisted and was hanged. In world history, my students analyzed the lyrics of the 1971 song, "Anacaona," by Cheo Feliciano.

Saartje (Sara) Baartman was born in 1789 in South Africa. By sixteen years old, she had lost both parents, her husband, and her infant child. She was eventually sold into slavery by Dutch colonists. On October 29, 1810, she was forced to sign a contract with her captives, the Cezar brothers, and a doctor named William Dunlop. The contract required that she would work as a domestic servant and travel across the United Kingdom. She would also be displayed for her shapely figure, the result of a disease in which adipose mass accumulated especially in her buttocks. They could not enslave her since the institution was by then illegal in Great Britain.

On November 24, 1810, she was exhibited in the Egyptian Hall at Piccadilly Circus in London. Abolitionists unsuccessfully sought to free her, but a court upheld the contract. Baartman became a popular sight to see, traveling across the country at different exhibits. In 1812, she was sold to an animal exhibitionist in France, where patrons could sexually abuse her for money. Remarks about her large breast and buttocks reached across the globe. Baartman died in Paris in 1815 at twenty-six years old. Her body parts remained on display up until 1974 in museums like the *Musée de l'Homme* (Museum of Man). In 1994, President Nelson Mandela requested that her body be returned to South Africa, which finally occurred in 2002. Baartman's trafficked person is but one example of the sexualization, fetishization, and commodification of Black women. Further, it is evidence of the prevailing Eurocentric and white supremacist standards of beauty and other norms, standards that have disrupted the traditional African cultures of women leadership and gender roles ,and instead replaced them with contemporary and anti-African systems of fatphobia, heteronormativity, homophobia, sexism, and other forms of body-shaming.

Teaching Truths

This past spring, Georgia joined several other states in passing its rejection of critical race theory, called the Protect Students First Act or HB 1084. The law prohibits the teaching of nine divisive concepts, including that the United States and Georgia are fundamentally and systemically racist. By design, classroom materials and instruction on race and other "controversial" subjects are limited; parents can complain to their student's principal about inappropriate or offensive lessons or materials and begin a process that punishes teachers and schools.

As a practitioner in teaching secondary social studies, I am most appalled by this new law. It prevents abolitionist, culturally responsive, equity-centric, and "ratchetdemic"[9] educators like my comrades and me

---

9 See Emdin, *Ratchetdemic.*

from embedded essential pillars in our classrooms to produce decolonized, communitarian learning spaces. The law strips us of our ability to develop critically conscious, culturally and racially literate scholars who are able to lead, serve, and thrive in a multicultural, globalized society. And the law violates our rights, the same rights our ancestors earned, which aid our liberation and combat moral decadence. In my classrooms, my philosophy is grounded in this mandate: "Create space for genius, and genius will emerge." The following curricular values and shared commitments spring from that foundation: criticality, identity development, intellectualism, and joy.

Criticality, as defined by Dr. Muhammad, "is helping students read, write, and think in active ways."[10] The concepts and connections that bring our curriculum standards to life are not intangible or irrelevant. History has often devastating connections to the living human beings in our classrooms. Their current conditions are direct outcomes of the historical events we teach. As a civics educator, I would be remiss if I simply taught the history and structure of our democracy without formulating a space for scholars to freedom-dream and engage. For example, students in my classrooms have completed civic action projects, as well as called and wrote letters to their members of the Atlanta Board of Education and the General Assembly. They have also conducted grassroots and political campaigns on key issues in their communities. This activism worries the status quo, even in 'progressive' schools.

One of the core tenets of culturally responsive education, even the less advanced diverse or multicultural education, is identity development. Genuine trauma-informed and differentiated approaches to instruction and teaching are employed. To realize my district's social emotional learning standards and "Learning for Justice's Social Justice" standards, I incorporated practices such as affirmations, art, music presentation and production, healing circles, and meditation. One example is a lesson on intersectionality, a framework likely to be targeted by the new law as a 'divisive concept,' according to a discussion at a state senate public hearing on Monday, February 7, 2022. The lesson includes reading the history and products of the Combahee River Collective, a Black womanist lesbian organization based in Boston, MA. Its members, from Audre

---

10 Muhammad, "Historically Responsive Literacy."

Lorde to Barbara Smith, introduced intersectionality, a tool for analyzed the exclusion of Black women and lesbians from the feminist movement and Civil Rights Movement.

Students learn about the range of identity categories and then use identity charts and art to describe and discuss their own identities. The conservative narrative is that intersectionality teaches minoritized scholars to believe their oppression to be absolute and unending, a depressing perspective. Instead, they build a scholarly community and develop personally by expressing themselves freely. They understood that their Blackness, youth, and other identities and experiences were not monolithic. The curriculum extends this aim; by centering African kingdoms and ingenuity, resistance, shared values, we develop an optimistic realism overlaying a communitarian, collectivist outlook. Indeed, my scholars' ancestors were the originators of socialism; they rejected the bastardized form of American individualism. As individuals and community members, they learn that "Identity is who you say you are, who others say you are... (and) who you desire to be."[11]

In an era where knowledge is misconstructed and misrepresented, accurate and nuanced information and resources need to be readily available. Although our scholars still need to develop critical thinking and research skills, they are well-versed in educating themselves through diverse forms of social media, from Google to TikTok. I admit that I introduce new concepts, knowledge, and topics. But by and large, our students are not empty vessels, not ignorant, indolent individuals. They bring a need, desire for some level of learning and thinking. New ideas are exciting. They rise to the occasion when we dismantle the racist lowered academic standards for beginning and developing learners. And they know what's going on around them and are curious about their present and future. Scholars readily bring new topics to the classroom—stories from across the pan-African diaspora, the war in Ukraine, the latest victim of state-sanctioned, police violence. They can explain and use common vernacular to teach each other.

We talk about learning loss and yes, there are deficiencies in their skills. But this truly denotes the major data loss, which is the primary concern of corporations like school districts and education companies

---

[11] Ferlazzo, "Author Interview with Dr. Gholdy Muhammad."

that depend on corporatist standardized testing. Our young people are learning and developing both 'soft' and 'hard' skills, independent and despite violent institutions of learning. The learning exemplars and products I have witnessed reveal this truth. They personally understand anti-Blackness, government, gentrification, and intersectionality. I regularly give academic terms to their lived experiences and cultures. In using their background knowledge, strengths, and personhoods to develop their skills, I'm a facilitator of learning and co-learner. Herein lies the reality of a decolonized classroom. Indeed, Dr. Muhammad states,

> [b]ecause our recent standards have been so skills-driven, knowledge has fallen by the wayside in a lot of schools, and that can strip away the joy that comes from simply learning new things about the world. But the Black Literary Societies of the 19th century valued knowledge as a vital part of a person's development. 'So I'm pushing this idea of intellectualism,' Muhammad says, 'of treating young people as if they are scholars and intellectuals and thinkers.'[12]

Identity and intellectualism come first, skills will follow. The result are classrooms co-led by young philosophers, using their curiosity and inquiring natures to discover authentic history. Notice how that depiction diverges from the one that motivates much of these laws: that biased teachers who were radicalized at private, liberal universities are indoctrinating our scholars with critical race theory and divisive concepts. How extremely off-base.

In social studies, educators should not simply deliver content but facilitate scholarship, thereby adding to the field of study at any grade level. Any good lit review has diverse sources for readers to explore. And any good social studies course allows for the open exploration of their scholars, who should have access to a multitude of interpretations and perspectives. During their independent learning processes, these scholars will develop their own understandings of knowledge from existing sources. Therefore, what we present to them and enable them to access matters.

To remedy the failures of my own learning of social studies throughout my career education, public and private, I taught American and global

---

12 Gonzalez, "Historically Responsive Literacy."

slavery differently than how I learned it. I refused to begin with slavery in Black history. I constructed a Black-centric framework to study and present American and global slavery. As a result, students of all backgrounds deconstructed their misconceptions and filled in key gaps in their learning. White figures and narratives like President Lincoln are decentered. Students broaden their learning about the brutality and resistance, including about the largest slave revolt (in New Orleans 1811) and contextualize contemporary phenomenon, such as the Trump/MAGA as a "whitelash" to the Obama presidency, a recurring historical occurrence similar to the end of Reconstruction or the race massacres in Wilmington, Atlanta, and Tulsa. They also understand, in another rebuke to Kanye's worldview, that their ancestors resisted white supremacy and oppression at every turn. It was counter to their way of life.

Our ancestors agitated and disrupted at every turn, from centuries-long wars on the continent, to rebelling and leaping from ships, to subtle and explicit methods on plantations. Ample evidence suggests that their revolution has slowly eroded systems of oppression, which persist in formidable ways but can be found on the offense historically. For example, the Stono Rebellion of 1739 in South Carolina led to the first anti-literacy laws. Our ancestors learned in secret, eventually ending slavery with their own hands in Haiti and the United States. In addition to the aforementioned slave revolt, another source of rebellion was Yaa Asantewaa, queen of the prosperous Ashanti Empire, also called Asante, in now modern-day Ghana who resisted British invasion until she was imprisoned in 1921 and Emperor Menelik II of Ethiopia, who defeated the Italians at the Battle of Adwa on March 1, 1896, the only African empire to resist European imperialism until at least the mid-20th century. These two pan African revolutionaries and their progress or victories helped inspire future Pan-African leaders, from Steve Biko to Kwame Nkrumah to Ellen Johnson Sirleaf.

As I personally explored the topic of police and prison abolition, I studied Angela Davis's *Are Prisons Obsolete?*, Michelle Alexander's *The New Jim Crow*, the U.S. Department of Justice's report on the Ferguson, Missouri police department, and other texts my professors and mentors provided me. Thus, I introduced my scholars to these culturally responsive works. They explored the multifaceted factors of mass incarceration and the school-to-prison pipeline as a continuation of previous learning about the evolution of institutionalized slavery. Together, we engaged philosophically and in real-time with our human rights and duty to disrupt. Mind you, my scholars have participated independently in Black Lives Matter and March for Our Lives protests, boycotts, a walk-out against their principal, and more good trouble. In their DNA lies the innate ability to resist against anti-Black oppression and inequity, any threat to their human rights. Further, they have developed the ability to critically analyze and often respond to dominant narratives about the past, like the positive effects of exploration in the Americas or imperialism in Africa or inaccurate causes of the Civil War.

The myth of the American Dream and American exceptionalism dissipates—a conclusion that often crystallized but might not have originated—in my classroom. American physicist Richard Feynman said, "The problem is not people being uneducated. The problem is that people are educated just enough to believe what they have been taught, and not educated enough to question anything from what they have been taught."[13] Teachers are not absolute and supreme holders of all knowledge, pouring into the empty minds of their students (i.e., what Paolo Freire labels the banking model of education). Healthy skepticism and critique of existing norms and systems - critical thinking skills - are desirable outcomes of the learning process.

When students can challenge their Eurocentric, white supremacist curriculum, they learn about emancipation as a result of Black resistance, the Civil Rights Movement and the involvement of Black women struggling against sexual violence by white men, as well as learn about the failures of *Brown v. Board of Education* to account for the equitable (not integrated) education Black parents actually wanted. Nuanced, intersectional interpretations and preparations allow for students' scholarship founded in a wide range of historic sources and voices. Just as students use techniques like S.O.A.P. to analyze sources, educators must curate resources that appropriately address the inquiry, "From whose perspective are we telling history?"

Joy is the secret spice of a Black-centric classroom. It looks different everywhere; the joyful community my scholars and I cultivate cannot be

---

13 Feynman, Twitter, May 29, 2021.

duplicated or replicated. Texas high school social studies teacher Jania Hoover reminds us that

> Black joy and Black love are central themes for understanding Black history. Simply put, without a focus on Black joy, Black history is incomplete. When we teach oppression and struggle without also teaching the joy of resistance, for instance, we miss the mark. Joy is a part of the human experience. When we separate Black people's struggles from their humanity, we see them as less than human. When we see them as less than human, it becomes easier to justify continued racial disparities in society.[14]

They know the struggle. Repeated lessons on grit and hard work fall short because many of our scholars are the stones the builders refused, roses that grew from concrete. They have lived and persisted.

Thus, mantras and Black history lessons limited to racial oppression hinder rather than propel their vast imaginations and joyful thinking. When I looked at and learned my scholars, I often see and feel their pain and trauma. They have experienced loss and violence, even more so with access to social media. I can't help but imagine the impact of violence against Black people and youth on their psyches. They must see themselves, as I do, in Trayvon Martin, Tamir Rice, Toyin Salau, Secoriea Turner, or the scores of young people gunned down in or snatched from their neighborhoods. They must face daily their mortality and the harrowing reality of white supremacy. And yet, the Black boy joy and Black girl magic born in the academic space sustains my praxis and my hope for education. With their own spice, however, educators can include some of the elements I incorporate. For example, students created raps and spoken word pieces to demonstrate the oral story tradition of West Africa. They curated music playlists to summarize their learning in government. We learned dances from across the diaspora and competed in Black music karaoke. Teams made Tik Toks for campaign messages and other PSAs. Outdoor learning often ended with playing with chalk and eating wings. Our celebrations of Black August, Latinx Heritage Month, Black History Month, Women's History Month, and others are marked by art, music, love, and community building. You can't fake it, either. If anyone, our students are emotionally intelligent.

---

14 Hoover, "Don't Teach Black."

This generation of scholars know how to advocate for themselves by insisting you respect their name pronunciations, pronouns, and learning styles. Rightfully so. With a quickness, they pick up on energy and vibes. Attempts to prioritize joy, social emotional learning, relationship building, you name it, must be authentic and genuine. Students also develop joy for learning when they have buy-in. This generation of scholars is opinionated. They reject what doesn't work for them and excitingly engage with what does. Choice boards, class government positions, collaborative lesson planning ensure a decolonized, student-centric learning space. Ultimately, as we share in this phenomenon, my scholars need classrooms grounded in healing and joy, protected at all costs.

Moreover, our classrooms and schools themselves are places of extreme curriculum, policy, and other forms of anti-Black violence. Their unsafe conditions impede teaching and learning. This truth is a painful one we must swallow. Like the fugitive pedagogists before me, I resist daily the egregious impact of the cercal state in education. I disrupt the school to prison pipeline with restorative practices, colonized curriculum with decolonized teaching and learning, oppressive education with criticality, identity, intellectualism, and joy. This endeavor is one I share with my scholars and comrades in education. In fact, our scholars are the best intellectuals and co-conspirators for the task ahead. Dr. Muhammad emphatically states,

> Black history tells us that educators don't need to empower youth or give them brilliance or genius. Instead, the power & genius is already in them. Genius is brilliance, intellect, ability, & artsy that [has] been flowing through their minds & spirits across generations.[15]

As a result of a Black-centric, decolonized classroom my scholars of all backgrounds have access to a representative and rare reservoir of intellectualism. In addition to the above, we have explored pan-African history dating back to the beginning of humanity, the racist treatment by the United States of Haitians during their eighteenth century revolution and connections to the deportations of Haitians today, the Great Migration and the oppressive experiences of Northern cities, AAVE and hip-hop/rap as legitimate rather than marginalized forms of communication and

---

15 Muhammad, Twitter, April 21, 2022.

expression, the use of highways like the Dan Ryan in Chicago and I-85 in Atlanta to separate Black and poor people, the role of agitators and disruptors like Ida B. Wells and other Black women who led movements that excluded them, the injustice and justice of land ownership from Oscarsville (now known as Lake Lanier) to South Africa, and so much more. We learned about the lives and legacies of Amy Jacques Garvey, the women of the Haitian Revolution, Claudette Colvin, Nannie Helen Burroughs, Mekatilili wa Mensa.

Consistently, students revealed a hunger for Black history—that even in their generation at predominately Black schools with almost entirely Black teachers—failed to satisfy. In his exit interview, one senior remarked, "I did not learn about the deeper and hidden history of Atlanta, Georgia." Herein lies an instructional dilemma; given limited resources and time, I grappled with the balance with local and global Black history, as well as with historical and contemporary topics. For example, our exploration of the local neighborhoods of Mechanicsville and the West End were not done justice. My presentation of this history here could go on for the remainder of this book. We know the long-winded nature of history teachers, after all! Here in this chapter, I desired to share at least a portion of the scholarly criticality and joy characteristic of my classrooms.

Today, I champion and engineer culturally responsive teaching and restorative practices as an equity coordinator for a small school district. I continue to facilitate learning as a tutor and history instructor outside of the public-school classroom. I also organize, develop curriculum, consult on curriculum and instruction, and strategize on policies. Like many leaders in education, I am concerned about the impact of classroom censorship on our educators and students, particularly on their engagement with Black history and studies. Given our duty to disobey unjust laws, my comrades and I have led the fight against classroom censorship and other inequitable laws and policies, despite the attacks. This approach is not original but rather guided by my ancestors and aligned with the spirit of Black radical pedagogy. As a "non-traditional" teacher, I had to catch up on my preparation before I formally entered the classroom.

The first book I read as a substitute teacher was *Teaching to Transgress* by bell hooks. I continued with Dr. Gloria Ladson-Billings's, *The Dreamkeepers*, as a student in Georgia State University's Social Studies M.A.T. program. Then came, *Why Are All of the Black Kids Sitting Together in the Cafeteria?* by Dr. Beverly Daniel Tatum. There are the books, *Multiplication is for White People,* by Lisa Delpit; *Culturally Responsive Teaching and the Brain,* by Zaretta Hammond; as well as, *We Want to Do More Than Survive,* by Dr. Bettina Love. Dr. Chantee Earl and her colleagues raised the Black educator-activist in me, sparking a productive anger that has produced culturally responsive teaching in the classroom and organizing in the community.

I am the founder and former co-chair of Gwinnett Educators for Equity and Justice, which advanced policies and practices for racial equity and justice in education during the summer of 2020. Over the course of two school years, during the worse of the anti-CRT culture war, we built and curated a high school ethnic studies course, successfully called for the removal of the Superintendent after a quarter of a century, flipped the mostly white and Republican Board of Education with the election of the first Black woman, facilitated culturally responsive professional development for leaders and teachers, and led the way to an increase in restorative practices and social-emotional learning for all scholars. I am also a co-chair of the K16 Teach Truth Coalition. Since 2021, we have organized protests and rallies, delivered testimony at hearings and virtually, and led a statewide call to action. Our workshops guide educators in navigating and resisting the new law. Our public campaigns correct the record on teaching the truth in our schools.

As educators everywhere struggle to understand new expectations and consequences, we offer suggestions and directions. Educators can use a plethora of resources to develop their cultural competency/humility and to ensure culturally responsive instruction. We must support them in understanding this shift as doing differently rather than doing more. School leaders must advance cultural responsiveness and equity with policies, procedures, and practices that center minoritized students and protect educators. Most importantly, we can combat confusion, fear, and division by organizing. Educators, students, families, and community members must stand in solidarity and join organizations, both specific to their roles and in unison.

The K16 Teach Truth Coalition is a multi-racial/multi-ethnic, multi-generational network of educators, education professionals, and other rightsholders in primary, secondary, and tertiary educational institutions. We partner with student organizers, parent advocates, policymakers, lawyers, allies in other states and industries, with the common goal of liberatory education for all our students. To any educator or rightsholder frustrated with our situation or disgusted with the injustices of the classrooms, passionate about abolishing classroom censorship or the school to prison pipeline: join an organization and get active. Our movement for educational equity needs you. As a Black man, I am fully aware of how white folks fetishize Dr. King and how Black folks pray to replace him. Kwame Ture declares only one way to honor the beloved leader: "You want to be like King? You want to truly honor King?! You must ask yourselves the question, "if King were alive today what would he be doing?" And I can tell you just as night falls day, if King were alive today, he would be in an organization working for the masses of his people."[16] To transform our schools from white supremacist institutions to healing and liberating environments, to pay educational reparations to our Black and brown scholars, we must organize and build together. In the face of these laws and educational injustices across time, it will take a movement to maintain a truly equitable and edifying education for all.

My freedom dream all along has been what I want for the scholars on my roster: a just and liberated world in which Black kids can grow up as themselves, can thrive tremendously, a world in which eight- or nine-year-old Anthony can proudly reach his mountaintop, whatever and wherever that may be, as healthy and as well as he can be. I am fighting for my scholars, my community, and people, and just as importantly, I am fighting for me and my radical, energetic imagination. One day, a young Black boy like me won't have to just dream and can just *be*.

---

16 Toure, Twitter, March 13, 2021.

BIBLIOGRAPHY

Bernard, Ian. "Queen Nanny of the Maroons (? - 1733)." Black Past, March 1, 2011. https://www.blackpast.org/global-african-history/queen-nanny-maroons-1733/.

Brownworth, Victoria. "LGBT HISTORY MONTH Angela Davis, Revolutionary." *Windy City Times*, October 24, 2021. https://www.windycitytimes.com/lgbt/LGBT-HISTORY-MONTH-Angela-Davis-revolutionary-/71602.html.

Charlemagne, "West, Kanye. KW/CTG Interview." Interview by Charlemagne tha God, April 18, 2018. https://youtu.be/zxwfDlhJIpw.

Editors, History.com. "Frederick Douglass." HISTORY. A&E Television Networks, October 27, 2009. https://www.history.com/topics/black-history/frederick-douglass.

Emdin, Christopher. *Ratchetdemic: Reimagining Academic Success*. Boston, MA: Beacon Press, 2021.

Ferlazzo, Larry. "Author Interview with Dr. Gholdy Muhammad: 'Cultivating Genius.'" *Education Week*, January 28, 2020. https://www.edweek.org/teaching-learning/opinion-author-interview-with-dr-gholdy-muhammad-cultivating-genius/2020/01.

Feynman, Richard. Twitter, May 29, 2021. https://twitter.com/proffeynman/status/1398492567017197573?lang=en.

Fields-White, Monee. "The Root: How Racism Tainted Women's Suffrage." NPR, March 25, 2011. https://www.npr.org/2011/03/25/134849480/the-root-how-racism-tainted-womens-suffrage.

Frederick-douglass-heritage.org. "Frederick Douglass and the Abolitionist Movement," November 20, 2013. http://www.frederick-douglass-heritage.org/abolitionist-movement/.

Givens, Jarvis R. *Fugitive Pedagogy : Carter G. Woodson and the Art of Black Teaching*. Cambridge, Massachusetts: Harvard University Press, 2021.

Gonzalez, Jennifer. "Historically Responsive Literacy: A More Complete Education for All Students: Interview with Goldy Muhammad." *Cult of Pedagogy*, August 2, 2020. https://www.cultofpedagogy.com/historically-responsive-literacy/.

Hoover, Jania. "Don't Teach Black History without Joy." *Education Week*, February 19, 2021, sec. Social Studies. https://www.edweek.org/

teaching-learning/opinion-dont-teach-black-history-without-joy/2021/02.

Howard, Mikelle. "(Sara) Saartjie Baartman (1789-1815)." BlackPast.org, September 22, 2018. https://www.blackpast.org/global-african-history/baartman-sara-saartjie-1789-1815/.

Ladson-Billings, Gloria. *The Dreamkeepers: Successful Teachers of African American Children*. San Francisco, Calif.: Jossey-Bass Publishers, 2009.

Muhammad, Gholdy. Twitter, April 21, 2022. https://twitter.com/gholdym/status/1517250548835229696?s=21&t=yu6UGIkPRh8G3m2BsHoodA.

———. "Historical Black Excellence Provides a Blueprint for Reimagining Education." ASCD, February 20, 2020. https://www.ascd.org/el/articles/historical-black-excellence-provides-a-blueprint-for-reimagining-education.

———. Twitter, March 13, 2021. https://twitter.com/JazzyDaddyDolla/status/1370922783698530307.

Pitchon, Allie. "Female Warriors Who Led African Empires and Armies." HISTORY, February 8, 2020. https://www.history.com/news/african-female-warriors.

The Voice. "The Race Problem: Miss Willard on the Political Puzzle of the South," *The Voice*, October 23, 1890. https://scalar.usc.edu/works/willard-and-wells/the-race-problem---miss-willard-on-the-political-puzzle-of-the-south.

Toure, Twitter, March 13, 2021, https://twitter.com/JazzyDaddyDolla/status/1370922783698530307.

Woodson, C. G. "The Celebration of Negro History Week, 1927." *The Journal of Negro History* 12, no. 2 (April 1927): 103–9. https://doi.org/10.2307/2714049.

6

Music, Math, and Malcolm X:
My Intellectual Journey of Truth

Douglas Henry Daniels

I knew hardly anything about going to college. On the eve of the Great Depression, my father went away to the University of Illinois, Urbana, but he had to drop out and return to Chicago when the depression wiped out his family's savings. He went to work and never returned to college. A generation later, my sisters went to teachers' college and became teachers in the public school system. So, I knew I was expected to attend college like them because I also excelled in my studies.

Besides my sisters' friends going to teachers' college, I knew only two people to go to college: one of my cousins attended the University of Illinois, Chicago. Another was a high school friend who excelled at math and probably received a scholarship to attend University of Illinois at Urbana. Otherwise, I knew no one who attended a university. Eventually he received a Ph.D. in math, but we lost track of one another. The expense of college and desire to get a job is what probably kept most from attending college.

In high school, I took advanced math and science courses, where my fellow students were college bound. In writing this essay, I thought about why I studied so much math and science in high school. Because of the Soviet Union's launching of the first satellite, Sputnik in 1957, the US schools emphasized the importance and study of science. I realized I did not like Physics and Chemistry, so I briefly thought about a legal career. I was fortunate to be enrolled in what were known as "star" classes in English and Social Studies for the best students who were likely to attend college. No one discussed or went to Ivy League or other name-brand schools, and only one attended the University of Chicago. Another student at our school went to the Air Force Academy. The rest went to small liberal arts schools in the Chicago area. This might have been so they could live at home.

I was Black in a predominantly white high school, and none of the white honors students ever asked me about my plans for college—ever. And I never discussed college with my parents or other high school students. Because they attended public schools, I assumed they could not afford "name" colleges and universities. While they seemed to discuss it with each other, it was also a rather private matter for them. We did belong to an honors society, however, and a handful took an exam and became National Merit Scholars.

We received—to my knowledge—no individual counseling about college, but the "star" students (as a group) were prepped for the college level exams we had to take for scholarships. I bought books on enlarging my vocabulary so I could increase my score. So going to college was a part of the program in the honors classes, but it was always general and rather abstract. No one coached us on how to fill out an application, or write an essay for entrance, or consider which school we should attend.

On one occasion after taking a scholarship exam, someone from that exam questioned me about my reading. The thing I recall most is his question as to what kind of magazines my family subscribed to, and I told him *Reader's Digest* and *Consumers' Reports*. He asked if we read news magazines such as *U.S. News and World Report*, and I had to answer no. This idea was a novel one for me. That might have been for the University of Illinois scholarship that I received—it covered tuition, but I am not sure.

In September 1960, I went where many of my Black friends enrolled: University of Illinois in Chicago, at Navy Pier, which had a flunk out rate of 50% for first year students. Some of my friends flunked out and others simply disappeared. They joined the military or went to work.

After one and a half years, I asked my mother for suggestions on where to transfer to complete my undergraduate degree, and she suggested the University of Chicago, where I applied and received a two-year fellowship. It required that I work during my third year, and the university always found a job for me. After a quarter of commuting from home, I asked about living in a dorm and the university covered the expense for two quarters. For my last year I lived in an apartment for a paltry sum of $115/month, which was split among three roommates.

After becoming a professor and raising three children who went to college, I learned how complicated the process of applying to college can be now. It was much simpler for me, and I marvel that I managed to get into a premier college at a time when Black students were not really welcomed. There were only seven or eight African Americans among the two thousand or so students at the University of Chicago (1962–1964). I majored in Political Science at the University of Chicago because I wanted to be a lawyer.

Because I did not get funding for graduate school, I joined the Peace Corps and was fortunate to be sent to Tanzania, where I taught primary school for two years. I also learned Kiswahili. At the time (1965-1967), Tanzania adopted a socialist path, creating Ujamaa villages, which were collectives. The government also forbade foreigners from teaching African history and geography because it thought they provided an incorrect perspective. The government explained that the European "explorers" were more accurately "visitors." I taught English, Science, Math, Art, and Physical Education, mostly in the seacoast town of Tanga.

This nationalism (that I experienced in Tanzania), along with *The Autobiography of Malcolm X*, sent to me by my parents, prompted me to study Afro-American and African history in graduate school at UC Berkeley, which offered me a three-year fellowship in 1967. This was the only university that I applied to that welcomed me in this fashion. When I applied for graduate school in 1967, things were much better for prospective African American students. For example, a friend, an Oakland attorney, explained to me how he went to UC. He was playing basketball (it was around 1966 or 1967) when a recruiter drove up, asked them (the young men) if they wanted to attend Cal, and gave them an application.

The History Department had just started a program in Negro History and Race Relations, offered by Professors Kenneth Stampp, Winthrop Jordan, Larry Levine, and Leon Litwack. They were influential in my study of social and cultural history. Of course, the civil rights movement influenced my interest in African American history. The Watts revolt occurred when I was overseas, but the Newark and Detroit revolts took place the year I returned to the U.S. in 1967, and while I was working in a VISTA program supervising volunteers in the Anacostia region of Washington, D.C. I thought the study of Black history would help me to understand the movement.

I was also exposed to the use of music as a tool to study history. My dissertation and first book focused on Black San Francisco in the nineteenth and early twentieth centuries. My subsequent books were a biography of Lester "Pres" Young, the famous tenor saxophonist, and a history of the Oklahoma City Blue Devils, a forerunner of the Count Basie orchestra. Subsequently I wrote a history of the oldest blues society in the United States: The Santa Barbara Blues Society. I also wrote about Berkeley's civil rights movement, covering the years from 1950 to 1965.

My interest in the history of jazz led me to apply for a Fulbright to study the music's crossing the Pacific from California to Honolulu, Manila, Yokohama, and Shanghai. The Fulbright took me to Yokohama, where I taught African American History and the History of Jazz to students at Yokohama City University, did archival research, interviewed musicians, and attended concerts and night club venues. I spent four months in Yokohama, and on subsequent occasions, I researched the history of the music in Manila and Shanghai. I returned to Yokohama several times over the next decade to attend the largest jazz festival in the world, the Yokohama Promenade. The festival lasts for two days and takes place in orchestra halls, in night clubs, and on street corners. This research provided a fresh perspective to the music's history, as most scholars have focused on the move from the South to the North and the West Coast and across the Atlantic. The Pacific phase of this history, I maintain, is no less important, as several Japanese and Filipino musicians were playing jazz by the 1920s. The music is deeply rooted in these sites.

7

Who Am I?[1]

Madeleine Moon-Chun

I wrote this when I was twelve years old, as I was reflecting on my summer trip (the summer prior to the pandemic) to South Korea. It was how I felt at the time as an eleven-year-old. I am fourteen now, and I have a more complex understanding of my identity.

Suji, South Korea.
The most down-to-earth, savvy place I've ever known.

Suji, South Korea.
My favorite place in the world.

I loved everything about the bustling city.
The identical apartments, laughing kids walking home from school, even the grocery stores!
I felt more at home here than almost anywhere else.
I loved the way buses were on every street and on every corner.

Standing on a bus with my mother and my brother, one afternoon after a day of fun, I felt as though this summer couldn't get any better.
But then an older man sitting across from where I was standing asked my mother why I was speaking English. Why I wasn't speaking Korean.
Even though my mom answered confidently that I was American, and that English was the language I was most comfortable speaking, I could not shake the feeling that he didn't approve.
It's funny, somehow, that you can be so prepared for something amazing to happen, but how unprepared you can be for something to go wrong.
After that, I thought about what the man said all the time, but I still didn't get it.

---

1 Written in seventh grade for Tom Painting's humanities class in 2020.

However, now that I am older and I have a better sense of our world, going back to that memory, I think I finally understand.

Some people here, in the United States, look at me and see me differently. Too many times, I've had other kids come up to me and ask if I'm Chinese or Japanese.
They don't seem to think that there are more countries in Asia other than China and Japan.
Every time, I answer that I am American, because I am.

But in Korea that day, I realized it can also go the other way. I'm not Korean enough to native Koreans, yet sometimes, I'm not American enough either.

My loss of innocence made me very different. I was no longer the little girl who thought everything was just how it seemed, no need to probe deeper. I began to see things I never saw or thought of before.
In a way, I am grateful for the scene in the bus all those months ago, for it helped me to see my true identity.
For a long time, I pondered those words, the very words that came from the old man's lips.
For a long time, I thought there was something wrong. With me. Most people say "Korean-American" like the "Korean" always has to come first. But I think, for me, it's a different case.

I am American Korean.

8

In the Hour of the Dragon: Nationalism, Feminism, and a Korean American Identity

Elaine Haikyung Kim

I spent my childhood and adolescence in the 1940s and 1950s living and attending school in Takoma Park and Silver Spring, then in working-class Maryland suburbs. I was born in New York City, but our family moved to Maryland when I was four years old because my father got a job working for the US Department of War, now the US Department of State. He had been in the US on a student visa since 1926, registering for classes first at the Lewis Institute in Chicago and later at Columbia University in New York for decades because the INS Act of 1924 prevented anyone born in Asia from immigrating or becoming naturalized US citizens. During World War II, the US Congress passed a special act allowing him and some other Koreans to obtain green cards, or permanent residency, because they had learned Japanese during the Japanese occupation and could read maps and other documents for the US war effort against Japan.

My brother and I were the only Asians in our neighborhood and school until high school, when I think there was a pair of Chinese sisters, making us four Asians among 1800 students. Sometimes I felt like an alien because the inside and outside of our house felt like different planets. In the early to mid-1950s, our two-bedroom house was a way-station of sorts for visitors and refugees from South Korea. Sometimes there were wall-to-wall beds that I had to climb over to get to the bathroom. Inside our house, conversations about Korea and its colonization—and later the Korean war—were important. Outside our house, none of my classmates had even heard of Korea. No one seemed to know or care much about Korea and Koreans until the Korean War (1950–53), if it was mentioned at all. "Korea" became synonymous with starving war orphans and desperate "war brides."

To my father, his Korean identity was everything. Like some other Korean immigrants of his era, my father loved encyclopedias, which he thought contained all the information necessary to understanding the West, if only one had time to read them. We had three or four sets, but the only volume he looked at was the "K" volume of each set, which invariably fell open to the entry on Korea. When my brother and I complained about being bullied and taunted at school as Japs or "ching chong chinamen," Dad would advise us to tell them we were Korean—as if that would have helped! He would rush over to open the encyclopedia and point out the sections describing how moveable type and gunpowder had been invented by Koreans and that marathon runner Sohn Ki-Joong had challenged white supremacy at the 1936 Olympics. Later, we found out that China took credit for gunpowder and the printing press because Korea had been under Chinese suzerainty when they were invented, and that Sohn's gold medal had been claimed by Japan when Korea was under Japanese colonial rule.

As far as I can discern, our mother was brought to Hawaii as an infant around 1903, when Koreans were being recruited to work on the sugar plantations by representatives of the Hawaiian Sugar Planters Association, which needed scabs to break the Japanese plantation workers' strikes for wages equal to those of white workers. Although she lived her whole life in the US, Mom was prevented by law from becoming a US citizen until the passage of the 1953 McCarran Walter Act. She spoke better English than Korean and was culturally American, or at least Asian American, but she could not vote. She was regarded and treated as a foreigner. Since there was no record of her birth or entry into the US, she had a displaced person's or DP passport. She never knew her birth father and had no siblings. She did not know of any extended family members—no grandparents, no aunts and uncles, no cousins. Her mother moved back to Korea at some point, leaving her completely alone in the United States. I think that she found her sense of community marrying Dad and embracing a Korean identity for herself. Sadly, she only visited South Korea for the first time in 1966, she was in her mid-sixties, when most South Korean women of her age wore Korean clothes and pinned their hair into buns held together with a *pinyo*. My mother had short, permed hair that she did not wear in the *ajuma* "bubble style," and unlike them she wore shirtwaist dresses and low pumps. Korean people stared and pointed at her, saying, "Look! An American." I wish she had never visited Korea and that she had instead passed away still thinking of herself as belonging to a community of Koreans.

I have sometimes wondered how Koreans in the United States during the first half of the twentieth century might have been different if they had been welcomed and embraced. I know that the early twentieth century social movements in China were supported by overseas Chinese, many of whom donated their life's savings as restaurant workers and laundrymen to their home villages as well as to Sun Yat-sen, the founder of the Chinese republic in 1911. It was clear that it was much easier to be discriminated against in the United States when the motherland was weak. Even when they suffered racist violence and discrimination, overseas Chinese could take comfort in the respect an appreciation of people in their home villages, to which they dreamed of triumphant return. For Koreans at the time, even such comforting dreams were not possible because the Japanese colonizers took over Korea and as well as the positions of power and influence that Koreans were not allowed to occupy. To return in triumph, Koreans had to first try to end Japanese colonial rule. It is no wonder that most of the overseas Koreans joined the national liberation efforts.

Nationalism appealed to overseas Koreans of all social classes. It also appealed to me, even though I had never been in Korea and had no ideas about it except for what was in the encyclopedia and from what Dad said about it. Since people constantly asked me where I was from, when I was going back, and why I spoke such good English, I felt like a foreigner who had to have a home somewhere else. I wanted to learn to speak Korean, but back then there were no programs or materials, unlike today when Korean popular culture has spread around the world and there are many resources for people from many countries clamoring to study the language.

In 1962, I went to South Korea for the first time, after I had just finished my junior year at the University of Pennsylvania, where I think I was the only Korean American undergraduate. I was with my dad. That summer, for the first time, I met people who looked like us, including many of Dad's extended family members. For the first time, I saw Dad being treated as an equal instead of being loomed over by people unused to foreign accents who I, as an American teenager, thought were snickering at him. Everyone seemed to understand his words and gestures perfectly, and he fit right in.

In early 1966, after I completed my master's degree at Columbia University, that bastion on Western civilization studies, I went to Seoul to work as a Lecturer in English at Ewha Womans University.[1] The year I spent living in South Korea between 1966 and 1967 has been vividly important to me ever since, not only because of all the new things I encountered but also because of what the experience taught me about myself, both then and later when I came to think about it.

Scarcely a decade had passed since the devastating Korean War that left four million people dead, an estimated ten million families separated, and northern and central Korea carpet-bombed and reduced to rubble during US air attacks against which Korea had absolutely no defense. All the same, I realize now that I saw Korea through the lens of US superiority, although I tried to conceal my attitudes.

I had my come-uppance, however, when I began to understand Korean patriarchy. Since Mom had never lived in Korea and all the stories about Korea I heard were from Dad, I was completely unprepared for the gender practices I encountered. First of all, I was twenty-three years old when I arrived in Seoul, or twenty-four years old by Korean age, which is calculated at the beginning of the lunar year. I did not know that for many Koreans at the time, a woman of twenty-four was thought of as being on the cusp of becoming an "old miss." I was told how girls who are too picky get pushed back like wilted cabbage to the back of the bin in the vegetable store. Worse, I was born in the Year of the Horse, which I was told was a bad year for women because horse women don't like to stay close to home and hearth like rabbits, monkeys, cows, sheep, chickens, pigs, and even snakes and rats. The only animals in the zodiac that were worse for women, they said, were dragons and tigers, and I was born in the hour of the dragon and the month of the tiger. Fortunately for me, I was told, I was not born in the Year of the Fire Horse. There are five types of each animal, according to the five elements of earth, water, metal, air, and fire, and Fire Horse women were believed to be "too strong," so strong that they often cause their husbands' deaths. They run around wildly, perhaps having extra-marital affairs and bringing ruin onto their households. It happened that 1966 was the Year of the Fire Horse, which only comes around every

---

[1] Ewha Womans University is a prestigious, private women's university in Seoul, South Korea. It was founded in 1886 by an American missionary, Mary F. Scranton. https://www.ewha.ac.kr/ewhaen/intro/foundation.do.

sixty years. Indeed, I noticed that there were no marriages at the wedding venues in my neighborhood until April that year, lest couples have daughters whom it would be difficult to marry off. Those who did have daughters that year sometimes lied that their babies had been born in the prior or subsequent year but were just large or small for their age. When I briefly worked as a volunteer in an orphanage in early 1967, I noticed that there was only one baby boy in an infant nursery filled with girls, and he was adopted during the short time I was working there.

My relatives wrung their hands because trying to find a husband for someone like me would be all but impossible. Unlike Americans, Korean people had no qualms about commenting on my appearance and offering unsolicited advice about what I could do to escape from my undesirable situation. "Your feet are so big! We call those feet 'thieves' feet.' You have to find shoes in the men's section." "You need to get a haircut and a perm." "You should never laugh too loudly or walk too fast." "Why do you have pierced ears? That makes you look Filipina or Chinese."

Instead of feeling embraced and accepted by fellow Koreans, I think they viewed me as slow and stupid because I could not speak much Korean. To many of them, I was only good for practicing English. I felt ugly, clumsy, and too big, even though at 5'3" and 120 pounds I was used to being considered small in the United States. Meanwhile, my older brother, who had graduated from Harvard and was in medical school—but whose Korean language ability was even weaker than mine—was considered a prime candidate for marriage to beautiful young daughters of wealthy South Korean magnates.

I tried hard to fit in, taking Korean language lessons and studying whatever I could find in English about Korean history and contemporary society. I came to realize later that what I was really learning—even when I was studying the language, which was geared to social and cultural hierarchy—was about Korean patriarchy. The customs and practices that I read and heard about were mostly Confucian and neo-Confucian practices from the most recent dynasty, the Chosŏn Dynasty.[2] Social and cultural practices from Koryo or Silla[3] times were obscured and pushed to the background. Almost everything I encountered about "Korean

---
2 The Chosŏn Dynasty lasted from (1392–1910 CE).
3 The Koryŏ Dynasty lasted from 918–1392 CE. The Silla Dynasty lasted from 57 BCE–935 CE.

culture"—whether about ancestor ceremonies or folk legends or everyday customs—was actually presented from a Korean patriarchal nationalist perspective.

Upon returning to the US, I transferred to the PhD program in English at UC Berkeley. I started school in the fall of 1968. Although there was only one other person of color, a Japanese American *sansei* from Southern California, in the graduate program, I saw for the first time many US-born Chinese and Japanese American undergraduates. One of my white classmates commented to me that they looked like "parodies of Americans." Seeing them was a kind of out-of-body experience because I felt like the proverbial "banana"—yellow on the outside and white on the inside. I was seeing the other Asian Americans as if I were a white person.

During my first quarter at Berkeley, I immersed myself in the familiar close readings of Chaucer and Milton, paying little attention to what was going on around campus. In the winter of 1969, I was emerging from a literature class when I heard someone say, "Are you Chinese or Japanese?" Tired of hearing this question, I whirled around to see, to my shock, a young Filipino American student. He said I should honor the Third World Liberation Front student strike and come with him to a meeting of the Asian American Political Alliance (AAPA). Used to being avoided, not sought out, for being Asian American, I followed him to the meeting, not knowing that my life would be changed forever.

I had experienced domestic racism as a child and adolescent. I had observed the unequal power relationship between the US and South Korea. But participating in AAPA helped me see the link between these two things. I learned about US wars in Asia and began to think about how US imperialism and racism were inextricably entwined. I became enraged about the many things that I was not taught, whether in public schools or in elite universities. Working with many others, I helped fight for and build the Asian American Studies program at Berkeley.

I had not formed deep friendships among my classmates from kindergarten to graduate school. Although they were five or six years younger than I was, I felt that the Asian American students I met were like my real classmates and AAPA was a little like a new family. I was happy that I found the possibility of being an Asian American.

Cultural nationalism is appealing as a personal and emotional response to social rejection. What helped me understand how I was limited by my own cultural nationalism was my encounter with Third World feminism in the 1980s. It is difficult to divest ourselves from the notions that have protected us in the past. We don't want to jump from the proverbial frying pan of white racism into the fire of Korean patriarchy. I know I still cling to some vestiges of my old thinking. I enjoy South Korean historical dramas, some of which might be patriarchal and might still appeal to my cultural nationalism. But at least I am aware of this tendency now.

In my classes, I did come across students who were enamored of Asian patriarchal nationalism. Some of them turn inward. Some who grew up feeling alienated and alone as I did might be attracted to nationalism to achieve a sense of community and belonging. But I believe that when they move on to the world of work, many of them will try to find ways to transcend nationalist thinking and dream instead of ways to make the world itself a better place.

Additional Notes on Professor Kim's Bio:

In addition to her numerous books and accolades, she has been active in community work and other forms of storytelling. She is associate producer of *Slaying the Dragon: Asian Women in U.S. Television and Film (1988)*, co-producer of Sa-i-gu: *From Korean Women's Perspectives* (1993), executive producer of *Labor Women: Asian American Women Labor Organizers* (2003). She is producer, director, and writer of the video documentary, *Slaying the Dragon: Reloaded* (2011). She is a co-founder of Asian Women United of California, the Korean Community Center of the East Bay, and Asian Immigrant Women Advocates in Oakland, California.

9

What I Wish I Had Known When I Was in High School: A Brief Reflection[1]

Ramsay Liem

In 1991 several years after a handful of Asian American students and I began meeting informally to discuss common interests, we launched the first seminar covering Asian American history and identity formation offered at Boston College. Subsequently, I taught the course each year until I retired in 2012. In retrospect, teaching that seminar was one of the most gratifying experiences of my tenure at the university for many reasons, not the least of which was the active learning I did along with my students exploring a severely neglected history of a complex and largely invisible sector of the American population. Our course somewhat paralleled the broader political movement among Asian Americans for representation in all sectors of the society including the Eurocentric literary, historical, and social science canons.

One constant in virtually every class of students was the moment when someone would blurt out in exasperation a version of "Why didn't' I know that? How come we never learned that in high school?" For some students it expressed feelings of betrayal; while for others, anger; and still others, depression. These were moments when repeated encounters of the exclusion of Asian Americans from the historical record suddenly registered as a violation of some students' prior assumption that American ideals of justice and equality extended to people like themselves. It was a bit like looking in the mirror one morning and suddenly realizing you do not see an accurate depiction, or any depiction, of yourself—a rude awakening.

But these were not only the reactions of my students. I, too, made similar and repeated discoveries of striking omissions in the academic

---

[1] I contributed this reflection when Dr. Hellena Moon, editor of this volume, asked me to support her efforts to introduce Asian American studies into the curriculum at her daughter's high school.

canon as I plumbed the social science and historical literatures for course materials.[2] When Dr. Moon asked me to contribute something to your own explorations of Asian America, I thought I would put myself in your shoes and ask myself—"What do I wish I had known when I was in high school?" Like my students, what might have shocked or disturbed me during my high school years had I been exposed to some of the hidden and neglected history of Asians in America? How might that knowledge have affected my self-image, understanding of the world around me, and future choices?

For context, my high school years were 1957–1961, no doubt so distant in time as to appear just this side of the Dark Ages to you and your classmates. But this moment was actually the prelude to a period of major social upheaval and radical challenge to the nation's institutions fueled by the civil rights and militant Black Power movements, national outrage over a seemingly endless, ideologically corrupt and brutal war in Vietnam, and a no nonsense and resurgent women's movement. The turmoil of this era was further stoked by the assassinations of John F. Kennedy, Martin Luther King, Robert Kennedy, Malcom X, and Fred Hampton, as well as the violent suppression of mass protests. These were unprecedented conditions that inspired a youth-led struggle challenging the virtual erasure of Asian Americans from the US historical record. In time, and often in the face of stubborn academic intransigence, these incipient efforts coalesced with a broader movement of anti-war and social justice activists to protest the historical erasure and ongoing struggles of Asian and Pacific Islander communities in America. This incipient and ongoing movement is responsible for providing the grist for the shocking discovery of students like mine of their censored history to query, "Why didn't I know that? How come we never learned that in high school?" Putting myself in their place, these are some of the things I can imagine wishing I *and* my classmates had known during my own high school years.

Do We/I Really Belong?

Growing up in Western Pennsylvania was a solitary experience for this Korean American teenager who had no idea why Koreans and other Asian Americans were so few in number in our area and probably had

---

2 I offered the first class in 1991 when relevant sources were limited.

only been granted a pathway to citizenship several years earlier. No US textbook offered any explanation, and mostly likely, few—if any authors or publishers at that time—even knew the answers. Consequently, being virtually the sole Asian American in my high school and neighborhood seemed like the natural order of things.

Had Asian American immigrant history been part of the US historical canon, I would have discovered that for more than one hundred and fifty years, immigrants or refugees from Asia were explicitly denied citizenship through the Naturalization Act of 1790.[1] For that matter naturalization or the granting of citizenship to newcomers based on residency requirements was explicitly designated for "white" people. Furthermore, over four and a half decades beginning in 1875,[2] successive immigration acts stemmed the flow of newcomers from all quarters of Asia culminating in complete exclusion in 1924.[3] The one exception was the Philippines, a US "territory" entitling its citizens' entry into the United States. In a self-serving ironic twist, however, in 1934 the Philippines was granted a commitment to independence to take place in eight years. This change in status eliminated the entitlement of Filipino/as to unrestricted immigration to America limiting them to a yearly quota of fifty!

The upshot of these exclusionary policies was the creation of tiny enclaves of Chinese, Japanese, Korean, Filipino/a, Indian, and other Asian newcomers like the ones in my hometown. Oblivious to this systematic out-casting of Asians, I experienced my racial status as the natural order of things consigning me to being a curiosity among my peers and considered perhaps as privileged to be among them.

Come but Don't Stay

Even more, I wish I had known that my teenage existence as an Asian curiosity ("are you Chinese, Japanese? What is Korean?") was the product of powerful forces both recruiting Asian workers to service a burgeoning US economic powerhouse as cheap labor *and* excluding them to placate

---

1 Imai, "Naturalization Act of 1790."
2 The Page Act of 1875 (Immigration Act) was a law enacted primarily against the Chinese, barring women and unfree laborers entry into the United States.
3 Immigration Act of 1924 (a.k.a., Johnson-Reed Act) set a quota on the number of immigrants entering into the United States, but it completely barred Asian immigrants from entering into the US.

white workers during times of political and labor unrest. The familiar cry to 'Get Labor First'[4] drew Chinese workers to help build the first transcontinental railroad that would integrate a rapidly expanding US industrial economy, Japanese, Filipino/a, and Korean laborers to transform the production of sugar cane in the Hawaiian Islands into a profit-making industry, and workers throughout East and South Asia for land reclamation and stoop labor for the country's burgeoning west coast agricultural heartland. But, often in response to the very success of Asian workers, the rhythm of 'Get Labor First' was also punctuated with periods of virulent and violent 'driving out' spurred by labor competition, political opportunism, and mob-like hysteria.[5] Some of the most horrific racial atrocities in the nation's buried past are to be found in violent attacks on Chinese laborers and their entire communities. Subsequent reformations of these early ethnic enclaves in metropolitan areas like San Francisco and Los Angeles afforded camaraderie in the face of these assaults if not reliable security. They continue to do so today as evident in the <u>mobilization of community</u> responses to a dramatic rise in anti-Asian violence.

Little did I know during my high school years that the handful of Chinese restaurants in our area were much more than oddities for locals searching for a bit of the exotic; nor that entry into the United States and entitlement to citizenship for Asian newcomers would be denied for decades to come in spite of early court battles waged by Chinese, Japanese, Korean, Indian, and Filipino/a workers contesting the 1790 Naturalization Act.[6] There is nothing in this hidden history that confirms a popular stereotype of Asian Americans as passive and accommodating.

Nor Did I Know That...

It would take a world war and the ongoing struggles of Black Americans to create the political conditions necessary to crack open the doors to immigrants from Asia. China, the Philippines, and India were permitted a token one hundred entrants beginning in 1943. As US allies during WWII, it would have been untenable for Roosevelt to claim the United States was fighting fascism abroad while maintaining a policy of Asian exclusion at home. From 1945–1948, the <u>War Brides Act</u> enabled

---

4 Takaki, *Strangers*, ch. 2.
5 Pfaelzer, *Driven Out*, xv–xxix.
6 Takaki, *Strangers*, Ch. 3, 5, 7, 8, 9.

Asian women married to US servicemen to emigrate to the United States.[7] Similarly, following the Korean War Armistice signing, an estimated 6,000 women from Korea entered the United States as war brides. But it wasn't until my fourth-grade year, 1952, that token immigration quotas were also extended to Koreans and Japanese. The McCarran-Walter Act of that year also ended the 162 years during which Asians were denied citizenship by naturalization![8] Notably, this symbolic opening of US borders to immigrants from Asia occurred on the cusp of the landmark <u>1953 Brown v Board of Education</u> Topeka Supreme Court decision outlawing segregation in public education and an intensifying challenge to racist and exclusionary institutions throughout US society.

Challenges to institutional exclusion and racism by unrelenting activism in the Black community created the grounds for the <u>1965 Immigration and Naturalization Act</u> that finally ended unequal and merely symbolic quotas on immigration from the Eastern Hemisphere.[9] Coincidentally, this was the year of my graduation from college. At the time I had no idea that it coincided with this ground-breaking legislation that, contrary to some nativist expectations, would spur the rapid expansion of Asian American communities via chain migration, the entitlement of newly minted US citizens to sponsor immediate family members. In retrospect, the sizeable Asian American communities that most take for granted today are remarkably recent creations for those in my generation.

Protest by Asian immigrants, contradictions in the US posture during World War II, and the determined struggles of other people of color were essential to creating the conditions that would eventually alter the monochromatic landscape of my high school years.

Why Was I Even Here in the United States?

During my high school years if someone had asked me why my very different looking and sounding parents were in this country, I doubt I could have answered fully. I knew that my parents' concerns about conditions in their homeland, Korea, figured prominently in their lives—the struggle for independence from <u>Japanese colonial rule</u>, short-lived liberation at the end of WWII, military dictatorship in the south aligned with

---

7   Lyon, "War Brides Act."
8   Hong, "Immigration Act of 1952."
9   Public Law No. 89–236.

an occupying US military government, and a <u>divided nation</u>.[10] But I really had only an inkling of the circumstances surrounding my parents' presence in the United States.

The gap in my knowledge of my family's history became apparent to me during an incident my junior year at a classmate's home. After dinner, my friend's father began asking me questions about my background, my nationality (I suspect he thought I could not be an American), and the Korean War. I have no doubt he meant well, but I felt 'under the gun' because I did not have clear answers to many of his questions. I must have murmured something to the effect that Koreans were still recovering from a disastrous war when he exclaimed that "wasn't I grateful that Dean Acheson had saved Korea from communism?!"[11] I wish I had known then that 'saving Korea' had glossed over the following:

1. a US proposal to the Soviet Union to divide Korea at the 38th parallel immediately at the close of World War II, a country with 2000 years of shared history, language, and culture
2. a United Nations backed US proposal to hold separate presidential elections in the south that further solidified the division
3. a US-educated Korean who was brought back to Korea by the US war department to become the leading presidential candidate, and
4. US command of allied forces during a Korean War that saw the death of a tenth of the civilian population largely from indiscriminate US saturation and napalm bombing, millions of internal refugees, and the destruction of 80% of the cities, towns, and villages in the north.[12]

That war continues to this day held in check by a mere truce (cease fire) agreement while untold numbers of Korean family members including <u>tens of thousands</u> in the United States remain separated from one another

---

10 Savada and Shaw, "South Korea under United States."
11 Kagan, *How Dean Acheson*.
12 Numerous, often contentious volumes have been published about the Korean War. For a starting point of reading, see Cumings, *The Korean War*.

Had I known this and much more about the 'forgotten' and never-to-be ended Korean War, I might have replied to my host that Acheson's contributions to anti-communist fervor that was to guide (misguide) US foreign policy for the rest of the century, cost the Korean people immense suffering and insecurity and robbed them of unified nationhood and the right to self-determination that the United States so jealously guards for itself. Then, five short years following the end of WWII, Korea became the site of the first hot war of the Cold War as civil conflict between left leaning and right-wing Koreans became engulfed in the contest for global hegemony between the United States and the Soviet Union.

My parents were already permanent residents in the United States during this tortured period, having been part of a colonial era generation of Koreans seeking international support for Korean independence from Japanese colonization. Their subsequent opposition to Korea's division and US supported anti-democratic forces in the south, and participation in an overseas movement for Korean reunification soon became their motivation to remain in this country. My family's story is emblematic of a small but active group of early Korean immigrants who have rarely if ever been included in popular or academic accounts of US history. Like so many others who comprise the complex Asian and, more accurately, Pacific American community, their exclusion from the "American story" can destine them to invisibility, exoticizing, or, at moments of social unrest, scapegoating. The anti-Asian violence in the present moment sadly has numerous though still largely hidden precedents in the past.

Violence at Home as well as Abroad

For the most part, I can recall only a handful of episodes of overt racism during my high school years. I suspect my fortune was due to my being the only outsider, more a curiosity than a threat. Others during the buried past of Asians in America were less fortunate and experienced outbursts of white rage as scapegoats during periods of economic contraction and heightened labor competition. A striking example is the "Driving Out" I mentioned earlier. As the mid-eighteenth century gold rush petered out and Chinese laborers were no longer needed to forge the most dangerous passage ways for the first transcontinental railroad, Chinese itinerant workers drifted westward settling in small enclaves in the newly opening West and Northwest. Simultaneously, a thriving newly industrialized economy entered what some have called the first significant recession in American history.[13] Anti-Chinese rhetoric began to surface reflecting but also appeasing mounting anxiety among whites. On the heels of widespread cries like, "the Chinese must go!," politicians penned the Page Act (1875) effectively eliminating the immigration of Chinese women to the United States and then codified the first policy excluding newcomers from a foreign nation explicitly identified by name, China.[14] Although Chinese workers constituted no genuine threat to white laborers given their limited numbers, Chinese settlements in California and other western states became targets of an unprecedented reign of terror and vigilantism abetted by local officials and media outcries. Unknown to the general public to this day, this period of anti-Asian violence has been erased from the US historical record much as the recently exposed 1921 Tulsa Massacre of African Americans had been until recently.[15]

Collective memory is jealously guarded to preserve national narratives preferred by ruling powers and vested interests. Contesting the "official story" is no mean feat as evident in the decades of struggle engaged by young Japanese Americans, their supporters, and eventually a broad swath of the Japanese American community to bring to light the shameful internment of Japanese Americans during WWII and to demand reparations.[16] That struggle along with many others to challenge institutional racism and correct the historical record would surface a decade following my graduation from high school in the form of a maturing Asian American movement.

Buried Even Deeper in History

Buried deeper in the history are examples of the tenacity of Asian newcomers' determination to resist exploitation in spite of their limited numbers and resources. Some immigrants turned to the courts to fight discrimination enshrined in law as in the case of the 1790 Naturalization Act that reserved naturalization for whites only. Others facing mob violence during the "driving out" also fought back in the courts but resorted to arms as well, while Asian field laborers joined forces with Mexican

---

13 Garraty, *Unemployment in History*.
14 Matsumoto, "Chinese Exclusion Act."
15 Tulsa Historical Society and Museum.
16 Niiya. *Preserving Japanese American Stories*.

farmworkers to wrest wage increases from powerful landholding associations. The stories of "paper sons and daughters," aspiring immigrants claiming to be children of Chinese American citizens, reveal the resourcefulness of Chinese newcomers determined to overcome the panoply of nineteenth and twentieth Century exclusionary immigration laws.[17] And no less remarkable are the "No No Boys" who answered "no" to two items on a loyalty questionnaire distributed to Japanese American males interned during World War II.[18] As US citizens warehoused in the camps, they refused the further insult of having to declare their loyalty in the face of the racist internment of their community.

Had I *and* my classmates known about and been inspired by this history, I suspect I would have been more grounded and confident as the sole Asian American during my high school years. And I might also have anticipated a future moment when others like me would envision Asian American solidarity in the wake of intensifying civil rights and Black power movements and what was to become a mass peoples' movement opposed to the second hot war of the Cold War, the Vietnam debacle. Indeed, a decade following my high school years, the country witnessed the birth of an Asian American movement when a new generation of Asian American youth joined forces with Black and Latinx students at San Francisco State College (now University) to demand open admissions for local working class students and a revised curriculum relevant to the needs of Asian American, Black, and Latino communities.[19] This was a pivotal moment for a contemporary generation of Asian Americans to learn about and build on past struggles for justice, equity, and recognition by earlier generations of Asians in America.

Knowing is not Enough

These and many other forgotten or never-told stories from our communities belie the questionable promise of the American project to "...form a more perfect union..." in which "...all men [sic] are created equal...." The erasure of histories of disunion and inequality creates perpetual outsiders hyper susceptible to scapegoating and potentially lethal abuse

---

17 Ngai, "Legacies of Exclusion.
18 Niiya. "No-No Boys."
19 Umemoto. "On Strike!"

when national insecurities are stoked. The history of Asian exclusion and driving out is but one example mirrored today in the virulent animus toward southern border crossers and the proliferation of pandemic hate crimes against Asian Americans. This xenophobia and scapegoating only promises to intensify as outspoken advocates of white supremacy further infiltrate the nation's institutions and public discourse compounded by US fears of diminishing global hegemony and a surging Chinese economic powerhouse. To be written out of the canon of American history is not only intellectually dishonest, but it also reinforces prejudices about who belongs and who does not and, therefore, who is a potential target during periods of heightened national anxiety.

When students in my Asian American Studies courses were shocked to discover an Asian *American* history, they felt cheated by those responsible for their prior educational experiences – a teacher, curriculum administrator, or high school principal. But this personal sense of violation often gave way to a realization that communities like theirs had been systematically erased from the US national narrative. This *structural* feature of the educational system conspired to cast Asian Americans as the "other" in the invidious divide between "us" vs "them," raising a host of difficult challenges: why are these boundaries drawn, what socio-political conditions intensify or mitigate them, who benefits and at what costs to others, and most importantly, what is to be done? These questions are not for an individual, a single course, or an entire curriculum to answer. They signal an urgent need for a far reaching, inclusive social movement built upon and guided by the experiences and insights of all those who bear the brunt of erasure. Today, years after the last of my students have matriculated, one of the most gratifying rewards of my work as an educator has been to discover that in different ways, many of them are engaged in that very project.[1] Hopefully, you, too, are or will soon be among them.

---

1 Two inspiring examples can be found in the contributions to this volume by the editor, Hellena Moon, and contributor, Judy Yu. They are scholar-activists who played a pivotal role in creating and enlivening our Asian American history and identity course at Boston College.

BIBLIOGRAPHY

Imai, Shiho. "Naturalization Act of 1790," in *Densho Encyclopedia*, ed. Brian Niiya, Densho Publishers, 2013. https://encyclopedia.densho.org/Naturalization%20Act%20of%201790.

Takaki, Ronald. *Strangers from a Different Shore.* Boston: Little Brown and Company, 1989.

Pfaelzer, Jean. *Driven Out: The Forgotten War against Chinese Americans.* Berkeley: University of California Press, 2008.

Lyon, Cherstin M. "War Brides Act," *Densho* Encyclopedia.ed. Brian Niiya, Densho Publishers, 2015. https://encyclopedia.densho.org/War%20Brides%20Act.

Cumings, Bruce. *The Korean War: A History.* New York: Modern Library, 2010.

Garraty, John A. *Unemployment in History: Economic Thought and Public Policy.* New York: Harper & Row, 1978.

Hong, Jane. "Immigration Act of 1952," *Densho Encyclopedia*, ed. Brian Niiya, Densho Publishers, 2020. https://encyclopedia.densho.org/Immigration%20Act%20of%201952.

Matsumoto, Mieko. "Chinese Exclusion Act," *Densho Encyclopedia*, ed. Brian Niiya, Densho Publishers, 2020. https://encyclopedia.densho.org/Chinese%20Exclusion%20Act.

Savada, Andrea Matles, and William Shaw, eds. "South Korea under United States Occupation 1945-48," *South Korea: A Country Study.* Washington: GPO for the Library of Congress, 1990.

Kagan, Robert. "How Dean Acheson Won the Cold War: Statesmanship, Morality, and Foreign Policy." Washington, DC: Carnegie Endowment for International Peace, September 14, 1998.

Public Law No. 89–236, "An Act to Amend the Immigration and Nationality Act and for other purposes," Oct 3, 1965.

Tulsa Historical Society and Museum. "1921 Tulsa Race Massacre." https://www.tulsahistory.org/exhibit/1921-tulsa-race-massacre/.

Niiya, Brian. "Preserving Japanese American Stories of the Past for the Generations of Tomorrow." *Densho Encyclopedia*, ed. Brian Niiya, Densho Publishers, 2020. https://densho.org

Ngai, Mae. "Legacies of Exclusion: Illegal Chinese Immigration During the Cold War Years," *Journal of American Ethnic History* 18, no. 1 (1998) 3–35.

Niiya, Brian. "No-No Boys," *Densho Encyclopedia,* ed. Brian Niiya, Densho Publishers, 2020. https://encyclopedia.densho.org/No-no%20boys.

Umemoto, Karen. "On Strike!" San Francisco State College Strike, 1968–69: The Role of Asian American Students," *Amerasia Journal* 15 (1989) 3–41

10

My Dearest Ancestors, Children, & Future Generation

Judy W. Yu

As I close my eyes and remember my childhood, I recall my parents teaching me that silence symbolizes respect in our Chinese heritage. Now as an adult with my eyes wide open, schools are teaching me that silence equates to invisibility in our American culture. I reflect upon the representation of silence between my two worlds and realize that I am privileged by the power of silence. I hear the silence of my Chinese ancestors who have built America and left behind their untold legacies of pain and glory. Their silenced voices and spirit continue to live in my present. Their voices help me connect with a fragmented past to fight for our survival – this is my promise to them.

— Yu's Journal 2005

Voices of children chanting "ching-chong" resonate in my mind as their stinging chimes have become imprints of my school memories. Since the age of five, I began to witness and experience the repercussions of systemic inequities based on a person's race, class, linguistic accents, and citizenship status in K–12 classrooms. Through my eyes, I saw the spiritual killing of minority children on the playground when attacked by racial epithets. On the street, my Asian friends and I were victimized and assaulted for being "chinks." In high school, teachers omitted the history of Asian American pioneers from their lesson plans because "we just can't study everybody." I have used these collective memories of racialized discourse and social injustices as my intellectual armor to decolonize my mind of the imperialistic ways of knowing.[1] Through these testimonies I hope to re-conceptualize my responsibility as an educator and to contribute to the reconstruction of American education in order to illustrate the continuing injustice and to create possibilities of change and equity for all.

---

1   Omatsu, 2003. Tuhuiwai Smith, 1999.

Growing up as a first-generation Chinese American from an immigrant family in the crossroads of Brooklyn communities with African Americans, Hasidic Jews, Irish Italians, and Latinx in New York City, my construction of knowledge has been enriched by my experiences in an urban context. In my working class and immigrant family, we paid homage to schools and entrusted teachers to educate us in fulfilling our greatest potential. My trust in schools and teachers, however, dissipated when I began to experience an academic and personal dissonance in my K-12 education.

As I grew older, my personal experiences at home and academic experiences in school erupted with tensions of inequalities through my observation in school curricula and teacher practices when I did not see and learn about myself, culture, community, and the diversity of people that made up my worldview. Instead, I saw the privilege of "whiteness" as a victim of inequalities rather than a valued member of US society. I realized that being white and speaking English in and out of school validated people as "real Americans." As a result, during my schooling years, I began to depart from my Chinese identity and native language. Inadvertently, these disruptive experiences have left me disconnected with the purpose of schooling and my desire to learn and engage in school as it related to my lived experiences as a Chinese American student from a low-income/working class background.

This journey motivated me to enter the teaching profession as a first-grade teacher after college. I pursued my Master of Education at UCLA, Teacher Education Program. I became a first-grade teacher where I developed an Asian American studies curriculum that included materials such as children's identity poems, first grade students' interviews with their parents about their immigration journey to California. I also included challenging topics such as stories about Chinese sojourners and laborers who risked their lives to build the transcontinental railroads across the United States so that they can offer a better future for their own children. We talked about the Japanese American incarceration during WWII and read stories such as *Baseball Saved Us*[2] and *The Bracelet*[3] to illuminate the atrocities, but also to highlight our humanity to fight for justice. We also

---

2 Mochizuki, *Baseball Saved Us*.
3 Uchida, *The Bracelet*.

painfully spoke about the story of Vincent Chin and created a display for our Asian American History Museum for K-5 School title, "Dear America, Why was Vincent Chin Killed?"

I decided to leave the classroom after five years in East Los Angeles, CA to pursue my Doctorate in Education degree at Teachers College, Columbia University. My goal for obtaining a doctorate was to provide me with the toolset as a researcher and an educator to create systemic pathways to develop culturally relevant curricula and to integrate Asian American studies into the K–12 curriculum.

My inquiries about traditional schooling and its curriculum brought me back to New York City as an after-school instructor for low-income Chinese American youth at a community-based organization in New York City's Chinatown in my graduate school days. Within a year of teaching and working with Chinese American youth, their personal testimonies gave me evidence that the reproduction of inequalities within the discourse and socialization of school, curriculum, and teacher practice continues aggressively today. My students' candid voice of disengagement in school gave us a point of entry to examine the academic and social injustices in our public school system. My students have ignited in me a stronger sense of compassion to listen and to learn about their dreams for a better life and their hope to create a school and community that are about justice. Our time together in and out of school have inspired our collaboration to challenge ourselves, other youth, teachers, and educational leaders to dare change a system of educational inequalities. We want to re-construct the relevancy of our public-school education to validate our own unique and collective experiences as part of America's growing and diverse history as Chinese Americans. This is our story.

Justice in Our Education

That was my mission about a decade ago, but now, fast forward my life and America's to the present day in 2022, as we have faced a global pandemic of COVID-19. Our nation has lost over 560,000 lives.[4] Nationwide, Black people have died at 1.4 times the rate of white people.[5] Media reports have illustrated that during COVID-19, Black people were denied

---

4 CDC, April 24, 2021
5 Covid Racial Tracker, 2021

health care services in hospitals due to the doubting of their health situation by medical staff; and as a result, it has led to numerous fatalities.[6] In addition to Black people's experiences with medical racism, there has been more visibility of the ongoing police brutality against our Black community before and in midst of the pandemic with the death of George Floyd, Breonna Taylor, Ahmaud Arbery, and Duante Wright to name a few lost souls.

Simultaneously, over 3,800 anti-Asian hate incidents have been reported across the country according to a national database organized by StopAAPIHate.[7] New York City saw an increase of 223% in Asian hate crimes in 2021.[8] Words of hate were incited by former president Trump referring COVID-19 as the "Chinese virus" and the "Kung Flu." As the pandemic spread, the rise of anti-Asian hate crime and xenophobia soared. On March 16, 2021, eight people were killed at Asian spas in Atlanta, Georgia, six of whom were Asian immigrant women.

Covid-19 unveiled a twin pandemic in the United States of COVID-19 and racial violence. As educators there is an urgency for us to reflect and to act now on being socially responsible on what we teach in our classrooms. We need to look at the historical legacy of racism against people of color, specifically against Black, brown, and Asian American communities. As educators, we have a responsibility to teach truths in our US history, scholarship, and stories in K-20 classrooms and begin to share our counterstories.

White supremacy is deeply embedded in our American education system. White supremacy is a belief system that posits white people are inherently superior to people of other racial and ethnic groups; as a result, this belief system dehumanizes people of color and positions them as othered and the "inferior" race.[9] Research illustrates that our K–20 curriculum and pedagogy is pre-dominantly white, Anglo-Eurocentric, focusing only on the achievements, cultures, history, and values of white Anglo-European American men.[10] To move away from the dehumanization of a white supremacist and Eurocentric curriculum, it is important

---

6 Guardian, 2020; Harvard Medical School, 2017
7 2021
8 NYPD, 2021
9 Tchen, *Yellow Peril*, 2014. Wilder, *Ebony & Ivy*, 2013
10 Sleeter, *Un-Standardizing Curriculum*, 2005. Yu, *Changing the Narrative*.

for our increasingly multicultural society to implement an ethnic studies curriculum and pedagogy that is critical, diverse, humanizing, and community-responsive to challenge the power structures of the status quo.[11]

In my own teaching and work, I use the tenets and framework of ethnic studies and counter-storytelling to build on the collective history and stories of Black and Asian Americans that have been erased in scholarship and public knowledge. By reclaiming our US history and stories, we are validating our ancestral histories and lived experiences as part of the American story and history. Ethnic studies is the interdisciplinary study of the political, social, cultural, and economic experiences of minoritized groups. It closely examines race, ethnicity, class, gender, and sexuality to understand how such groups have been affected by systems of power.[12] We use counter-storytelling to capture the experiences of race, racism, and racial realism through our storytelling, narrative, and lived experiences. Using the ethnic studies tenets and counter-storytelling framework in building Black and Asian American history in K–20 education, we are pushing the edges of methodology that have not been traditionally done before in teacher education and educational research.

Many teacher education programs are reproducing colonial education and ideas of white supremacy in their foundational coursework and clinical training, and as a result, this knowledge base becomes a foundational worldview in framing our current K–12 standardized curriculum and teachers' pedagogy. By *building racial rolidarity across Black and Asian American history in K–20 education*, I ask all of us to challenge and disrupt the common narratives in teacher education and K–12 curricula frameworks that have serious implications for racial inequities and that have traumatized generations of students of color.

My hope for the next Asian American Pacific Islander generation is that you cherish and honor our generational stories, our ancestors' courage, and their sacrifices to fight for racial and social justice. As you move forward into the world, I hope you always remember that Asian American and Pacific Islanders have been brilliant, brave, and loving people who have consistently centered their deep love for their children, families, and community. I hope that one day you can see that our humanity is forever

---

11 Fernandez, *Decolonizing Professional Development*.
12 Butler, *Gender Trouble*.

interconnected with others and that we are stronger and better when we love one another and come together.

With Hope & Heart, Judy W. Yu, Ed.D.

BIBLIOGRAPHY

Butler, Judith. *Gender Trouble: Feminism and the Subversion of Identity.* New York: Routledge Classics, 1990.

Center for Disease Control. "Center for Disease Control Mortality Covid19 Overview." 2015. https://www.cdc.gov/nchs/covid19/mortality-overview.

Fernandez, Anita E. "Decolonizing professional development: A Re-Humanizing Approach."

Equity & Excellence in Education 52, no. 2/3 (2020) 1–12.

Guardian. "For Black Americans, COVID-19 is a Reminder of Racism." February 22, 2021. https://www.theguardian.com/commentisfree/2021/feb/22/black-americans-covid-19-racism-us-healthcare

Haley, Alex. *The Autobiography of Malcolm X: As Told to Alex Haley.* New York: Ballantine Books, 1992.

Mochizuki, Ken. *Baseball Saved Us.* Illustrations by Dom Lee. New York: Lee & Low Books, 2018.

Omatsu, Glenn K. "Freedom Xchooling: Reconceptualizing Asian American Studies For Our Communities." *Amerasia Journal,* 29, no. 2 (2003) 9–33.

Smith, Tuhiwai L. *Decolonizing Methodologies: Research and Indigenous Peoples.* London: Zed Books, 1999.

Sleeter, Christine E. *Un-Standardizing Curriculum.* New York: Teachers College, 2005.

Tchen, John K.W. & Dylan Yeats, eds. *Yellow Peril! An archive of anti-Asian fear.* New York: Verso, 2014.

Uchida, Yoshiko. *The Bracelet.* Illustrations by Joanna Yardley. New York: Puffin Books, 1996.

Wilder, Craig S. *Ebony & Ivy: Race, Slavery, and the Troubled History of America's Universities.* New York: Bloomsbury, 2014.

Yu, Judy. "Changing the Narratives: Asian American Ethnic Studies in My 1st Grade Classroom." In *Planting the Seeds of Equity: Ethnic Studies and Social Justice in the K–2 Classrooms*, edited by Agarwal-Rangnath, (90–95). New York: Teachers College Press, 2020.

11

Why Trying to Fit in Is the Problem

Moon-Ho Jung

My family never sat around and talked about history. But there were lots of historical tidbits that got mentioned over and over. I remember my family talking about how brutal Japanese colonialism in Korea had been. There was one particular story of Japanese officials ripping the fingernails out of Korean Christians that was told often and in graphic detail. I knew very little about the history of Japanese colonialism, but I was taught from an early age that it had been sadistic and inhumane. To this day, whenever Japanese colonialism is mentioned, I think about fingernails.

The United States, on the other hand, received a far better and lighter treatment in our household. It was a blessed country, a Christian country, the land of freedom. It was the United States that had liberated Korea from Japanese colonialism. And that image co-existed somehow with our family's daily encounters with white supremacy in the United States. We encountered a lot of overt racism in Michigan in the 1970s and 1980s. Being called a "chink" was almost a daily occurrence. One day in elementary school, it got so bad that I came home crying. My mom's advice: "Tell them you're Korean."

I also grew up at a time when multiculturalism was making inroads in America's schools. We used to have potlucks at school, where my brother and I had to represent Korea and Koreans everywhere. In third grade, because I wasn't used to wearing traditional Korean pants with drawstrings, the back part of my pants had fallen down. I had no idea. Exposing my Korean butt to my classmates and teachers marked my earliest exposure to multiculturalism. My teachers reinforced and reproduced that idealized image of American diversity, calling the United States the "melting pot," a "salad bowl," and so forth. Kimchi was our colorful, if pungent, contribution to that beautiful American salad.

But what if we see and engage the United States otherwise? What if we recognize the United States not as a multicultural nation welcoming diversity but as an empire rooted in white supremacy. It took me a long time to figure that out, but once I began to see empire in US history, I could not unsee it. That past is all around us. From that perspective, studying history can become exhilarating and liberating, a way for us to find our identities unmoored from white settler notions of Americanness. By studying the past, I gained the confidence to try to understand who I am and who I want to become, in terms that can confront and refute the US empire's self-righteous and self-congratulatory myths.

Generational Myths of Multiculturalism

"Where are you from?" It is a politically loaded and racially coded question that many Asian Americans dread. We usually respond with bitter humor or muted apology because that question, intentionally or not, places Asian Americans on the defensive, as if we need to explain *our* presence in *their* country. In the most benign terms, the question is a symptom of a dominant mythology that would have us believe that the United States is a "nation of immigrants." The question could be extended to, "Where is your family from?" At some point or another, it seems, we can all identify a family member or an ancestral figure who dared to "immigrate" to the United States.

In that vein, most Americans, including Asian Americans, generally like to narrate their history along generational lines. The first generation immigrates; the second-generation rebels against their immigrant parents to become more "Americanized"; over time, future generations become more and more "American" and fully "assimilated." It is an anti-historical way to narrate history, where everyone's history begins anew with the "immigrant," a transhistorical figure who continually embodies the American spirt of individual success. The descendants of white settlers who founded the United States—those who can trace their lineage to the *Mayflower* and the like—become eligible to join the Daughters of the American Revolution (DAR) and other patriotic organizations to rejoice in their unquestioned Americanness.

I don't play the generational game anymore, although I am more forgiving around Korean Americans. Many Korean Americans are obsessed with generations—first, 1.5, second, third, etc.—to figure out how "Korean" or "American" we might be. In those instances, I will play along.

I will answer politely to their direct question, "What generation are you?" But when others, especially white folks, ask that question or its variation—"Where are you from?"—I no longer get defensive. I pivot to offense because I know that we cannot narrate our history along a generational model. "I don't know," I say. "The United States came to Korea, called us 'gooks,' and killed millions of us. America came to us first, so what generation does that make me?"

Most Americans would probably find my answer offensive because it is that global context of US imperial violence that narratives of US history are supposed to erase. That is why conservatives have been waging war against the teaching of Ethnic Studies, Critical Race Theory, and critical *anything* for generations. They believe that history is something to be worshipped and celebrated, mostly to justify and perpetuate the racial and colonial order that their white settler ancestors created. Senator Ted Cruz, for example, recently denounced Critical Race Theory as "an extreme and divisive theory that pits children against other children, divides us based on race, and teaches a false and revisionist history of our nation." Explosive in their potential, critical minds are dangerous things.

In the version of US history that I learned growing up, Asian Americans were virtually invisible. I cannot recall the textbook we used in AP US History, but I can guess when and where Asian Americans must have appeared first. The Chinese were most likely mentioned in reference to the California Gold Rush or the building of the first transcontinental railroad. That aspect of Asian American history can fit neatly into the epic drama that has supposedly defined and made America: Chinese immigrants, hoping to make it rich in America, crossed the Pacific to live out their American Dream. The United States is indeed the "nation of immigrants."

Fed such saccharine versions of history, I wrote about the joys and frustrations of my "bicultural" identity in my college applications. Thankfully, as far as I know, that essay is not available anywhere. One of the earliest debates in the field of Asian American Studies revolved around such notions of personal identity. In 1971, psychologists Stanley Sue and Derald Sue proposed three personality archetypes—the Traditionalist, the Marginal Man, and the Asian American—to characterize the different ways that Asian American children adapted to reconcile familial traditions and American norms. Asian Americans were always striving to fit in, unsuccessfully, a predicament that translated into perpetual feelings of alienation.

When I got to college at Cornell University in 1987, I became captivated, stunned, and confused by what was being billed as the Korean-Black conflict. Beginning with a boycott of Korean greengrocers in Brooklyn in 1988 and erupting in three days of violence in Los Angeles in 1992, the Korean-Black conflict was all over the headlines. How did the acquittal of four white LAPD officers in the beating of a Black driver lead to a wholesale attack on Korean-owned businesses? That racial logic seemed to make no sense, but race itself never made sense per se. I read the *New York Times* obsessively.

For reasons that confound me today, I decided to major in Government at Cornell. My courses in the major did not engage race critically or historically. In a course on US constitutional law taught by a self-proclaimed conservative professor, his lecture on World War II and civil liberties essentially rationalized the mass incarceration of Japanese Americans. At the time, I did not have the language or the knowledge to challenge what he was saying. Feeling alienated and alone, I walked out of that lecture, but I doubt that anyone realized that I was leaving in protest. As I was walking out, I made direct eye contact with the professor. I wish I had given him the finger right then and there. I knew that language.

My higher education began only after I completed my major. In my last three semesters as an undergraduate in 1990 and 1991, as the so-called Korean-Black conflict intensified, I took courses that helped me make sense of the world. I could not get enough of Africana Studies, Asian American Studies, and History. Reading W. E. B. Du Bois, Vincent Harding, Malcolm X, Maxine Hong Kingston, and many others transformed my worldview and drove me to ask questions that I had not known to ask. Reading and writing had a new purpose. Beyond getting a good grade, I was beginning to wake up to new political possibilities, to new ways of seeing the United States.

I soon abandoned my plans to apply to law school. I decided to pursue graduate studies in History, a discipline that had drawn only big yawns in high school. At one time, I thought history was irrelevant. Why study the past, which we cannot change, when we can make a difference now? I am sure many of you may be asking that question. But we can, and must, change the past—or, more precisely, how we interpret the past.

We cannot surrender the past to white colonial settlers who miraculously have become "pioneers," "immigrants," and "Americans" in history textbooks and Hollywood films. There is way too much at stake.

America Never Was America to Me

After Barack Obama's victory in the 2008 US presidential election, lots of Americans congratulated themselves. Many proclaimed that the election marked the beginning of a post-racial moment in US history. Not long after that election, I was doing some research at the National Archives, right outside of Washington, DC. As I was walking back to my hotel room one day, I noticed a big yellow school bus in the parking lot. It was full of high school students, probably on a field trip to the nation's capital. When they saw me, some of the kids started screaming out the window: "Jap!" and "Chink!" and "Kamikaze!" Before I could think, my right middle finger shot up to the sky. That was not a post-racial moment.

Obama's election, which seems so long ago now, appeared to inaugurate new possibilities. In comparison to most presidential candidates, he could talk about race intelligently. But he also had to pay homage to American myths of racial inclusion. In March 2008, in a speech that threw his former pastor under the bus, Obama talked about "this nation's original sin of slavery." "Of course," he added quickly, "the answer to the slavery question was already embedded within our Constitution—a Constitution that had at i[t]s very core the ideal of equal citizenship under the law; a Constitution that promised its people liberty, and justice, and a union that could be and should be perfected over time."

I see and teach US history very differently. I do not see slavery as a forgivable sin in an otherwise glorious experiment in democracy. Instead, I believe we have to press harder, to think deeper, to recognize that the US Constitution laid the foundation to colonialism and slavery at the heart of American democracy. Although the Founding Fathers self-consciously left out the term *slavery* in the Constitution, they purposely inscribed provisions to strengthen the institution. Through the infamous three-fifths clause, the foreseeable ban on slave trade prohibitions, and the fugitive slave clause on persons "held to Service or Labour," the Constitution did not raise questions on slavery. Without question, American democracy was founded in part to preserve and protect chattel slavery.

As I prepared to work on a dissertation project in the 1990s, I wanted to explore how Asian American history might relate to the history of slavery. My dissertation, which eventually became my first book, explored the historical origins of "coolies," a racial epithet projected onto Asian workers for centuries. The term became potently popular in the era of slave emancipation, when slave owners and their representative governments searched desperately for a labor force to replace and supplement enslaved Black labor. Racial representations of Asian workers as "coolies," I argued, led to their recruitment (unlike Black people after slavery, they were cheap and submissive) and their exclusion (unlike white people, they were too cheap and too submissive), beginning with the Page Law (1875) and the Chinese Exclusion Act (1882).

My first book project also compelled me to place the image of the United States as the "nation of immigrants" in historical context. Five years after the Civil War in 1870, Senator Charles Sumner of Massachusetts proposed to remove the word *white* from the 1790 Naturalization Act. His colleagues defeated his proposal by attacking Chinese "coolies" as racially unfit for US citizenship—"a race without love of liberty," a lawmaker claimed. In the process, members of the US Congress insisted that they were defending the true, legitimate "immigrants" who had created America, "our progenitors," as a New York representative argued, "the white people who earlier or later came from Europe."

Through a critical engagement with the past, I came to see the present, my own identity, in a radically different light. I came to understand that the pitting of Black people and Asian people has been pivotal to reproducing white supremacy. I also came to see that the exclusion of Asians from the United States was not an exception to or a betrayal of America's inclusive traditions. It was, in fact, fundamental to that notion of the American nation, a racial project that equated whiteness and Americanness. The answer to our feelings of alienation was not to try harder to fit in. The answer was to appreciate why that was a game we were bound to lose, always. We needed to change the rules of engagement.

As I was finishing my first book, President George W. Bush waged his global "war on terror," a perpetual state of war through which the US state essentially claimed the authority to incarcerate, torture, and kill anyone living on our planet. That a Korean American, John Yoo, authored the Bush Administration's infamous "Torture Memo" sanctioning brutal tactics against "unlawful combatants" was horribly embarrassing and utterly predictable. Bush liked to appoint persons of color—remember Colin Powell, Condoleezza Rice, Alberto Gonzales?—to do his dirty work. That was multiculturalism at work. A new generation of American war criminals might have looked more diverse, but their crimes against humanity dated back to the origination of the United States.

Perhaps the most insidious aspect of the US history I learned in high school was the absence of the US empire and Indigenous peoples. We surely learned about the Northwest Ordinance (1787) and the methodical process that allowed "voters" to petition for statehood, for example, but that history of American expansion and American democracy conveniently skipped over a fundamental detail: Indigenous peoples lived on those lands claimed by white settlers. "Manifest destiny" lives on. "US history, as well as inherited Indigenous trauma," Roxanne Dunbar-Ortiz argues, "cannot be understood without dealing with the genocide that the United States committed against Indigenous peoples." If it is anything, the United States was and is an empire.

It is from that foundational premise that I conceived and wrote my recent book, *Menace to Empire*, an exploration of how the racialization of Asians as threats to US national security came to be crucial to advancing the US empire. In particular, I traced "sedition" to its colonial origins that categorized anticolonial expressions and anticolonial movements as criminal acts. During the height of the Philippine-American War in 1901, for instance, the US Philippine Commission issued the Sedition Act, which made it "unlawful for any person to advocate orally or by writing or printing or like methods, the independence of the Philippine Islands or their separation from the United States whether by peaceable or forcible means."

The US military, full of veterans of Indian wars in North America, waged a genocidal war in the Philippines to secure the US empire. But Filipinos continued to mobilize against the US empire, organizing anticolonial movements that the US state attempted to monitor, criminalize, and repress. By seeing peoples in and from Asia as racialized and radicalized subjects of the US empire, not as immigrants aspiring to become Americans, my new book suggests the need to frame anti-Asian racism, including racial violence, as quintessentially American, an expression of and a justification for US claims to sovereignty across the Pacific and around the world.

That unyielding racial logic would evolve into the US national security state as we know it today, an unparalleled behemoth subjecting racialized and radicalized peoples around the world to unrelenting violence, all in the name of "national security." Demonized over the last century as "anarchists," "communists," "gooks," and "terrorists," Asians have been cast as "un-American" and "anti-American," those who needed to be killed and contained to protect the racial and colonial order that is the United States of America. In that context, insisting on the "Americanness" of Asian Americans can never meaningfully address a deeper history of empire and white supremacy. Until we can make sense of that history, we will not be able to understand why anti-Asian racism remains such a violent force menacing the world we live in today.

Conclusion

We, as human beings, cannot make sense of who we are without some kind of historical consciousness. We draw connections to our ancestors, to historical forces that precede and exceed our personal existence. Studying the past is a personal act, but it is also a political act. History, as I see it, is ultimately a means to generate collective visions of identity, community, and justice. Shortly before his assassination in 1965, Malcolm X challenged his Black audience to stop identifying themselves as "the American Negro" or approaching racism as "an American problem." Racism, he said, was "a problem that is so complex... that you have to study it in its entire world, in the world context or in its international context, to really see it as it actually is." Identifying as an "American" was politically limiting; identifying with Black and Asian peoples around the world held unlimited potential.

We need to study the past to find worlds of new possibilities, to figure out who we are and who we can become. History, as taught to me through high school and beyond, unfortunately had the opposite effect. It conveyed a patriotic story of inclusion and assimilation that demanded that we try to fit into the benevolent "nation of immigrants," the greatest nation on Earth. I wish I had known that it was possible to reject that history, to challenge my teachers, to demand that we reckon with the United States as an empire rooted in white supremacy. Knowing at least that much now, I will be trying to reckon with that history of empire and white supremacy for the rest of my life.

At the University of Washington, I (Moon-Ho Jung) teach a big lecture course titled, "Race and American History." In the subsequent pages, you can find a list of the readings I assigned the last time I taught the course (Autumn 2021).

HSTAA 231: RACE AND AMERICAN HISTORY
Autumn Quarter 2021
University of Washington

INSTRUCTOR
Moon-Ho Jung (he/him)
204D Smith

DESCRIPTION
We will survey U.S. history, from its beginnings to today, by exploring how race has enabled conceptions of the American nation and empire and shaped everyday practices and social interactions among different peoples. How have racial concepts, racial representations, and racial practices fundamentally defined power dynamics in the United States? From slave revolts to the Black Lives Matter movement, how have various individuals, communities, and organizations framed and pursued racial justice?

TEXTBOOKS
Roxanne Dunbar-Ortiz, *An Indigenous Peoples' History of the United States*. Boston, MA: Beacon, 2014.

Tera W. Hunter, *To 'Joy My Freedom: Southern Black Women's Lives and Labors after the Civil War*. Cambridge, MA: Harvard University Press, 1998.

George J. Sánchez, *Boyle Heights: How a Los Angeles Neighborhood Became the Future of American Democracy*. Oakland, CA: University of California Press, 2021.

Malcolm X, *The Last Speeches*. Atlanta, GA: Pathfinder, 1989.

Course Packet Readings

1. George Lipsitz, "The Possessive Investment in Whiteness," from *The Possessive Investment in Whiteness: How White People Profit from Identity Politics* (Philadelphia: Temple University Press, 1998), 1–23.

2. "Declaration of Independence (1776)" and "Constitution of the United States (1787)," in Melvin I. Urofsky and Paul Finkelman, *Documents of American Constitutional and Legal History*, second ed. (New York: Oxford University Press, 2002), 54–58, 85–97.

3. "Naturalization Act, March 26, 1790," in *The Columbia Documentary History of the Asian American Experience*, ed. Franklin Odo (New York: Columbia University Press, 2002), 13–14.

4. Walter Johnson, "Reading Bodies and Marking Race," from *Soul by Soul: Life Inside the Antebellum Slave Market* (Cambridge: Harvard University Press, 1999), 135–161.

5. "*Dred Scott v. Sandford* (1857)," in Melvin I. Urofsky and Paul Finkelman, *Documents of American Constitutional and Legal History*, second ed. (New York: Oxford University Press, 2002), 366–372.

6. "*Plessy v. Ferguson* (1896)," in Melvin I. Urofsky and Paul Finkelman, *Documents of American Constitutional and Legal History*, second ed. (New York: Oxford University Press, 2002), 539–543.

7. Excerpts from *Takao Ozawa v. United States* (1922) and *United States v. Bhagat Singh Thind* (1923), from Ian F. Haney López, *White by Law: The Legal Construction of Race*, revised edition (New York: New York University Press, 2006), 176–182.

8. Peggy Pascoe, "Miscegenation Law, Court Cases, and Ideologies of 'Race' in Twentieth Century America," *Journal of American History* 83, no. 1 (June 1996): 44–69.

9. Barack Obama, "A More Perfect Union," March 18, 2008.

https://constitutioncenter.org/amoreperfectunion/docs/Race_Speech_Transcript.pdf.

10. Ana Mari Cauce, "We the People: Diversity, Equity and Difference at the UW," April 16, 2015. https://s3-us-west-2.amazonaws.com/uw-s3-cdn/wp-content/uploads/sites/10/2015/04/23170031/diversity-equity-and-difference-speech-transcript.pdf.

11. Robin D. G. Kelley, "Polycultural Me," *Utne Reader* (September-October 1999). http://www.utne.com/politics/the-people-in-me?pageid=1#PageContent1.

12. Kenneth J. Cooper, "I'm a Descendant of the Cherokee Nation's Black Slaves. Tribal Citizenship Is Our Birthright," *Washington Post*, September 15, 2017. https://www.washingtonpost.com/news/post-nation/wp/2017/09/15/im-a-descendant-of-the-cherokee-nations-black-slaves-tribal-citizenship-is-our-birthright/

13. Donald J. Trump for President, "Immigration Reform That Will Make America Great Again," 2016. https://www.nytimes.com/2019/07/17/magazine/white-men-privilege.html?searchResultPosition=4.

14. Claudia Rankine, "I Wanted to Know What White Men Thought about Their Privilege. So I Asked," New York Times Magazine, July 17, 2019. https://www.nytimes.com/2019/07/17/magazine/white-men-privilege.html?searchResultPosition=4.

15. Weiyi Cai, Audra D. S. Burch, and Jugal K. Patel, "Swelling Anti-Asian Violence: Who Is Being Attacked Where," *New York Times*, April 3, 2021. https://www.nytimes.com/interactive/2021/04/03/us/anti-asian-attacks.html.

16. Jon Wiener, "The Predictable Backlash to Critical Race Theory: A Q&A with Kimberlé Crenshaw," *The Nation*, July 5, 2021. https://www.thenation.com/article/politics/critical-race-kimberle-crenshaw/.

17. Naomi Ishisaka, "Contrasting Coverage of Gabby Petito Case and Missing and Murdered Indigenous People Shows 'Absolute Injustice,'" *Seattle Times*, September 27, 2021. https://www.seattletimes.com/seattle-news/contrasting-coverage-of-gabby-petito-case-and-missing-and-murdered-indigenous-people-shows-absolute-injustice/.

12

Liberation Through Identity: "We Are Lucky to Be Free"

Takeru Nagayoshi

"You Are Lucky to Be Free"

This is what my *okasan*, my mother, told me when I came out to her at fifteen. There was no rejection. No line of questioning. No denial, or pity, fear, or disappointment. A simple declarative claim—an acknowledgement without doubt and an affirmation of the biggest secret I had kept to myself up until that point.

Up until that point, I was taught by society that being gay is bad. A scourge. A defective trait. An impediment to any chances of success and happiness, should I choose to live in full unapologetic truth. Up until that point, my truth was my cage.

"You are lucky to be free." Up until that moment with *okasan*, I could not fathom my identity as any other way, let alone as an answer and path to liberation.

As queer people, we become acutely aware at early age that society was never designed for us. We have existed in the margins, at best as anomalies to tolerate and accommodate, and at worst, as targets of persecution. But where I saw limitations, my mother saw endless sky: A child so underserved by the palette given to him, that he had to bring all colors of the rainbow and draw outside the canvas.

Okasan assured me that I get to chart my own path forward—one unencumbered by the rigid rules that govern how young boys ought to act and be. Many men struggle with the pressures of gender roles and traditional forms of masculinity, but accepting my queerness means I can also choose to operate outside this template. I can explore and express myself with true authenticity. I am free.

Our identities not only define—but liberate—us. This is what my *okasan* taught me.

In the classroom, my mother's wisdom echoes loudly. It's the pedagogy I chose to teach my students and their multiplicity of identities that inspire our space.

Our identities hold liberatory power, and when we encourage our students to explore and express them, not just in earnest but through hope and with limitless wonder, we empower them to live in their truth and in freedom.

But I am often surprised that my students do not always share this view about themselves. Where I see endless sky, many of them see limitations.

When students write their college essays, for example, I'm intrigued by the details they share about their identities and background, but I'm also taken aback by the shame and resentment that seems to underscore how they discuss them. A girl feels embarrassed by her Haitian accent, rather than celebrating the linguistic diversity she possesses. A boy recounts every slur he endured for being Chinese, instead of the community of Asian friends he made through shared culture and ethnicity. A student laments how their parents will never accept their sexual orientation, ignoring the progress and attempts toward understanding their family has made. These observations are particularly noticeable among my students of color, or those from low-income and other minoritized backgrounds.

One student—we'll call her Octavia—had trouble explaining her interest in criminal justice reform. Her first draft droned on about abstract notions of justice, but without revealing anything about her. As was customary when I workshop their college essays or write recommendations, I interviewed Octavia. I asked about her identity, her family, and her community. I asked her about experiences, high and low, that helped shape her values and will help direct her future.

Through this conversation, I learned that neither of Octavia's parents went to college. Her mother, an immigrant from Cape Verde, does not speak any English, while her father works late-night shifts to support the family. Her sister became pregnant in high school and her brother was convicted of felony.

Octavia also shared about the time an officer handcuffed and banged her body on the pavement in front of her peers. According to this school, this punishment was justified because of Octavia's apparent disrespectful behavior. She was thirteen. After she shared this story, we sat in silence and in tears.

Octavia's final draft focused on this experience—how it shed light on police brutality, how it ignited her empathy for George Floyd, and how it connected her to the countless Black and brown people victimized by the criminal justice system. By embracing her identity and exploring the endless sky beyond the adversities our identities may imply, Octavia crafted an understanding of self that connected her to worlds beyond her.

—

People from oppressed or underrepresented backgrounds are quick to recognize the weight of their identity. People can reinterpret their identities, however, as they struggle to leap beyond its adversities.

For many young people figuring out their place in life, the need to focus on this adversity is part of the design—an unfortunate battle scar helping make sense of their word, an "inspirational story" we adults expect of them. But when we only push our kids to examine their hardships without imagining what's beyond it, we clip their wings and limit them to the single story of their past, not of their infinite futures.

Liberation through identity is not only acknowledging the totality of who we are, but also daring to dream outside of our adversities.

It's the pedagogy of creating psychological safety and the audacity for students to center truth and honest self-reflection. It's the pedagogy of empathy, where we listen to and accept one another in service of our shared humanity and common purpose.

When we understand and accept our truth, our power cannot be taken away. As educators, we have the capacity to nurture this power and the responsibility to nurture it wisely. We have the joy of getting to embrace our children for who they are and telling them with full imagination and wonder: "We are lucky to be free."

PART THREE:
GENERATIONAL STORIES, CONVERSATIONS, & HEALING TRAUMAS

13

Ebony in the Ivory Tower

Adia Butler & Dr. Lee Butler

I (Adia) have spent my entire life being Black in predominantly white spaces, including my K–12 schools and undergraduate schools. According to the statistics of the school district I attended, a learning gap between Black and white begins in middle school. It should, therefore, be no surprise that my racial identity didn't start consciously affecting me until middle school. The challenges to being Black became even more severe in high school. As I became more socially conscious, the impact of being Black in a predominantly white school system grew. The more aware I became of my Blackness in a white-preferred world, the more the whiteness of my peers stood out to me in how their whiteness was perpetuated by their words and actions. Whether their actions were deliberate or unwitting, it became more difficult to get through the days. My father, who is very African-centered, meant my home life stood in sharp contrast to my school life.

I was always one of a few or the only Black person in the classroom. I was hyperaware of the pressure put on me as the inadvertent, and quite frankly, unwilling, "spokesperson" for the race. Rather than bringing my father's African-centeredness to my school presence, my awareness of extreme whiteness led to my being withdrawn or silent. The result: Don't be too loud, or else I'm the Angry Black Woman. Don't call out racism in any form, or else I'm too sensitive and a wilting flower. Don't talk about race unless warranted (like during the Civil Rights unit in American History class), or else I'm the Black girl who makes everything about race.

My father had similar experiences during his secondary education during the early to late 1970s. Also attending predominantly white schools, he has clear memories of walking the fine line of being Black in a white-preferred world. Coming of age in a post-Civil Rights America, he sees the challenges I faced in middle and high schools as remarkably similar to my experiences from 2012 to 2018. He regularly tells the story of his high school guidance counselor who tried to steer him away from the elite private liberal arts colleges in which he sought to enroll. He describes this time as "molding him for mediocrity."

The attitudes of the white-preferred world created conflict within and caused me to feel I had to defend my identity and articulate facts of being non-white in America. Naming the facts in the Obama era, ironically, would get *me* branded as a racist for seeing color at a historical moment that described America as a "post-racial society." My father was highly critical of America's desire to posture itself as post-racial while simultaneously ignoring the microaggressions that President Obama had to endure. Although I tended to be more vocal on the rare occasion of classes focused on Black history, my general posture was silence, particularly in the presence of people who refused to understand the dynamics of race.

Not unlike my father's experiences of being "molded for mediocrity," my negative high school experiences become the primary lessons that influenced my life in college. Yet, even on a campus that prided itself on diversity and inclusion, the student body was still 73% white. As a campus of white liberalism, the white-preferred attitudes often proved to be more heinous and harmful than right-wing ideology. The discomfort I felt throughout secondary education turned into a rage that I bottled up in class and unloaded in private. I vented the pressure in out-of-class conversations with my Black friends and the white friends I felt I could trust. Whenever I did call someone out in the moment, a nagging in the back of my head yelled at me to shut up because I was being *that* Black girl, perpetuating *that* stereotype. Even in writing classrooms, where I felt most comfortable despite the lack of racial diversity, I was profoundly aware that the challenges to my being will never end.

I recall countless instances that accentuated my high lessons of a white-preferred society. My freshman year roommate was racially mixed but white-passing. Her heritage was Indigenous American and European. Her hometown had very few Black people, which made me one of a few African Americans she had contact with. I often wonder, would her mother have treated me differently if I was not Black. As a writer and poet, I was subtly challenged as a Black person writing fiction and prose. I am still flabbergasted by those who thought giving Black people easier access to education was the answer to eradicating institutional racism. While my father is clear to speak of some of the benefits of affirmative action, he is clear to identify that African Americans have not been the leading beneficiaries of affirmative action and the efforts to roll back affirmative action policies is racism's continuing legacy. In a class dedicated to discussing depictions of race and gender in children and young adult literature, I was astounded by the freely spoken, but still acknowledged, anti-Indigenous slur followed by a claim that microaggressions are not a big deal. There was a further claim by the same person that non-white people who experience microaggressions overreact.

There were misperceptions and misinterpretations that made Black people invisible. I recall a class presentation where a selected poem, very clearly about a Black family being attacked by the KKK, was enthusiastically interpreted to be about Hanukkah because it mentioned lamps and oil. The misinterpretation continued by relating the poem to the musical *Hadestown*. When I, as the only Black American in the class, spoke to the Black American experience of racial terrorism, I was shut down and silenced. Who could imagine that someone would believe that "Negro" is the N-word? White-preferred society empowers people to believe what is inappropriate to be acceptable, like a white person choosing to respond to me using Ebonics and a Blaccent. In public spaces, and especially the classroom, I would always code-switch and only speak "standard" English dialect outside of my dorm room.

When one of my professors asked about the infamous Will Smith slap, a question that my father refused to comment on, I allowed one person to give their opinion before I took over the conversation completely. I could not hold my peace on that day. A little over a month later, the same professor assigned "slideshow karaoke," where students created slides about a set of topics that would be randomly assigned to other students to present. Instead of developing my presentation on why Five Guys is better than McDonald's, or why *Ferris Bueller's Day Off* is the greatest 80s movie, I decided to create a presentation about reparations. A "liberal" white person was given the presentation to perform and make humorous for the class. The second she saw REPARATIONS in big capital letters and a picture of Huey P. Newton on the title slide, she became visibly uncomfortable. Throughout the presentation, she could barely read the slides I so carefully curated; she stood silent for seconds at a time before motioning for the professor to switch to the next slide. Her white liberalism was dumfounded by one simple word that challenged her liberal posture for ten minutes and, for the first time in the semester, silenced her.

Living through secondary and post-secondary educational systems of being forced to listen to misguided interpretations, of being questioned, judged, and gaslighted/gaslit by liberal white people, I am hard-pressed to believe white-preferred society will ever change. Regardless of what I do or say, it seems that I will always be invisible to white liberalism.

Closing Thoughts: First Person Plural

Adia wrote in the first person and I, Dr. Butler, in the third person in order to keep her experience front and center. I, Dr. Butler, put it through a strong edit, which makes the essay us, but the fundamental framing is all her! It was difficult to see/hear how strikingly similar our stories are, despite the nearly fifty years separating our experiences. In whose lifetime will we actually see a change? Is it possible to see such change when things seem to keep moving deeper and deeper under the surface until they become indistinguishable except to those it directly affects?

14

Creative Expressions: An Interview Between a Teenager and His Mom

Kyle Little and Lahronda Welch Little

Introduction

"Mom, I have made a decision - I am going to act." Such a declaration from my son, Kyle, was not a surprise. Quite frankly, ever since he was a small child, he has acted and entertained our family. With a ready smile and incorrigible sense of humor, Kyle holds a pragmatic view of the world, particularly from his vantage point as a student in a public suburban school system that is predominantly African American.

What is also true about Kyle is his courage and propensity to try new things. Ever the artist-philosopher, my son employs a critical eye on social and educational systems. It is not lost on him that by virtue of his placement within these systems that he himself is implicated—in fact, we all are. Kyle manages his criticisms of education systems that, according to him, lack imagination through various forms of creative expressions, such as content creation for social media and drama. In the following conversation, Kyle and I uncover how he came into the arts and how his artistic expressions help to facilitate self-realization and academic achievement.

Lahronda: What inspires you?

Kyle: What inspires is seeing young people do great things. I enjoy seeing average people make do out-of-the-box choices and do amazing things.

Lahronda: Who comes to mind?

Kyle: Gaten Matarazzo on Stranger Things. He has a condition called Cleidocranial dysplasia, or CCD. He was diagnosed with it when he was younger, and he didn't let it come between him and his dreams. He has accomplished quite a bit at a really young age. That's pretty inspiring.

Lahronda: When you're inspired what are you led to do? What are your creative expressions?

Kyle: When I'm inspired, I guess it all just depends. Typically, I do things I normally probably wouldn't do. If that makes sense.

Lahronda: What is something you've done recently that you normally wouldn't do?

Kyle: I joined my drama club. That wasn't a thought at all before this school year. But then I guess being around that a theater environment inspired me to join.

I took advanced theater my Sophomore year of high school, and that was my first time doing something like that.

Lahronda: As you learned more, what is it about theater attracted you?

Kyle: Learning about the history and just the fact that you can be any thing you want to be. When it comes to art, the arts, it can be anything you want, especially acting.

Lahronda: It sounds like, for you, acting akes your life more expansive. Would you say that?

Kyle: Yes, I agree with that. I never knew the arts was as big as it was. There's so much you can do even if you're not an actor. But yes, I see acting as a way through which you can just, no matter what it is you want to be, or any dreams that you've had, or anything, you can do it. You can.

Lahronda: What are your other creative outlets?

Kyle: YouTube is one. I've found social media to be a blessing. It can be bad in some ways, but I see social media as a good thing. It really depends on what you do on social media, but it can also benefit people in certain ways.

Lahronda: What ways?

Kyle: As in like confidence. It can really boost your confidence. And it opens a lot of doors.

Lahronda: When you say it boosts your confidence, I agree. Some people like being anonymous, though, because confidence can steer one in different directions. What is the positive aspect of one's confidence being boosted? And what kind of door are you looking to open?

Kyle: In doing YouTube, the more I grow a lot of new opportunities that could come up such as like businesses who recognize that I can get a lot of people on my side. Which means they would possibly want me to showcase their products and get people to purchase. Also, people like to "hop on the wave."

Lahronda: Do you like that?

Kyle: I mean, it's cool.

Lahronda: I think the word you're looking for is "influencer."

Kyle: "Influencer," that's it. You have a huge influence on people if you're a content creator.

Lahronda: A lot of people create content, but everybody's not an influencer. What is it about people, in general, that make them an influencer?

Kyle: There are a lot of things. But mainly, if you're just being organic. Just being you and being real. Don't try to fake anything or be something you're not to get people on your side. People can tell if you're being you or not. I feel like being an influence is you putting your thoughts beliefs out there. Then people can choose whether to be with you or not.

Lahronda: Organic. That's a good word. Were you a YouTuber before or after you became interested in acting?

Kyle: I say it really happened around the same time now to be honest. I started YouTube when I was in sixth grade, but it was just for fun.

Lahronda: You were in the sixth grade?!

Kyle: Yes. When I was in sixth grade, I was making videos in my room, and I would post them. I didn't have any quality and no editing skills. I didn't know what I was doing. I just turned on the camera and talk. Just insane.

Lahronda: You posted it on YouTube?

Kyle: Yes, but all the videos are gone. I wanted a gaming channel. I remember when I was in sixth grade, and there was this game called Fortnite. All the kids were playing it, and I always wanted to be a YouTuber. So, at the time, I didn't know how to work my PlayStation because we had just gotten it. I would use my phone and record the TV as I was playing the game. Then I would just commentate the game. Since then, I have learned to like about YouTube. When I was a sixth grader, I was excited to just *act* like people were watching my videos.

Lahronda: You acted like people were seeing your videos?

Kyle: Yes, I'd pretend I was some big time YouTuber, and say, "oh, you guys like or subscribe." No one was really watching them, it was just fun to do. Then around 10th grade, that's when I became really interested learned how to edit and decided to start my YouTube channel back up.

Lahronda: You have always just had this intrinsic confidence. It was interesting to watch you, even as a baby. You were never seemed to be shy. Can you ever recall a time in which you were not confident?

Kyle: There's definitely been moments. But I always overcame being shy by doing out-of-the-box things. Like I remember when you had just became the assistant pastor at a church, and it was our first youth meeting. My first youth meeting, I didn't really know anyone. But the youth minister needed somebody to pray at service for Youth Sunday, and I just decided to do it. I was kind of nervous, but I did it anyway.

Lahronda: As a toddler and very young child, you used to be so silly. In every one of your pictures, you never gave a regular smile. You always gave us the silliest face. You were always in entertainment mode. Just a natural. Do you remember being silly?

Kyle: Yes, but I don't really know where that came from. To be honest, that's just how I always moved. I just always did whatever felt right. And like, if somebody was taking a picture, then it was like, I guess I'll just smile for the picture.

Lahronda: Let's look at this a bit more critically. Until maybe a year ago, getting you to do your schoolwork was like pulling teeth. Then something clicked. What happened? Because about that same time is when you started the videos. Would you say there is a correlation?

Kyle: When I started the videos, maybe. But school was always not my thing. Not that I couldn't do it, it just was never a big interest. I could do "this school stuff," but I figured that I just have two more years left, so let's just finish these out.

Lahronda: Why wasn't or isn't school you?

Kyle: Because it's just, it was so like standardized. School is very standardized. I guess that's when I fell in love with the theater. When I say standardized, I mean, everything is by the book. Every kid in the world it seems is learning the same curriculum. I mean the same thing, same curriculum, same time. School never really sat right with me; it got to a point where I just wouldn't do work.

Lahronda: Say more about that. You said school never sat right with you.

Kyle: In elementary I was fine with everything. But then I began to question everything concerning school in middle school. It's all so punitive. If your child doesn't go to school, parents go to jail. Everything comes with punishment if there is no follow through. That seems wrong to me. Some parameters are good, but most of them are not.

Lahronda: What are the good things about school?

Kyle: Developing people skills, social skills, and your problem-solving skills. For example, I always viewed math as not learning the actual material but developing the skill to problem solving by getting around it. When you're in school, you will do one unit for one week and then the next week you're on to a completely different unit. You learn the material, take the test, and then forget it. This is the case for most subjects, except for like English Language Arts (ELA) and social studies. I've never felt that I *have to* learn a particular thing. It's more of "how can I get past this?" Most of school learning is a means to an end. The skill to get past difficult things is what I was always focused on.

For me, school is not necessarily useful.

Everything in elementary school that you learn, then ELA, and basic science and all that is useful. But from middle school, I can't really recall much of it. I have always "why did I learn that? if I was only going to touch on it for a week and then never bring it up again."

Lahronda: It sounds like school as you have experienced it has not been practical.

Kyle: School as a system - reporting to class by this time, lunch at that time, et cetera, has never sat right with me.

Lahronda: Then you get to theater...

Kyle: And then it's like an escape. Like a getaway. It's just a whole different world.

Lahronda: Would you say that once you took theater and you started the started YouTube that school then became...

Kyle: ... it became bearable. It became something I didn't mind doing, unlike before. I don't mean to sound like school was completely bad. I always had friends, always. I was good in that state, but just school in general was never really fun. I used to say to say to myself, "I really got to get up and go to this." And not that I hate school; I don't hate it. I think the system could be better. When my freshman year came along, we were in quarantine, and then I started thinking of school as an opportunity to develop other skills rather than just do schoolwork.

Lahronda: What other skills?

Kyle: Like solving social problems—you can build that skill in school. You know, you're always going to have your school bullies and things like that. I always thought that you needed to learn how to deal with people early on, as early as you can. Bullies are not going to go away.

Learning how to work with people, I always saw that as a good thing.

When I was in quarantine school was actually very difficult because all of the social leaning was cut out and all that was left was academics. No friends. Everything was cut off. It was kind of my most difficult year in school.

Lahronda: Now that you're a little older, do you feel that academics are more useful?

Kyle: Social studies and history, those are useful, because learn about the government and different societies. School is most useful in terms of like just growing up and being a human.

And developing the skills to get past certain obstacles is a good outcome. That comes out of doing.

Lahronda: That's interesting. I imagine a lot of young people feel that way. I remember when you were either in kindergarten or first grade, I went into your room, and you were in your closet. You had set up a little classroom. You said, "I'm teaching the kids." You remember that?

Kyle: I think I was in first grade. Being a teacher is a big role. And I thought, I always thought that being a teacher was cool until I got to middle school.

I learned that just because you know a certain subject front and back does not make you a teacher. If that makes sense.

Lahronda: Makes perfect sense, and you're right.

Kyle: I feel like to be a teacher is a lot more than just knowing how to do something. You have to know how to talk to kids. As a teacher, you counsel and teach. You're not just telling kids what to do and how to do it, and then make them go do it. I always saw the good teachers as the ones who knew how to treat people and knew how to talk to people. Great teachers *know* people.

Lahronda: Who was your first-grade teacher? Was it your first-grade teacher that inspired you to create that classroom?

Kyle: My first-grade teacher was that teacher that we had a problem with. The teacher that inspired me wasn't even a teacher that I had. It was a teacher that I saw on TV – on Reading Rainbow, a TV show I used to watch. It was this guy who taught; he was African-American. They would go on crazy field trips and things like that. But I think that is what made me look at teaching in a whole different way.

I had one teacher when I was in seventh grade ELA. His name was Dr. Smith. He was probably my most memorable teacher that I had in terms of being a good teacher. Then my eighth grade ELA teacher, Ms. Ms. Dawkins. I feel like those were teachers that did not just know the topic, but actually knew how to teach. Good teachers are hard to come by. Whenever there's a good teacher, it's always, a good thing.

Lahronda: What have you learned about yourself?

Kyle: I learned from certain people that I have "warm energy." People have told me that they enjoy watching my videos because I always smile. It's always a genuine video. I'm just in my room, talking to a camera, like I'm talking to them. That's what I've learned about myself. And all of this is a journey. I've only just started not too long ago, so I'm not that far into it. But I'm hoping to learn more.

Lahronda: Do you find it difficult to watch yourself?

Kyle: I actually like watching myself. Before I upload, I watch the entire video through. I'm very picky about what I post. Because if I watch it back and I realize that I have just created something just to get a video out only to stay consistent, then I'll delete it. I don't want those types of videos on my page.

Lahronda: You sound like an artist. Oftentimes, when an artist creates something, it's beautiful to the public. But to the creator, it does not measure up.

How does your view of the world impact what you create?

Kyle: Well, mainly I like to create positive videos. Looking at the news, like it's just a lot of crazy stuff that happens. When you click on my channel or you see a video of mine, I want you to see something positive.

So, I guess my view on the world pushes me to make positive videos.

Lahronda: Beautiful.

And you mentioned earlier, quarantine. What was your outlet when you were in quarantine?

Kyle: I felt kind of dull. I still went to basketball practice, and I guess that was an upside. Like that was cool. But other than that, on like a day-to-day basis, I just kind of felt disconnected. I would wake up at like seven in the morning. By 8:15, open my computer, and it's like 30 people in the class. No one really says anything. It's just the teacher talking to you for like 15 minutes and then you leave. They explain the topic, you leave, and then you do your work. Next, you pop in for your next class, like hour and a half later and do the same thing. It was a huge adjustment.

During this time, I also learned how to edit videos. Learning a new skill was very helpful during this time.

Lahronda: What are the demographics of your school? Let's talk about that for a minute.

Kyle: I say 70% is African-American. About 15-20% Hispanic. Then Asian and White.

Lahronda: You've never been in a predominantly white space, have you?

Kyle: In first grade (private school) was predominantly white. But other than that, I've mainly been in African-American spaces.

Lahronda: Do you think that has made a difference in how you see yourself?

Kyle: I have never done things for other people. I have never bought certain clothes because everybody else was wearing them. I think I still would have probably been pretty much the same Kyle.

Lahronda: What a minute, Kyle, remember when I was a youth pastor?

Kyle: Oh, yeah that was a predominantly white environment. So, yeah, that's, probably my only time. I think I was there from fourth grade to seventh grade.

Lahronda: And how was it? How did being at Bethel influence you?

Kyle: I guess it just kind of exposed me to different people and like knowing how to act in certain places. And it exposes you to different types of different cultures. Being there made the transition to where we are now smoother.

Lahronda: Are you uncomfortable in predominantly white spaces?

Kyle: No, not really. I've never really been uncomfortable in any space with people. By that, I mean, I've always just been able to adapt.

Lahronda: Do you code switch?

Kyle: Yes. When I'm at school I talk differently than when I'm at church.

Lahronda: Code switching is not a bad thing?

Kyle: It depends if you're a completely different. There is a way to code switch and still be true to who you are as a person.

Lahronda: How do you intend to hone your skills in acting going forward?

Kyle: I guess repetition. I don't get a lot of reps when it comes to acting. I mainly monologue in my room because I don't have anybody to act with. And then there is drama club. Because of a mistake I made at the beginning of the year id drama club, I'm not a main actor. But I am learning all the behind-the-scenes stuff.

Lahronda: What was the mistake?

Kyle: I didn't fully analyze my script before I auditioned. I looked over a few roles, and then I saw that there was this main role. The play is called "Wrestling Season." I'm not built like a wrestler, so it doesn't really make sense for a casting director to cast me in a wrestler's role.

Now going forward, I analyze the script.

Lahronda: Final question, what did your dad and I do right and what did we get wrong where your creative expression is concerned?

Kyle: Placing me in different environments. Growing up I wasn't an introverted type of kid and growing up we went to different places. We were at church and a lot of public events. So, I got to really observe and learn people. I feel like that was a good thing.

Lahronda: But did we get wrong?

Kyle: I mean, I don't see anything wrong with me. Not saying that I'm perfect or anything. I have flaws, of course. But I can't think of anything you all did wrong, per se.

Lahronda: All right, Son.

Kyle: Okay.

One of the greatest gifts as a parent is watching our children come into their own and listening to how they bring their ideas to life. We do not often get to witness how one charts one's own path; we are only privy to the outcome. What Kyle has modishly shared, with his quippy sayings and relaxed demeanor, is a peak into his world as it is unfolding. What a gift! I learned a few things that I did not know about my son, such as LeVar Burton being an inspiration. I also discern a young person who is self-possessed and grounded despite the past couple of years of being quarantined during his last year of middle school and first year of high school. Listening to Kyle, I am even more convinced that 1) we will continue to uncover the effects of the COVID-19 pandemic for some years to come, and 2) music and various other art forms are essential for a well-rounded education. Said differently, art is a potent gateway to mental and spiritual health and an apt coping strategy through which one can foster resilience and fortitude.

15

"Centering" Yourself Before You Log On: Black Girls, The Enneagram, and Self-Care in the World of Social Media

Christal Bell & Danielle Buhuro

Introduction

We immediately do this when we open our eyes in the morning. We do it again while eating breakfast. We do it again as we are driving to work. We do it again while at work. Then, again over lunch. By the end of the day, we are on it again. Lastly, before we close our eyes at night, we must take another scroll on it before we fall asleep. What is this "it" that keeps our mind consumed from sun rise to sundown? Two simple words: social media. Much of our life is consumed with social media. Never mind CNN, MSNBC, or Fox News—this is the first place we turn for news on current events. Instead of simply picking up the telephone to call family relatives, we log on to Facebook to check their status updates. Instead of printing our photos and placing them meticulously in hefty, durable store-bought plastic photo albums, this is the place we go to upload all our photos directly from our camera phones in virtual photo albums online. Facebook. Twitter. Instagram. Snapchat. Social media platforms continue to take over our world! But what happens when social media begins to negatively affect a young Black girl's identity and self-esteem? What happens when racialized sexism in the digital world goes viral? What happens when social media causes and produces negativity, toxic and unrealistic views of self-esteem? Pediatric Chaplain, Rev. Dr. Christal Bell, shares that it can birth levels of toxicity.

When one thinks of a toxin, the idea of a physical poison probably comes to mind. However, toxins can be attributed to social and emotional factors as well.[1] This trifecta that can occur can not only be damaging but lethal. Dr. Bell shares that the psychological effects of negative social

---

[1] Chin, "Environmental Toxins."

media impact can manifest false narratives and unrealistic notions of oneself and image. These false narratives birthed from toxic comments and untruths on social media cause disruption to one's mental health. We are inundated daily with images, memes, videos, and other social media content that if not careful can distort not only a person's worldview, but also sense of self. To shift this narrative, Dr. Christal proposes that a social media detox at times is necessary to reset. While there is not one prescribed one way to "detox" in this sense, the following suggestion is given.

1. Limit your time on electronic devices.
2. Surround yourself with people who uplift your worthiness.
3. Be mindful that filters and false advertising.
4. Remember a person's self-worth is not dependent on likes, shares, or retweets.

While we are specifically focusing on young Black girls for the nature of this work, the above "detox" reminders transcend race, gender, sexual orientation, and generation.

When Hate Becomes a Status Update: Racialized Sexism in the Digital World

Sarah Pink and John Postill were the first virtual ethnographers to study social media as its own unique mini virtual ethnography apart from other online entities.[2] They were also central in highlighting how social activism impacts the study of social media ethnography. In 2012, Postill and Pink moved to Barcelona for a period of one year and observed the use of social media in various local and national protests.

While Postill and Pink are acknowledged for publishing ethnographic work on social activism via social media, Danielle proposes viewing the #BlackLivesMatter movement as the first ethnographic work on social activism via social media in the United States. The #BlackLivesMatter movement was initiated on July 13, 2013 in response to the George Zimmerman verdict. George Zimmerman, neighborhood watch volunteer, fatally shot unarmed Black teenager, Trayvon Martin. His death sparked a national debate on racial profiling and civil rights. Zimmerman was found

---

2 Postill and Pink, "Social Media Ethnography."

not guilty of second-degree murder, and he was also acquitted of manslaughter, a lesser charge.

After the verdict was announced, three radical Black organizers — Alicia Garza, Patrisse Cullors, and Opal Tometi — created a Black-centered political will and movement building project called #BlackLivesMatter. The #BlackLivesMatter Movement takes into consideration the intersectionality of oppression. "Black liberation movements in this country have created room, space, and leadership mostly for Black heterosexual, cisgender men — leaving women, queer and transgender people, and others either out of the movement or in the background to move the work forward with little or no recognition. As a network, we have always recognized the need to center the leadership of women and queer and trans people. To maximize our movement muscle, and to be intentional about not replicating harmful practices that excluded so many in past movements for liberation, we made a commitment to placing those at the margins closer to the center."[3]

The challenge however is that while Twitter and Facebook were initially strengths utilized by three LGBTQIA women in 2013, these same virtual platforms have ironically become weapons just a few years later. According to a recent study by Yale, social media has a direct negative impact on the identity formation and self-esteem of young, Black girls. Their study, involved online focus groups of twenty-seven Black girls ages fourteen to eighteen from fifteen different US states.[4] According to co-author of the Yale study, Dr. Ijeoma Opara,

> We learned that Black teen girls navigate social media being aware of gendered racism, which they are victims of, while also being aware that they are seen as less desirable than their White teen counterparts... This is disheartening that young Black teen girls experience this type of discrimination at an early age and can undoubtedly impact their self-esteem, their views of Black girlhood, and ultimately impact the type of partners they choose to be with who may not honor or respect them.[5]

---

3 "Herstory - Black Lives Matter."
4 Belli, "Yale Study."
5 Belli, "Yale Study."

A present-day example of how racialized sexism in the social media world can lead to low self-esteem can be seen in the case of creative Tessica Brown.

"I Am Not Your 'The Gorilla Glue Girl'": The Digital Lynching of Tessica Brown

A present-day example of this can be seen in the case of Tessica Brown, whom social media oppressively labeled "Gorilla Glue Girl," after she mistakenly used Gorilla Glue to style her hair one day. The most devastating consequence of sharing this on the internet, however, is the trauma of ridicule that Black women experience.[6] Furthermore, Brown has repeatedly asked not to be nicknamed 'the Gorilla Glue Girl,' especially since the label has taken a toll on her children. Her eleven-year-old daughter was ridiculed by her classmates at school.

The question we have grappled with is, "What if Brown would have been successful?" What if Brown would have succeeded in utilizing the Gorilla Glue product to style her hair?" I venture to say we would have labeled her a genius! Anyone in the creative arts or entrepreneur field will tell you that if one experiments with a product and it is successful, people will automatically label you with positive attributes of being courageous, inventive, and prolific before your time. However, when one is unsuccessful in the same experiment, he/she/they are immediately labeled the opposite with denigrating terms like stupid, dumb, or crazy. Worse yet, in the world of social media these oppressive, self-damaging words go viral.

The video of Tessica Brown's hair mishap is nothing short of a digital lynching. As of February 19, 2021, the video had been viewed 37 million times. Because of the high number of views and shares of the video, we venture to say that the viral critique of Brown was not only pointed towards her, but to all Black girls, thus inciting a racialized sexism trauma to Black girls alike. When we use the language of digital lynching to describe the fate of Tessica Brown, many Black folks reading this project can relate or maybe even be triggered given the United States' sordid history of lynching Black people.

The act of lynching was popular in the United States during the Jim Crow era. The period of Jim Crow (1865-1954) seemed to pick up where

---

6 Fakuade, "The 'Gorilla Glue Girl.'"

African enslavement left off. While Africans and American Americans suffered great physical and psychological abuse as slaves, White Christian slave masters always committed to leaving their enslaved property *alive*. Beaten, tortured, and lambasted, at least and enslaved one could say he/she still had breath. The killing of a slave was considered a threat to slave owner's economic success as slaves were deemed property needed to mind cotton fields and care for domestic duties in the house. With African enslavement being outlawed via the Emancipation Proclamation and later, Juneteenth, former slaves had a new terror to grapple with –death. While those once enslaved enjoyed new liberation and freedoms, it was all very short lived, temporary compared to the new conundrum those once seized in bondage were forced to face. The Jim Crow era brought a new paradigm shift with it that meant Africans and American Americans were no longer property to "cherish", but now indispensable like animals –one could be killed with no threat to success. According to James Cone, Black bodies were no longer valued once Congress passed the Reconstruction Act in 1867, granting Black men citizenship rights. Cone states,

> Many felt that it was one thing to lose the war to the North but quite another to allow ignorant, uncivilized "n——s" to rule over whites or even participate with them in the political process. White supremacists felt insulted by the suggestion that whites and blacks might work together as equals. Whether in the churches, colleges, and universities, or in the political and social life of the nation, southern whites, who were not going to allow their ex-slaves to associate with them as equals, felt that if lynching were the only way to keep ex-slaves subservient, then it was necessary.[7]

The lynchings of Black bodies for White people's own political success in the 1800s and 1900s parallels the lynching of Tessica Brown and other Black girls and women on social media for digital media's participation in a culture of white supremacy.

White people attempted to maintain their social status in the same way that the culture of white supremacy maintains power through technology and in digital space. The lynching of Black girls' digital bodies supports the privileged status of white culture in the digital world of social

---

7 Cone, *Cross and the Lynching Tree*, 4.

media. The lynching of Black bodies represented a divine experience for many white people, further asserting their over Black bodies. According to James Cone, after witnessing "Birth of A Nation" (1915), a film which sought to justify lynchings of Black bodies and portrayed Ku Klux Klan lynch mobs as much-needed and celebrated superheroes, many white movie-goers in the South reported encountering "a 'religious experience' that 'rendered lynching an efficient and honorable act of justice' and served to help reunite the North and South as a white Christian nation, at the expense of African Americans." In the same sense, we argue that the digital lynching or killing of Black girls' digital bodies bolsters the culture of white supremacy and helps justify the dangerous belief of God's divine will in subjugating Black girls and women.

Black Women: The Most Abused Group on Twitter

Unfortunately, as Black girls mature into adulthood, the social media world becomes even more violent towards Black women online users. According to a study conducted by Amnesty International, Black women are the most abused group on Twitter. "The data shows Black women were 84 percent more likely than White women to be disproportionately targeted." For example, "one in ten tweets mentioning Black women was abusive or problematic, compared to one in 15 for White women. Women of color were 34 percent more likely to be targeted." Furthermore, this social media hate is not restricted towards only Black women. Amnesty International found that "while Black women received more abusive tweets compared to White women, Latinx women are more likely to get threats of physical [violence]; Asian women faced more ethnic, racial and religious slurs; and mixed-race women faced abuse across all categories including sexism, racism, physical and sexual threats, the study found." In light of this, how can Black girls and women practice self-care in light of racialized sexism in the world of social media? I suggest utilizing The Enneagram Personality Test as a resource for self-care.

"Centering" Your Head, Heart and Gut – Examining The Enneagram's Triad Centers

We love personality assessment tests. They become wonderful resources for persons to reflect on their strengths and growing edges. Personality tests don't lie. They tell the honest truth about one's personality, characteristics, behaviors and drives. The key to personality tests is remaining open to the results. The urge to respond with, "That's not me!" after results are given, becomes the entry point of an Oprah Winfrey "Ah Ha" moment. There are several personality tests that exist. One can engage a free Myers-Briggs Test (www.16personalities.com), or a 5 Minute Personality Test, or The Enneagram. While I have a fond appreciation for all of them, we lean more towards the Enneagram Test for the sake of this project. While many models exist, for the sake of this work, the image below has been created for this purpose.[8]

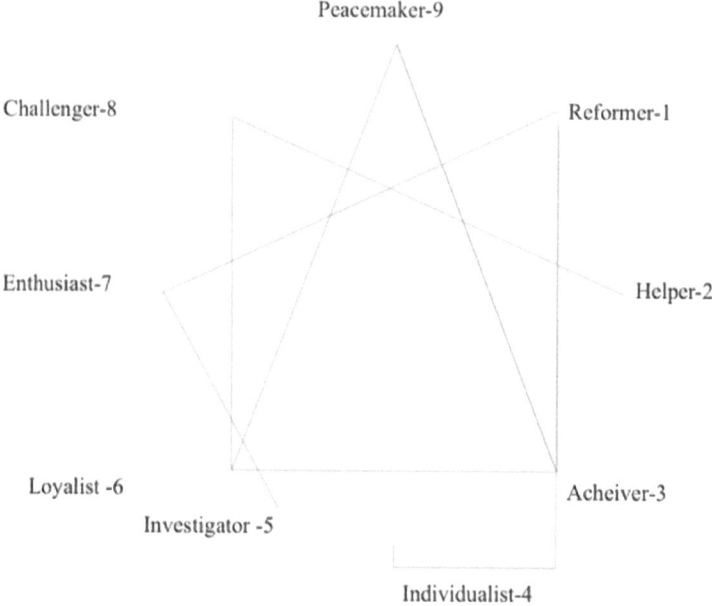

The Enneagram Personality test suggests that there are nine particular personality types that exist. See "The Enneagram with Riso-Hudson Type Names" to the right. All persons, regardless of race, ethnicity, gender, socio-economic status, sexual orientation, etc. identify as one of these nine types. According to the Enneagram Institute.

We have found that most develop *one* of the nine types dominating their personality, with inborn temperament and other pre-natal factors being the main determinants of our type. This is one area where most

---

8 This enneagram diagram we are using here was designed by Dr. Christal Bell.

of the major Enneagram authors agree—*we are born with a dominant type*. Subsequently, this inborn orientation largely determines the ways in which we learn to adapt to our early childhood environment. It also seems to lead to certain unconscious orientations toward our parental figures, but why this is so is still being questioned. In any case, by the time children are four or five years old, their consciousness has developed sufficiently to have a separate sense of self. Although their identity is still very fluid, at this age children begin to establish themselves and find ways of fitting into the world on their own.[9]

The enneagram is divided by three centers: The Heart Center, The Head Center, and The Gut Center. It is believed that these three centers are what drives a person's thoughts and actions. People generally lead with one of these three centers depending on which of the nine personality types they score as after taking the Enneagram test. Types 2, 3 and 4 lead with the Heart Center. It is believed that folks leading from the heart center wrestle with issues of shame. Types 5, 6 and 7 lead with the Head Center. People leading from this center wrestle with fear. Types 8, 9 and 1 lead with the Gut Center. People leading from this center struggle with appropriate use of their anger.

When we talk about self-care, we center the conversations around external activities that persons can engage in such as exercising, cooking, playing with a pet, gardening, or talking with a friend. While these activities are useful, we believe it is more advantageous to engage in what is inner reflective work. For me, how person's respond to crisis, oppression or other happenings in the world is directly influenced by one's inner workings, one's personality types, one's innate driving centers of fear, anger, and shame. Thus, self-care must take into consideration the power of internal reflective work.

In response to the current crisis of social media and how Black girls are attacked in digital space, we believe Black girls can practice self-care before logging on by first tuning in to her enneagram type center. They can then work on reflecting how their center can either serve or hinder them/her when she/they log on to social media. The narrative enneagram suggests that persons reflect on their personality type and corresponding driving center from three parts of their being:

---

9 "Introduction to the Ennegram."

One's Mind
One's Body
One's Spirit

We believe that if one can ground themselves by processing what their center is saying or potentially will say to their mind, body, and spirit before they log on to social media; they can better care for themselves when they experience an oppressive status post, photo, or video. Danielle would like to feature some real-life case studies to demonstrate how this process works in practical terms.

"Centering" Yourself Before You Log On...

Now we are going to have some fun practicing some self-care for our social media world! First, take a free Classical Enneagram test here: https://www.eclecticenergies.com/enneagram/test. Next, grab a journal and write down which of the nine types you scored as given the results of the test. According to the image above, which center category does your type fall into: the anger Center, the shame center, or the fear center? Below are some case studies on characters that embody one of the three Enneagram centers. After you are done reading, we invite you to take in the wisdom and insight highlighted from whichever is the center you scored as on your enneagram test and journal your responses to the reflective questions.

In the reflection questions accompanying each case study, choose the reflection path that resonates with you the most in questions three and four.

Terika Thomas
Terika Thomas is nineteen years old who goes by "she/her" pronouns. She prides herself in being a social justice activist. She loves to confront oppression in all its forms. She's a loner, stays to herself even though she knows a lot of people and many folks—those in oppressed conditions—feel drawn to her. Terika's father is president of a social justice organization. Her mom ran an after-school feeding program for children who are food insecure. Unfortunately, her mother died suddenly when Terika was young, and she has wrestled with unprocessed grief for several years. She's angry at God for taking her mom at a young age. Terika always speaks her mind and has a knack for being brutality honest. Her biggest challenge is Facebook. She always finds herself in a Facebook debate in which she's got to have the last word. She stays on Facebook at all times of the day and night, sometimes

developing tremors in her hands now because it's difficult to sit still. Terika took the Enneagram Test and scored as a Type 8. How does Terika practice self-care in the world of social media?

Reflective Questions:

Is there anything that's making you angry in these moments? Many times, anger is the friend of grief. What are you grieving in these moments? What are positive thoughts you can think right now? How can your anger serve you on social media in these moments? How can your anger hinder you on social media in these moments?

How does this anger feel in your body in these moments? How can you care for your body right now? What does your body need?

If your religious practice is that of a monotheistic tradition, like the young woman in the case study, do you resonate with her anger. If so, why? How do you remember [in your faith practice] that you are loved and that God is not angry with you? Write all the ways you're experiencing love from a *higher power* in these moments.

How does your belief system (humanism, naturalism, monotheism, etc..) show up in these moments? Are there ways that your belief system supports you, and, if so, how? Are there ways that your belief system causes conflict for you, and, if so, how? Write all the ways you're experiencing love in these moments?

Michelle Duncan
Michelle Duncan is twenty-three years old. She's smart, intelligent, and witty. She makes straight A's in school. Her mom is a well-known principal of a upper class suburban school. Her dad is a CEO of a computer consulting firm. Her mom and dad were strict disciplinarians and only demanded the best from her. Michelle always makes the honor roll. She's the oldest of four siblings. She loves shopping. She loves putting together a nice, conservative, clean outfit. Image means everything to Michelle. She has a heart of gold. She'd give you the shirt off her back if you were in need. Michelle is dependable and loyal. Her boss loves her at work. She always gets the job

done. Michelle loves to post cool Instagram pics showing posing at the latest event in town. She also loves posting her favorite meals for the world to see. Whenever she's got good news, she loves posting pics of her latest achievements. Unfortunately, a couple of her posts that she just knew were hot, only got a few likes so far. She's very disappointed. Michelle took the Enneagram Test and scored as a Type 3. How does Michelle practice self-care in the world of social media?

Reflective Questions:

Is there anything that's making you worried in these moments? Many times, worry is the friend of anxiety. What are you anxious about in these moments? What are affirming thoughts you can think right now and affirmation statements you can say to yourself right now? What are you ashamed about? How can your shame serve you on social media in these moments? How can your shame hinder you on social media in these moments?

How does this shame feel in your body in these moments? How can you care for your body right now? What does your body need?

Donna Sumter
Donna Sumter is 16 years old. She's a junior in high school and is worried about her future. Her family is financially struggling, and her mom works hard to make ends meet. Donna doesn't know if she wants to go off to college in another city. She was recently accepted to Clark Atlanta University in Georgia, but she doesn't want to leave her mom to raise her two baby brothers without any help. Donna's dad was the unfortunate victim of police violence and is currently incarcerated on bogus charges. Donna likes to log on to social media every now and again, but she becomes sad looking at pictures of her friends posting about the colleges they were recently accepted into to attend in a year. Donna has never lived away from home. She's wondering what she should be when she grows up. She's thought about being a pilot, but the fear of heights always robs her of her dreams. Donna took the Enneagram Test and scored as a Type 6. How does Donna practice self-care in the world of social media?

Reflective Questions:

Is there anything that's making you scared in these moments? Many times, scare is the friend of fear. What are you afraid of in these moments? What are reassuring thoughts you can think right now and confidence-building statements you can say to yourself right now? How can your fear serve you on social media in these moments? How can your fear hinder you on social media in these moments?

How does this fear feel in your body in these moments? How can you care for your body right now? What does your body need?

BIBLIOGRAPHY

Belli, Brita. "Yale Study Reveals Social Media Habits of Black Teen Girls and Guides Risk-Reduction Video Game." *Yale School of Medicine*, July 26, 2021. https://medicine.yale.edu/news-article/yale-study-social-media-habits-black-teen-girls-risk-reduction-video-game/.

Chin, Nancy P. "Environmental Toxins: Physical, Social, and Emotional," *Breastfeed Medicine* 5, no. 5 (2010) 223–4. https://www.ncbi.nlm.nih.gov/pmc/articles/PMC2966478/.

Cone, James H. *The Cross and the Lynching Tree*. Maryknoll, NY: Orbis Books, 2020.

Fakuade, Melinda. "The 'Gorilla Glue Girl' Never Wanted Her Nickname." *Vox*. February 19, 2021. https://www.vox.com/the-goods/22291160/tessica-brown-gorilla-glue-girl-tiktok-viral-surgery-manager.

"Introduction to the Enneagram." Enneagram Academy. Don Riso, Russ Hudson and the Enneagram Institute. Accessed May 23, 2022. https://enneagramacademy.com/enneagram/introduction-the-the-enneagram.

Postill, John, and Sarah Pink. "Social Media Ethnography: The Digital Researcher in a Messy Web." *Media International Australia* 145, 1 (2012) 123–134. https://doi.org/10.1177/1329878X1214500114.

PART FOUR:
LEADERSHIP, MORAL BRILLIANCE, & COMMUNITY ENGAGED LEARNING

16

Two Leaders Who Are Students of Relationships: A Conversation

By Lori Klein and Jonathan Klein

Lori
My brother Jonathan and I have led teams and organizations. We live on opposite coasts of the United States. For the past eight years, I served as Director of the Spiritual Care Service of Stanford Medicine at Stanford Hospital. Jonathan is the Senior Vice President of Multi-Family Services, as well as co-owner of Klein Property Management, a company in New Jersey. We rely on strikingly similar values and behaviors as successful leaders. Recently, we reflected on our journeys together. Here is our conversation on leadership.

Becoming Leaders
Lori
How and when did you know you wanted to be a leader? Describe your journey to your first leadership positions as an adult.

Jonathan
I wanted to lead and create opportunities for myself even as a kid. I brought the candy bars I sold to raise money for Boy Scouts to school, where some kids bought from me daily. The Scout masters had a hard time believing I sold so much candy without adult help. I continued to be an entrepreneur in high school, selling the newly popular IZOD shirts to schoolteachers as a reseller for a supplier, placing fliers in each teacher's mailbox. In the more traditional sense of leadership, I served as vice president of our Jewish congregation's youth group, then as a paid advisor, first to that congregation then to another.

Our congregation's youth group was a bright spot for me as a teenager. Being a non-athletic Jewish kid in a high school whose leaders tended to be athletes, I felt relatively invisible, on the margins. Still, one of my friendship groups included some of the smarter athletes, and one of them is my friend to this day. Maybe because I was a nice, helpful guy, I ended up on the Prom court. Looking back now, it's satisfying to realize your popularity or degree of happiness in high school does not predict your success later in life.

My big break came when I was eighteen years old. One night, Lori and I were talking at the neighborhood diner. The Manalapan town administrator saw us and asked if I wanted to produce the town calendar. He knew my photographs filled the most recent high school yearbook. A township staff person said I should talk with the owner of one of the largest local shopping centers about advertising in the calendar. Something clicked in my first conversation with him. I found the details of his real estate work fascinating. It became obvious that I wanted a mentor and he wanted to mentor someone. The next summer he asked me to work for him constructing two office buildings. By my early twenties, I knew enough to hire a team to build a million-dollar home. That first mentor is still part of my life today, both personally and professionally.

Building homes for wealthy clients could be stressful. Sometimes they asked us to tear out finished construction for the slightest real or perceived fault. Financially, it resembled a boom-and-bust cycle; boom when we first received payment, bust between projects. This economic instability did not work for my family, which now included my wife and baby daughter. I joined a New York residential real estate firm as an assistant property manager, even though I knew I did not want to remain a cubicle dweller for long.

I'm a massive people watcher and learn by observing. When I attended homeowner association board meetings, I figured out that the property manager could influence whether a meeting became adversarial or productive. I learned to set expectations proactively by giving progress reports on our company's work for the association. I figured out how to move a meeting along, how to shut some people down and encourage others to speak so no one person monopolized the conversation. Most of all, I watched my supervisors and when I had the opportunity, the senior leaders. I observed which behaviors were effective or ineffective.

I rose through the ranks. My experience building homes and navigating between clients' unceasing demands and contractors' insisting that workers be paid on time as they deserved made me fearless about resolving the smaller quarrels that come up in property management. I connected with my peers intending to become a leader among them. That doesn't mean I spoke to them with a tone of authority. Instead, I offered to answer their questions and helped them solve difficult situations with their assigned properties. This strategy worked. My boss promoted me once there was an opening because I already functioned in that supervisory role. In the circle of directors, I followed the same methodology, ultimately becoming the most valuable leader. I was in lower-level management for only a short time and was appointed the firms' president the year I turned 43, the same year my congregation elected me president. By then I had already served as president of my own homeowner's association. My proactive approach to projects, close observation, friendly helpfulness, and fearlessness about potential conflicts led to success in all three areas.

Lori

Even though Jon and I grew up together and I knew the general outline of his early successes and struggles, I appreciate learning how Jon's school days as an entrepreneur gave him confidence. During my childhood, I also led in formal and informal ways. At her first school conference, my mother learned my kindergarten teacher worried that I was the mother whenever I played house. My mom asked how this happened. When the teacher said I convinced other children I should be the mother, my mother said, "there's nothing wrong with that," and closed the discussion. At nine years old, I helped the older girls circulate a successful petition in 1969 that permitted girls to wear pants to school during winter months. I took my turn as ringleader in tormenting teachers we found boring.

In high school, I edited both the school newspaper and literary magazine. Despite these accomplishments, those four years dragged slowly. I had a few close friends, but as a "brainy girl," the 1970s version of a nerd, who often skewed the grading curve higher, I was not popular, even among the better students. Most of my homework bored me to the point I could only tolerate completing it while watching television or sitting in the kitchen with the family coming and going around me. I found some of the rules imposed on us frustrating and rebelled. For example, the administration required us to carry passes if we walked in the hallway during class times. For the April Fools' high school newspaper, I printed a blank hall pass with the principal's signature on it, which meant the legitimate passes had to be redesigned. The principal called me to his office and told me he was disappointed in me. When he asked what I thought he should do to me as a consequence, I said I didn't think he would do anything. He didn't punish me, probably because I recently had been named the first National Merit Scholar from our school. While I don't recommend defiance as a strategy, this incident probably predicted I sometimes would take calculated risks.

Both our parents led others. Our mother served as shop steward in the local teacher's union when they first employed the successful tactic of intermittent one-day strikes in the early 1970s. During the same era, our father helped found the Manalapan Civic Association, a service and networking club open to men and women, at a time when most such clubs did not admit women.

Our parents spoke truth to power. Our mother informed the school principal she would not comply with new school district rules that she found infantilizing regarding teachers' lesson plans. When fire damaged our large local farmer's market, our father chaired the Zoning Board which recommended new safety measures despite pressure from local businesspeople who thought them too expensive.

Our parents also mentored colleagues and subordinates. Younger teachers came to our mother for advice about curriculum, teaching methods, and maintaining discipline in the classroom without yelling. Our father encouraged his employees' development. In the most dramatic example of this, he hired one of our cleaning ladies to work in his office, first as a bookkeeper's assistant. He encouraged her education and training, until she acquired the skills to leave his accounting practice for a professional-level job in local government.

Some lessons from our parents I rejected. Our dinners also included nagging us children. Our father spent years of energy on grudges if he believed someone harmed him or his family. Our mother remained a schoolteacher despite feeling intellectually and professionally limited by it. Even so, I learned from listening to my parents' leadership stories.

Given our experiences, what might you do to prepare yourselves for adult leadership in high school? It's never too early to develop and preserve life-long friendships. Both Jonathan and I have friends in our lives now who we have known for decades. For me, this is true even though I moved 3,000 miles away from my hometown and place where

I attended university. Long-time friends give us stability through all the ups and downs of life. I also began to explore what brings me joy and found that writing, singing, dancing, reading, and deep friendships help me feel whole. Finally, high school can be a time to experiment with who you want to be in the world – how will you show up as a person and what dreams do you want to manifest?

Self-Supervision

Lori

I believe we need to supervise ourselves before we can effectively manage others at work. What personal traits did you cultivate?

Jonathan

Whether I was a property manager or president, I wanted to be a better leader than those I saw who led through negativity and aggression. I don't think it's professional to be irritable. If you speak sternly, and even that is rare, you don't have to raise your voice. In the twelve years I led one company, the staff would talk about the two to three times I shouted. Each of these times I had seen or heard a male employee attempt to intimidate a female employee to get some professional advantage. I want to treat my staff with the same respect I expect.

Someone told me early in my career, "you're afraid to give the bad news." I took that to heart. Now people say I tell the truth with no filter. Why filter it? I end up making bad decisions if I don't give the full story.

It's become more difficult over the years to leave work at work—and not bring it into my time to relax and sleep. Technological developments have made it easier for colleagues and clients to contact me about something small. When we carried beepers in the 1980s, our "off" time was our own unless there was a flood or fire. Now people text each other about everything, erasing all boundaries. Still, I try to get downtime during the weekend.

Lori

Unlike Jon, I can get irritable at work if I have too much to do, which is the norm working at a hospital, especially during a pandemic. Because I am not always at my best, the first person I supervise is myself by managing my emotions and assumptions, so that I am receptive and responsive rather than reactive.

Remaining curious helps me counteract my irritability, as well as my judgments and negative assumptions about other people. Curiosity helps me to put into perspective instant stories about why someone did not complete a task or seemed to use poor judgment. In my most recent role, my affection for my spiritual care team curbed my irritability, but I sometimes struggled when interacting with people from administrative departments assigned to support our work. I had to learn that becoming irritable or judgmental made solving a problem harder, because it sapped my intelligence or decreased a co-worker's desire to help. I also saw my assumptions about why people said or did something fall apart as soon as I became curious and asked for their story.

I'm willing to be vulnerable with my team. During the pandemic, each of us at times felt fear, frustration, worry, sadness, exhaustion, or resilient, confident, rested. Because I sometimes shared how I felt, other team members felt more freedom to express their emotions. This helped all of us stay in balance and enabled people to offer or receive support. Team members told me they appreciated my being authentic, even though they knew I also had to project confidence and optimism as part of my role.

Making Decisions and Changes
Lori
Some days as Director, I made dozens of decisions, large and small. How did you approach making improvements or decisions?

Jonathan
I think ahead in broad terms to understand what the outcome might be. As best I can, I quickly ascertain pros and cons then decide for the client or company. When problems come up, as they always do, I don't see barriers. Either alone or with others on my team, we figure out a work-around. When making decisions, our goal is: how do we strengthen individually and as a company?

Ideally, everyone in a company can suggest improvements. Once I entered senior leadership, I emphasized employee empowerment because that would give them the impetus to make worthwhile changes. Unfortunately, I quickly learned team members don't want to be empowered; they want to be told what to do. Not everyone wants to be a leader. So I appreciate the exceptional staff who can contribute at that bigger level, but don't expect it of everyone.

Lori
Like Jon, I involved my team in decision-making whenever possible. I aspire to be both humble and confident. Humble because I never can see a complicated situation from all angles, such as the best way for one chaplain to prioritize too many patients to see over a twelve-hour on-call shift. Whenever possible, I consult with at least one knowledgeable person on the team before making a decision.

At the same time, I retain confidence in my good judgment. An acquaintance once told me it is better for a leader to decide quickly, then apologize and pivot to a new direction if they were wrong, than it is for the leader to be indecisive. Not only has my experience confirmed this advice, I have also found that my team and supervisors trusted me more because I took responsibility and made changes to correct a wrong, original choice. My team also appreciated that I did not slow them down by overthinking. If they came to me with a reasonable plan, I was more likely to say, "let's try it and see how it goes."

Working at a large institution like Stanford Health Care, it is almost impossible to make significant changes quickly, especially if you need to rely on anyone outside your own team. My approach was to select a future vision, then picture a pebble that I could nudge toward that goal at every opportunity. This helped me celebrate small wins along the way instead of getting frustrated. The change I'm most happy about was integrating our spiritual care team more thoroughly into the care at bedside for patients, their family members, and staff. Dozens of small and large movements contributed to that shift over the course of several years, but we got there!

Listen and Be Approachable
Lori
Did your staff feel they could come to you with questions and concerns?

Jonathan

Listening is almost more important than talking. I say to people, "you're not going to get in trouble for asking a question. You'll get in trouble for not asking a question." I also tell my staff, "don't avoid telling me you're unhappy, then tell me you're leaving." I won't stand in their way, but I want to hear. If I know they're unhappy, maybe we can change something about their job duties that might be better for them and the company. This might be why my office in New York had the highest employee retention rate of any national residential real estate company.

You should always be approachable. I kept my office door open and had no problem stuffing envelopes with everyone. Most importantly, I take a positive approach to problems. One time the CEO asked me to attend a board meeting with a client homeowners' association. A property manager and their supervising director already were assigned to that meeting. I learned they had not prepared quotes for the board to review about the cost of repairs and renovations. At the meeting, before the board chair asked for quotes, I proactively set expectations, saying we were getting quotes and working with suppliers to obtain the necessary materials. This way, we looked like we were up to date on the work. After the meeting, I told the property manager and director that we would create action lists and talk weekly about their progress. I didn't criticize them; we just moved ahead. I think people know when they've messed up. There's no need to point that out to them.

Lori
Jon and I follow the same values in this area. My two most crucial pieces of advice about leadership: "listen with curiosity and be respectful," including valuing other people's experiences, culture, and innate wisdom. Sadly, because too few workers are treated consistently with respect, just doing this already puts me in the category of "good supervisor."

Early in my tenure as Director of Spiritual Care at Stanford Hospital, a colleague told me, "You might think that someone stopping by your office to talk interrupts your work, but that *is* the work." I encouraged staff, students, and volunteers to come by—with questions or requests—to discuss challenging situations. There were some days I had to remind myself that the "interruptions" *were* the work, but mostly I benefited as much from my open-door policy as anyone on the team. I learned if a team member was struggling with someone before the problem festered. I answered questions that prevented mistakes and facilitated our work. I celebrated small victories. Most of all, I built trusting relationships with any willing partner.

When I became Director of Spiritual Care, I entered the most powerful employment position I have ever held. With staff and students, we had more than twenty people on our team, almost two hundred if we included volunteers. At the same time, we were required to staff the hospital with a chaplain or chaplain student 24/7 and expected to handle the most emotionally fraught situations with skill and grace. I never felt more vulnerable to failure. People who choose to do spiritual care in a hospital tend to be passionate about the work, but there are still tasks few enjoy, like the night or holiday shifts. To help maintain a devoted team and because I wanted to care directly for patients, I signed up for some of those shifts. I answered the office phone when our administrative assistant was absent. I did enough of almost every type of job in our department so I could effectively train new hires. This approach is often described as "servant leadership." I think this *is* leadership.

Working with Leaders Above You
Lori
We also report to our supervisors! How did you conduct yourself so that your boss saw you as both a valued employee and a leader?

Jonathan
I make myself indispensable to the people above me by offering to fulfill some of their job responsibilities. This allows them to step back and work on a new project. I learned how my bosses thought, what they prioritized for the company's success. Then, if another business or organization approached me to partner on a project or resolve a problem, I could speak for my supervisor. My boss approved of my taking this initiative and I always let him know what had transpired. Over time, other organizations knew to approach me because I understood what was best for my company.

Lori
Like Jon, while I respect my supervisor's authority, I can also be bold. I came to meetings with my boss with a list of questions seeking their

advice and brief updates about my team. This startled some who had a set meeting format, but they appreciated I did not want to waste their time. In discussions, I'm not afraid to disagree. I assume they are paying me for my well-informed opinion as well as my willingness to implement plans whether I agree with them or not. I've never been punished for this behavior; in fact, I think it helps leaders above me give me more responsibility and autonomy.

Someone told me a long time ago, "never let your boss be surprised." For years this meant I let my supervisor know if I or someone on the team had done something that could have a negative impact. I did not want my boss to ask me to explain a complaint they'd heard from someone else. More recently, a supervisor told me he also wanted to know if I or someone on the team did something wonderful; he didn't want to look foolish if someone complimented me and he didn't know the context.

Supervising, Evaluating, Mentoring, Partnering
Lori
How do you help your staff grow and develop?

Jonathan
I'm a fan of the "ABC" mode of management: you spend 80% of your time with "A" employees, optimizing their strengths and compensating for their weaknesses. If an employee is not a good writer but excels at client relations, why try to make them a good writer? Get someone else to do the writing. You don't want "C" players on your team but there's nothing wrong with "B" employees. You need some utility players who can fill supporting roles in several areas,

I don't understand the purpose of a yearly evaluation; I review my employees' weaknesses weekly. To do that, I mentor them, talking about their opportunities to improve and how to work through problems. I ask where they feel they are weak, then partner them with someone who is stronger or give them training if I think they can improve.

Maria (one of Jonathan's long-term employees, who he called during our conversation)
I started working with Jon when I was twenty years old. Now I'm turning thirty-nine. I began as a receptionist and now work as a management executive. Jon has had a huge impact on my life, guiding and advising

me about my career and personal matters. He gave me the "rights and wrongs" of a situation but left the option up to me. Now I make my own decisions and inform him. When we first went to board meetings together, Jon spoke—and I listened. Now we both speak. He treats me more like a partner than an employee.

Jonathan
Even while I realize most people want to be led, from the beginning of my own career, I've kept my eye out for people who want to be leaders. For example, most property managers treat the assistant property manager assigned to them like an administrative assistant. I treat them like a future property manager. I delegate pieces of the job to them and then help them get better at it. I've received calls from former employees, sometimes many years later, asking for advice or a letter of recommendation. I offer myself as a mentor for life.

Lori
Like my brother, I think yearly evaluations create unnecessary worry for most employees and do not foster professional development or team functioning. If I noticed or heard about someone performing well, I usually recognized that employee publicly right away. If I learned someone performed poorly or not up to their usual standards, I talked about it privately with the employee as soon as possible, while everyone's memory is fresh.

Carl Rogers, a founder of humanistic psychotherapy, said, "individuals have within themselves vast resources for self-understanding . . . ."[1] Rogers encouraged his clients to use those inner resources. This approach inspires me. If a chaplain made an error in judgment, could not effectively handle a family dynamic, or missed a deadline, my first question was, "what would you do differently next time? Even if the employee did not know, my initial trusting questions made them more open to my guidance.

Concluding Thoughts
Lori

---

1 Rogers, *A Way of Being*, 115.

Appropriately expressed in a work environment, I believe love—the kind of love that articulates, "I desire your flourishing as a human being"—is indispensable for a successful team. Even though Jon and I work in different industries, I think both of us put *flourishing*—for our teams, ourselves, our organizations—at the center of our approach as leaders.

References

Rogers, Carl. *A Way of Being*. Houghton Mifflin. Boston, MA: 1980.

17

How Do We Teach Moral Brilliance?

Nathan Reddy and Nadinne Cruz

Here is my (Nathan) discussion with Nadinne Cruz, a Filipina American scholar-activist who pioneered the service-learning movement, a movement which strove—and continues to strive—to integrate community engagement into university education throughout the United States and the world. As someone who is a scholar of service-learning myself (particularly as it relates to working with youth and my own Asian American identity), I regard having this discussion as a pivotal point in that journey. I expand more on my own journey elsewhere in this anthology, and that story of service-learning may not even have happened if it weren't for the pioneering efforts of service-learning activists like Nadinne. In my mind, I include this discussion as an honoring of that legacy and a "passing of the torch." I am beyond honored to have received it here. One thing I would like to note before you dive into the discussion is that *the torches are plentiful*—limited only by the imagination—and up for grabs. It is my hope that this discussion conveys this truth to you, the reader, and that you consider taking one yourself. I believe that our responsibility as scholar-activists—in fact as people—is to the next generation of people, and I hope this discussion serves as a reminder of that ultimate purpose.

In this discussion, we reflect on what storytelling means and what it means to us. We specifically reflect on a story told by Cruz that grounds the questions we raise. That is the story of Le Chambon. Le Chambon is a rural French commune whose members made it a haven for Jewish people fleeing the Nazis during World War II (1939–1945). Nadinne describes the central quality the people of Le Chambon possess as "moral brilliance": their capacity to know what is the right to do, to decide to do it, and to attend to the hundreds of daily details of organizing and living with their choice to give refuge—over a sustained period of time—to people who would have otherwise perished with the many thousands in the Holocaust. Using the people of Le Chambon as our model, we explore how we can cultivate moral brilliance in our universities, our communities, and ourselves. In full disclosure, the title of this chapter is posed as a question because we do not offer a definitive answer. Rather, we are working towards an answer through discussion, and we invite you to ponder with us what it means to practice moral brilliance, as well as what a pedagogy for moral brilliance might entail.

Nathan Reddy (NR): "May my story unwind like a long thread." This is a quote by Leslie Marmon Silko from her book *Ceremony* that you reference in one of your speeches that you shared with me.

Nadinne Cruz (NC): Yes.

NR: Coincidentally stories are one of the main themes of this anthology. Can I ask the story behind why this quote resonates with you?

NC: Hmm. When I was growing up, a lot of family gatherings focused on uncles and aunts telling stories. For the longest time I always felt that what happens in families with things as common and ordinary, at least in my experience, as storytelling, is diminished by its ordinariness. And so, it struck me when I read Trinh T. Minh-ha and then thereafter began to look at various forms of stories as narratives that provide a structure for speaking out of truth. Not truth with a capital "t," but truth-telling. I think part of what she said was that storytelling "one of the oldest forms of moral truths." That's what she was saying, "moral truths." And of course, by adding an "s" and making it plural, implicit in that there are many truths, and it's contested. But storytelling requires an audience, those who hear the story, the one who tells the story, and in that sense it's a dynamic interaction whereby who is listening matters to who is telling the story. I think in my own experiences, telling my truths in this field of civic engagement and service-learning and so forth, I tended to speak depending on who my audience was. The words and phrases I would choose, would depend on who the audience is and what I think they wanted to hear. But anyway, I am curious too. In your experiences, what does storytelling mean to you? How have you experienced storytelling?

NR: In an article I wrote (and a revised version as a chapter in this anthology),[1] I share a story about my own, I guess racial consciousness, as it relates to being Asian American and the hate crime that happened at Cornell University. Something I knew about that story was that it was relatively controversial because I was open about Asian Americans, young Asian Americans and what it means to be an ally as it relates to Black Americans. Me coming to terms with what allyship means, that was through the story that I crafted for myself. Now, I critiqued allyship because I felt like there was, especially in terms of service-learning, an implicit association between, you're not tying your struggle, or your liberation with someone else's if you're saying you're an ally. That's just my perspective, and that's a bit controversial. I learned to undermine the binary between "servicer" and "recipient of service" in the service-learning program I did at Cornell. Before I engaged with an Asian American community outside of campus, I identified as an "ally" to communities I felt I was more privileged than in one way or another, and I thought that meant rendering services to them because of my comparatively higher privilege. Through service-learning, I learned that works to normalize that higher privilege in some ways instead of working to undermine it. I think undermining it means diminishing barriers, between "servicer" and "recipient of service," but also other barriers like class, race, gender, and sexuality. Of course, that's easier said than done, because as Trinh T Minh-ha wrote, "categories always leak." So that's a struggle in itself.

NC: Yeah, I thought in your story, it seemed like it was doing many things at the same time. There is a narrative, a storyline, a beginning, middle, and end. Like how you got involved, why, what happened when you got involved, what happened afterwards, so that's the storyline. At the same time, you were interrogating your involvement in it. How it ought to mean, or didn't mean, this and that, the way you had hoped. The questions that it raised, the challenges, and what it required of you to resolve some of those questions that arose while you were participating. In many ways, the storytelling served the purpose, or served the function of having a

---

1   This chapter, "Teh Bà Ta Hkèh Poo," is a revised version of an article that appears in Community Works Journal on the following website: https://magazine.communityworksinstitute.org/teh-ba-ta-hkeh-poo-sharing-stories/.

narrative that you interrogated but honored at the same time. A story in a way allows you to present it as an inconclusive narrative where it both states what happened and raises questions at the same time. And it allows you to be personal while not having made up everything either, it's not an illusion, and at the same time you are not presenting it as an objective act either. It's complex and I thought it was a wonderfully written story with all those elements in it. Which I think to me means you were able to do your truth-telling in it. At the same time, it was raising questions that, in a way, allows the reader to also think about "hmm, is that a question for me as well? How does that fit for me?" I did wonder about that because in a presentation on my thoughts on service-learning, that most people who work as an ally or in solidarity with a people's struggle would consider what they are doing as civic engagement or service or community outreach. They would call it, "I am working in solidarity with" or "I am working in allyship with others." I do understand allyship as a process in which I identify my location in a political struggle. I understand what others may be struggling with, and I draw a line between those two struggles and in that commonality is the space where allyship happens. Then I understand how my struggle for liberation, the category of peoples that I might be categorized with and their struggles, what that has in common with the struggles of another people. If I connect those two things, then I am in allyship with them, but it requires me to understand my location in some struggle, not only their struggle, but my struggle. When you connect the two, then there's allyship. As for solidarity, I think of that less as necessarily connecting the two struggles, but that I am simply declaring my support for and affirmation of the struggles of another group of people who are not a people I belong with. For example, I could say "I am in solidarity with Black liberation movements as expressed in Black Lives Matter." That's different from if I were to say, "I work in allyship with Black Lives Matter by working with Filipino liberation groups who connect what they're doing with BLM." I think that's a different thing and it's a lot more complicated and requires a lot more of us, but you started out with the question of storytelling, and I wondered why you were drawn to ask that question, or if you are hoping to go to another question.

NR: The reason I asked about storytelling is because the anthology is centered around truth-telling and I heard you mention that quote by Trinh T. Minh-ha in one of your talks, and so I just wanted to know your story behind why that resonated with you, and to some extent it resonated with me because that's how I understand things now, through stories.

NC: When I highlighted the people of Le Chambon in Southern France and the individual, Mang Ando, the peasant, who taught me a moral truth; I felt that it was more effective to tell their story in order to get that across than to say it as if I were just telling a historical fact. In a story like that of Le Chambon, I personalize it, because I can tell an audience why that resonated for me. For example, when I tell that story… when I first heard it, I felt I was haunted by that tale. I was haunted by a question after hearing the story of Le Chambon and their housing of several thousand Jews during World War II at the risk of their own lives. What haunted me was a question like this: what if we taught in colleges and universities in such a way that one of the outcomes of all that teaching is that everyone who graduated would be capable of doing what those people of Le Chambon did? What would we teach? How would we teach it? That was what haunted me. Ultimately, if what we want are individuals who can understand a challenge (i.e., take risks, have courage, act effectively, humanely, and ethically), and all those elements are in the story of the people of Le Chambon, they didn't have a university degree, so what is it that we're missing? If that's the outcome that we want. I'm wondering, maybe that isn't the outcome that we want—it's not necessarily for moral brilliance. It's for something else, and of course we know it's for something else.

NR: You mentioned the book *Where's the Learning in Service-learning?*[2] In a past conversation. It made the argument that service-learning was good because it benefits the student cognitively and in terms of their career and skill set. Am I far off?

NC: No. I think it was making the argument that we're not losing anything academic by engaging in service-learning. We shouldn't worry that there's a lack of rigor in the learning from service-learning by engaging

---

2   Eyler and Giles, Jr, *Where's the Learning*.

in it which was what they were trying to address. That was the worry. That once you take students out of the classroom and they're out running around in communities, they're engaged in projects it's going to "dumb down" the curriculum.

NR: It's interesting because you posed the question of what education did the community, Le Chambon, what education can lead people to be other-centered, as Martin Luther King Jr. said? I think it would be interesting if a service-learning practitioner was overt about their belief that an other-centered education is ideal. Especially since we are talking about solidarity and allyship, what greater allyship is shown by putting your life on the line for other people on the basis of humanity. Common humanity. It's interesting because they didn't get a university degree, but then the question is how should a university education instill those values?

NC: Don't forget, it was skillfully done because they achieved it. They achieved hiding people in a sustained way, over thousands of them, over three thousand of them over several years and got away with it. It wasn't like they just risked their lives; they did it skillfully. They hid people in beehives. They dressed them in ways that they could look like they were part of a farming community. It was very skillfully done, and there was a lot of collaboration and communication. There were arguments among them about how to do it, how to avoid the Nazis. It wasn't simple. It required cleverness, skill, commitment, and a whole lot of things we say we hope college graduates will be able to enact and embody. But we have to intentionally teach it. So, this truth-telling that is in the anthology; we can't expect that students know how to do it unless there are models for it. You have to have models. Sometimes those models are out in communities. In as much as we want to think that our excuse for being in communities is that we are out there to benefit them, in many ways a huge excuse for us to be educating students is for them to connect with people who embody moral truths. Or what I call "moral brilliance." It's not expertise like civil engineering or mechanical engineering. It's something else. I'm not saying that we throw out the things we learn in college to get our degrees; it's just that there's something missing. This truth-telling and liberatory process should be an important part for each learner's education, but we are not making space for it.

NR: Something that came across my mind was that there are a variety of pedagogies that I've seen in the world, at least from my understanding, that lead people to be extremely altruistic or self-sacrificing. Martin Luther King Jr.'s philosophies motivated people, both Black and white, to put their lives on the line. That's one source of liberatory education. But I also think about, well, the most extreme example, the Buddhist monks who self-immolated to protest. So that was another education. I don't know his name, but apparently, he self-immolated without moving a muscle.[3] That was from his own identity as a Buddhist. I'm unclear about this, what was the education of the community of Le Chambon?

NC: Well, I think that they were a very close-knit subsistence farming community that had for over hundreds of years, suffered persecution as Huguenots. They created a very tight-knit community. That doesn't necessarily guarantee that they would reach out to others, but they embodied their belief system. Or, they embodied their beliefs. But we don't embody our beliefs as a whole campus, for example with refugees. We don't say "well, we have X number of beds available during summer break." We don't use residence halls. Why don't we use them for refugees? We're not set up to think of campuses as a collective embodiment of civil society. It's as if it is something else. It's not quite that. In any case, I think there are many critiques of education as not being liberatory and therefore not a space where students are going to learn truth-telling. That's just not going to happen. Not as a core or focused part of the curriculum. It seems to me that part of the premise of this anthology is that students need to learn how to liberate themselves as learners, which is hard to do if you go into college thinking you're privileged. So, if you think you're privileged, you don't need liberation. I think that's another difficult thing. That's a very complex analysis, it requires complex analysis to understand that it is possible to be privileged and oppressed or privileged and not free.

NR: Being both privileged and oppressed is what a lot of young Asian Americans, that's how they characterize themselves.

---

3 An elderly Buddhist monk died by self-immolation in a well-known protest. See "Monk Suicide."

NC: Yeah, I read that in your story.

NR: Yeah, we have relative privilege but also the minority experience is still salient. I just think that that's an important insight that young Asian Americans have hit upon. The conventional wisdom is 'well, we'll leverage our privilege to help people." We are somehow higher in the hierarchy; I'm getting into that kind of recipient and beneficiary binary that I think traditionally comes with 'allyship.'

NC: That's tough to do, what you were saying, to be privileged and oppressed and to use one's privileges as something to leverage on behalf of those with less privilege. If Asian Americans are not themselves organizing in resistance struggles, mobilizing to deal with anti-Asian hate crimes for example, or workplace practices that would be considered oppressive, then it's hard to say, 'well I'm going to leverage my privilege on behalf of others who have less privilege' because we're not even organized. I'm just saying 'we' hypothetically. There are a lot of Asian Americans who feel privileged, but they are not themselves capable of being mobilized in political action because they have not a clue how to do political mobilization. They have not, in fact, participated in different forms of political organizing. There are all kinds of ways to do community organizing, there's labor union organizing, community-based, grassroots organizing, but if you have no idea how one's own group is organizing, I don't think you can leverage anything because you are just leveraging your own individual self, standing alone naked. That's not a collective power of anything. Where do students learn how to organize? For several years, I taught a community organizing course; and some of my former students are statewide, national, and international organizers. They learned how to organize. But that is not commonly taught in colleges and universities. We prefer student learners to be individuals going out there and benefiting communities, but we don't want them to be politicized by organizing on behalf of their own liberation. We would rather have them think about other people who need them, and how they can apply their own skills, and less about "how is my own group needing to fight against oppression and how do we do it." That's the basis of being an ally—when you can connect that struggle with another struggle. That's not benefitting somebody else. That's connecting my struggle with your struggle. It requires a whole lot more learning and education than is available through a typical service-learning course, project, or anything like that.

NR: I think you hit the nail on the head. And I know you don't identify as "Asian American," or at least I don't think so.

NC: Well, yes and no. It depends on what the context is. I mean, I'm Filipina American because I am an immigrant from the Philippines. But then people today are saying 'well, is that Filipino American or Filipinx,' just like Latinx, which has a different political connotation. And what does it mean for a Filipino American who identifies as an Asian American? In terms of the collectivity of Asians, people identified as Asians, and the interconnectedness of their histories of oppression as immigrants coming to this country based on race, ethnicity, etc., I am also Asian American. I think of that identity in a political context. Understanding the continuity of themes across many different groups who are categorized as Asian and their fight and struggle against injustices in this country. Anyway, I just wanted to say that I do identify as "Asian American."

NR: Ok, that's good to know. So do I. I also feel like I'm Indian American but also Asian American. I also identify as South Asian American because that's a different racialization. It's interesting, I'm racialized differently from East Asian Americans but we share a lot in terms of the model minority stereotype.

NC: I have to show my ignorance here, when people say "South Asian American" then do they include India and Pakistan?

NR: Yes.

NC: And when they say "Indian American" they don't include Pakistan?

NR: Yeah, then it would be "Pakistani American."

NC: Oh, ok.

NR: Can I just raise one more thing?

NC: Yeah.

NR: We've been talking in a broad sense about the education that college students, especially Asian Americans but all college students, what type of education leads them to build identities related to social change and contributing to the social good? Do you think that's not necessarily something that colleges and universities want to cultivate in their students? Because of the potential in creating citizens who are actually–I think there is an ideological reason that having students learn through community engagement might be against their long-term interests.

NC: Whose long-term interests, the students or the university?

NR: The university.

NC: Hmm, I haven't heard that one. As long as it's not being politicized against the best interests of the university, I think more often universities like to tout their community engagement as a way of communicating to neighboring communities that they are good for them because they are always fighting against the criticism that the university is a giant among smaller power neighbors and that they are not benefiting those neighbors. Especially when it comes to 'oh the university is buying up all these houses.' Now housing prices go up, because the university is buying up houses for faculty and staff and converting some of it for their own university uses, so that's one criticism. Or that their students are noisy and a pain in the neck, we have to live with that. So the university keeps using engagement as a counter, 'we're good, we benefit the community.'

NR: I guess I'm trying to say that I have a theory that universities encourage student activism but channel it through individual advancement.

NC: That's true.

NR: They encourage citizenship but there are aspects of citizenship that I think they don't necessarily want to cultivate in their alumni, and part of that I think is having a collective consciousness or an organizing consciousness, creating more community organizers.

NC: That's true. They would rather have individual heroic figures that they can write up about as individual heroic alumni. But not like some group, or some alumni have organized or mobilized getting out the people of color vote in places like Arizona or Pennsylvania, which some of my former students have done.

NR: One last question. What is your favorite book and without giving out too much detail, why do you recommend it?

NC: Wow. I don't think I can give you a favorite book. I have a corner of my bookshelf where I have stacked or shelved books that have meant something to me over time. Because I'm seventy-three, I have had many more decades than you on earth, it means that over so many years there can't be a book that, oh my gosh, just opens the world for me.

NR: Every year, Cornell has a book they send to all freshmen to read, and that's like the community read. What would you suggest for the next class if you could choose that book?

NC: I guess I would go back to Jamaica Kincaid's *A Small Place* because it's small, it's a story, but it's packed. It raises a lot of questions.

To the Readers: The Nadinne Cruz Community Engagement Professional Award recognizes an exemplary Community Engagement Professional who has demonstrated collaboration with communities focused on transformative change, a commitment to justice-oriented work, and an impact on the larger movement to build ethical and effective community engagement locally, regionally, nationally, and internationally. Consider applying or notifying someone else about the award if they may be interested!

A final note: Nadinne and Dwight E. Giles, Jr. authored an article in response to the seminal service-learning book *Where's the Learning in Service-Learning?* that I mentioned in our discussion. The article is called, "Where's the Community in Service-Learning Research?"[4] While the former addressed the benefit of service-learning for students, the latter

---

4 Cruz and Giles, "Where's the Community."

broaches the question of how communities benefit from service-learning, if at all. Reading this article actually introduced me to Nadinne's work, and I highly recommend it to everyone for whom reading this chapter has led to more questions, perhaps more questions than answers.

BIBLIOGRAPHY

Cruz, Nadinne I., and Dwight E. Giles, Jr. "Where's the Community in Service-Learning Research?" *Michigan Journal of Community Service Learning* 7, no. 1 (2000) 28–34.

Eyler, Janet, and Dwight E. Giles, Jr., *Where's the Learning in Service-Learning?* San Francisco, CA: Jossey-Bass, 1999.

"Monk Suicide by Fire in Anti-Diem Protest," *New York Times*, June 11, 1963.

18

Fighting Racism with Solidarity: #knowyourBIPOChistory

Akemi Kochiyama

Keep expanding your horizon, decolonize your mind and cross borders.

—Yuri Kochiyama

We're gonna fight racism with solidarity.

—Huey Newton

In early 2021, a year into the pandemic and increasing Anti-Asian violence, I listened to Ta Nehisi Coates talk about Black and Japanese American Reparations at the Shinso Ito Center for Japanese Religions and Culture at University of Southern California. He talked about the model minority idea being a "contradiction in terms" and yet such a powerful and pervasive stereotype that seems relevant to anti-Asian racism in the past and now. At the end of the talk, the moderator asked Coates to talk about pervasive racism and imagining a way for our nation to move forward. Coates responded with questions of his own which I found useful. He asked,

What is the story we are going to tell? What are the communities we want to build?[1]

All this made me think about my own story and the communities of which I have been a part and want to build. In this present moment, I am deeply concerned about the rampant and highly publicized racial violence against Asians. At the same time, I see the opportunity for all of us to understand the deep and harmful impact of racial and cultural stereotypes on the myriad forms of violence against all Black Indigenous

---

1 Coates, "Reparations Past and Present."

People of Color (BIPOC)[2] communities and marginalized people. We have an opportunity to reimagine the kinds of community we want to build.

I am a fourth generation Harlemite of Japanese American and Black descent and daughter of a Black Panther. I grew up in Harlem in the 1970s in a large multicultural family with a broad and diverse extended community of friends and activists within a culture/politics of Black Power and anti-imperialism. My Japanese American family has resided on 126th street for nearly one-hundred years. My understanding of the history of multiracial/multicultural solidarities is extensive, personal, and political.

In thinking about the history of racism and violence in America, rampant attacks on Asians right now, silences and myths regarding past Black and Asian solidarities, and my own family's experience; I want to propose that the present moment is an opportunity to reframe our understanding of US history and to strengthen and expand radical solidarities and coalitions among Black Indigenous People of Color communities.

By learning and understanding our shared and overlapping experiences of racism, discrimination, harmful stereotyping, scapegoating and economic exploitation, as well as disenfranchisement in the United States and globally; we can begin to build empathy and solidarity and organize community-based and political coalitions that help us to more effectively address institutionalized racism, violence, and other systems of oppression that impact and harm our communities.

I want to begin with some US history and a story of how my grandparents, a second-generation Japanese American couple, landed in Harlem in 1960 and ended up participating in numerous movements for civil and human rights for the second half of the twentieth century. Their story is a powerful example from which we have much to learn. I will briefly share some of their seminal experiences in this country and how the people they met and the communities they became a part of informed and impacted their lifelong commitment to multicultural community building and social justice for all oppressed people.

---

2 I use the term Black Indigenous People of Color (BIPOC) here, rather than people of color (POC) to highlight and differentiate the unique experiences (genocide and chattel slavery) of Indigenous and Black (African American) people in the United States which impacts and informs the relationship to white supremacy for all people of color.

The Nakahara Family in San Pedro

My grandma Yuri was born and raised in San Pedro, Southern California in the 1920s. A child of patriotic first-generation Japanese Americans, she and her two brothers enjoyed a relatively comfortable and normal American childhood and adolescence until her father, a successful commercial fisherman, was arrested by the FBI at the onset of World War II. Along with many other Japanese American community and business leaders residing on the West Coast at that time, my great grandfather was unjustly accused of being a "spy" and incarcerated as "a prisoner of war" immediately after the bombing of Pearl Harbor.

Having no evidence to charge him, my he was released a few weeks later, emaciated and unable to speak. He died the next day. A few weeks later, Yuri's family was uprooted from their comfortable home and incarcerated, along with 120,000 Japanese American citizens, under President Roosevelt's Executive Order 9066, which was issued on February 19, 1942. Their homes, farms, assets, and belongings were seized by the United States government and never returned.

Yuri and Bill during WWII

As luck would have it, Yuri met her husband, my Grandpa Bill, a native New Yorker from Harlem, during World War II at an all-Japanese USO in Hattiesburg, Mississippi, where he was training at Camp Shelby, a segregated army base for Black and Japanese soldiers getting ready to deploy to Europe.

Like many other young Japanese Americans at the time, my grandfather was stunned by the American government's distrust of Japanese American citizens following the bombing of Pearl Harbor. He enlisted in the army largely to prove his loyalty to America and to escape internment camp. Bill ended up serving in the all-Japanese 442nd Infantry Regiment who later became famous for their heroics (the most highly decorated regiment in U.S. military history), fighting on the front lines in France and Italy during WWII.

Although my grandparents would not fully comprehend the racist implications of Executive Order 9066 until years later, their experiences during the war (including encountering Jim Crow in Mississippi) significantly impacted and informed a new sense of themselves as *people of color* in America as they began to build family and community in post-World War II New York City.

On top of their experience of segregation and discrimination during the war, upon arriving in New York City and embarking on married life, my grandparents would soon discover that Bill's status as a decorated veteran of the war did not entitle him to the same rights of the GI Bill as white veterans. Rather than receiving a low-interest mortgage for a house in the suburbs, my grandparents' only affordable option coming out of the war was low-income housing.

After spending the first few years of their marriage in the predominantly Black Amsterdam Houses in midtown Manhattan, my grandparents jumped at the chance to move to the Manhattanville Houses when it opened on West 126th Street in 1960. Having grown up in the Sheltering Arms Orphanage on West 126th Street, my grandpa Bill was excited at the idea of returning to Harlem, to his very block, to raise his family.

At the time, my grandparents' resources were so limited that they couldn't afford to rent a moving vehicle. So, they transported their family's belongings from the Amsterdam Projects on West 65th St to the Manhattanville Houses on West 126th by subway during a snowstorm in December. My grandpa Bill said it took numerous subway trips back and forth to complete the move and that even the youngest of the 6 children carried something.

For much of my life, I thought the Kochiyama family ending up in low-income housing in a predominantly Black community was unusual. Through conversations with Japanese elders over the years, I've learned that this was not the case. As a result of their disenfranchisement during World War II and encounters with severe discrimination, prejudice, and the inability to find housing, employment, and economic mobility after the war; many Japanese American families moved into low-income Black neighborhoods in Los Angeles and San Francisco, Detroit, and Chicago following World War II. In many cases, Japanese Americans were the beneficiaries of mutual aid from their Black neighbors who supported them as they re-entered a viciously anti-Japanese America following World War II.

Upon moving into the Manhattanville Projects on 126th Street and Broadway in Harlem at the start of the 1960s, my grandparents were excited to participate in the many opportunities to learn about, befriend, and work with neighbors and members of their community in Harlem.

Yuri, Harlem 1963

It was in Harlem that my grandparents first got involved in civil rights. It all started when they became members of the Harlem Parents Committee and enrolled themselves and their six children in the Harlem Freedom Schools and began learning about the history of Black people in America. Their education and involvement in these organizations led Yuri, Bill, and their children to participate in and support a wide range of community organizations and to get involved in African American, Asian American, and Third World movements for civil and human rights; ethnic studies, as well as anti-war efforts in Vietnam.

When I think about the history of solidarities and relationships between Black and Asian people and communities, there are many stories and examples I could tell. There is one particular relationship—between my grandma Yuri and Malcolm X—that I would like to share here.

· ORGANIZATION OF AFRO-AMERICAN UNITY ·

Mary Kochiyama

is a member of the
Organization of Afro-American Unity

Malcolm X .... Chairman

June, 1964

Yuri's OAAU membership card

In 1963, Yuri met Malcolm X—a meeting that she would later refer to as her "political awakening." Malcolm's friendship and influence dramatically changed her life and political perspective. She joined his group, the Organization for Afro-American Unity OAAU), to work for racial and human rights.

Through her lessons at the OAAU's Liberation School and exchanges with Malcolm, Yuri's political perspective became more radicalized and more international in scope. It moved her to become passionately committed to Black nationalist struggles (in Africa and in the United States), to support Puerto Rican struggles for independence, to have solidarity with Cuba and countless other international liberation and sovereignty struggles.

Malcolm X with Japanese journalists at Kochiyama Family home, 1964

On June 6, 1964, Malcolm X visited my grandparents' home in the Manhattanville Projects on West 126th Street, upon their invitation to meet with three writers from the Hiroshima/Nagasaki Peace Study Mission. These writers were on a world tour speaking against the proliferation of nuclear arms building. They were also *Hibakusha* (atomic bomb survivors) and wanted to meet Malcolm X more than any other person in America and asked Yuri to request a meeting.

My grandparents' apartment was packed to capacity with an international assembly of activists, artists, journalists, friends, and neighbors when Malcolm arrived. Gracious and warm toward everyone who approached him, Yuri said you could hear a pin drop when Malcolm began to speak.

He talked about his time in prison, about the history of colonialism in Asia and Africa, about the People's Republic of China, and his admiration for Mao Tse-tung. He then spoke about Vietnam. As Yuri recalled, the most memorable and important things he said that night were about Vietnam and the implications of American involvement there. He said,

"If America sends troops to Vietnam, you progressives should protest.... The struggle of Vietnam is the struggle of the whole Third World: the struggle against colonialism, neo-colonialism, and imperialism."

A few months later Malcolm embarked on hajj to Mecca. He sent my grandparents eleven postcards from nine countries over the course of that journey. My favorite one is the one from Kuwait. It reads:

"Still trying to travel and broaden my scope since I've learned what a mess can be made by narrow-minded people."

Postcard from Malcolm X, Kuwait 1964

Though she had only known Malcolm for eighteen months by the time of his death, his friendship and mentorship had a profound influence on Yuri's political perspective. It had transformed her from a liberal civil rights activist to an international revolutionary anti-imperialist.

I tell this part of my family's personal and political story as one example of many narratives and histories that exist and that give us an opportunity to reimagine Black *and* Asian interactions beyond conflict—and beyond stereotypes and prejudices that serve to limit our ability to really know each other or to build solidarity and effective movements that protect and serve us. Sharing and documenting our stories and counternarratives is a critical element of building solidarity.

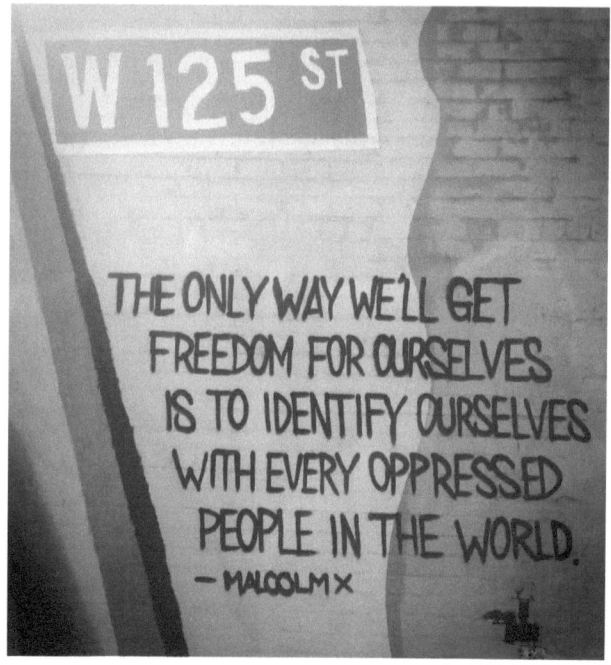

Quote from Yuri-Malcolm mural, Harlem, NY

To reimagine the past, present, and future of BIPOC solidarity in response to anti-Asian hate and racial violence in all forms and toward all oppressed peoples, I think the most important lesson I've learned from my family's story is how important it is to connect with *all kinds of people*.

Working, living, learning, and building community with people who are different from ourselves is critical to breaking down dangerous stereotypes and prejudices and help us all to develop a sense of mutual respect and an understanding of where our lives and experiences intersect and overlap.

Whether it's the "model minority" or the "dragon lady" or the racist Asian store owner or the Central American drug dealer, or the Black criminal; all racial and cultural stereotypes are dangerous and harmful and can have profound and violent impacts—when held by a police officer or a teacher or an immigration officer or a judge or a juror any, as we've learned, any person with a gun....

These stereotypes—perpetuated by the media and even in some of the most prestigious educational institutions—lead to individual acts of violence, but also to the perpetuation of systemic racism and violence in many forms. Whether it leads to shooting Asian women in massage parlors to murdering countless innocent Black and brown children in the street, or putting children in cages, or unjustly incarcerating millions of black and brown and poor people in prisons and detention centers across the land, or purposefully holding communities in multigenerational poverty; racial and cultural stereotypes in America all function to engender and perpetuate systemic racism, BIPOC conflict and violence.

There are many promising examples of organizations and BIPOC coalitions and communities doing important solidarity work now. There are national organizations like "*Tsuru* for Solidarity," advocating and mobilizing support for the rights of immigrants in detention at the borders. Another promising organization of solidarity-building is the "May 19th Project," a multicultural film collaborative which has produced fourteen educational videos about BIPOC solidarity in response to anti-Asian violence. Another great organization is the "National Nikkei Reparations Coalition (NNRC)," a coalition of Japanese American organizations and organizers mobilizing support of HR40 and Reparations for Black People.

As these organizations and the activists leading them are demonstrating, the present moment provides us with an important opportunity to reimagine our shared future and to be creative about our own practices in solidarity. I am hopeful that these efforts will continue to expand and grow as we continue to reimagine what authentic anti-racism and solidarity can look like and how we can better educate ourselves to be in solidarity in response to racism and violence against all BIPOC and oppressed peoples whenever and wherever it is happening.

"You have to act as if it were possible to radically transform the world. And you have to do it all the time." —Angela Davis

19

Speaking Up and Speaking Out: Living at Full Volume

Allegra Lawrence Hardy

The content of this chapter was originally offered as words of inspiration to the next generation of leaders as I was honored by Atlanta Girls' School with the Full Volume Award. As I prepared my remarks, I thought about the many lessons I have learned from raising three brave, dynamic girls who always use their voices and from spending countless hours with the amazing students of AGS.[1] I share these words with you because it is time to redefine society's expectations about what women should be and how we should use our voices.

Full volume is about expressing our best ideas and trusting that our audience has the capacity and grace to receive them. Full volume requires confidence. Many times, full volume is not easy or soothing to the ear. But very often, full volume is long overdue.

As a child, I lived my life at full volume. I come from a long legacy of Spelman women, and like them, I was raised to be a change agent. My mother, grandmother, and aunts accepted nothing less. I was overjoyed to enroll at Spelman and find an entire institution built to help me refine and amplify my voice.

But after graduating from Yale Law School, completing a clerkship at the United States Court of Appeals for the Eleventh Circuit, and starting my first job as an associate with a "Big Law" firm, something began to change. In many settings, I was concerned about taking up too much space in the room. I worried that I was out of place. At my Big Law firm, I was the only woman of color associate in any office of the firm. I walked into work each day feeling deeply uncomfortable. One mentor commented that I had allowed the world to take out a nail file and shape me into size.

---

[1] I owe a great deal of credit and a debt of gratitude to my friend, colleague, and creative collaborator, Tonya Adams Nelson. Tonya is a constant inspiration as she role models living life at full volume. This chapter would not be possible without her.

Employees at the law firm were strongly encouraged to join the social club located on the top floor of our building. It was said to be the place to network, the place where all the important conversations were had, and the place where deals were made. Of course, there was a hefty price tag associated with joining the club, and while I had started this well-paying job, I was more concerned about paying off a significant amount of student loan debt than joining the social club.

But I continued to feel pressure from my colleagues to join, and I felt the need to attempt to fit into my new environment. So, one evening, I sat down with my mother to go over my budget and see if it could be financially feasible for me to join the club. After running through various scenarios and calculations, we determined that because the membership fee included daily breakfast, I could reduce my grocery budget and shift those funds to pay for membership to the club.

So, every morning before work, I would go to the club for breakfast and sit in the same spot. Almost every day, the firm's managing partner also arrived for breakfast, and as I was the only woman of color associate at the firm, he greeted me by name each day. In response, I would shrivel up in my seat, tuck my shoulders in, and whisper, "Good morning." Each morning, I would give myself a pep talk and encourage myself to engage with him, but when the time came, I could not use my voice.

I was scared to take up space. But I knew better—my mother and grandmother had not raised a shrinking violet. Yet, each morning when the managing partner approached me, I felt so small. And I felt I was betraying the best parts of myself. How did I solve this dilemma? I went without breakfast.

Eventually, through many life experiences and opportunities, I began to rebuild the muscles attached to using my voice. I share this story, and these reflections, because I hope the next generation of girls and change agents avoids even a single day of swallowing their voices. The world needs the voices, the ideas, and the creative solutions of the next generation. We do not have a moment to lose.

At one point or another, we have all been told, "never give up," "be chill," "mind your own business," "don't sweat the small stuff," "don't take what is not yours," or most chillingly, "be seen, not heard." These ideas are commonly shared in society, but unfortunately, without our knowledge, they force us to lower our volume, to shrink, and to feel small.

I challenge you to flip the script and do the complete opposite of what society tells us to do—live your life at full volume. I have learned these lessons by following the examples of this incredible generation of young women leaders, and I share these lessons with you today:

Give Up.

You are reading this correctly—give up. Despite what society tells us, there is power in giving up.

Give up and let go of your need for recognition, for acceptance, or for someone else's approval. The energy you spend hoping and longing for recognition, acceptance, or someone else's approval is better spent somewhere else.

Also, give up on uncompromising journeys. When we are not attached to a specific outcome, we open ourselves up to a more authentic way of being because we are living in the moment—with no expectations of end results or traditional social rewards.

Give up your need to be smug, glib, or clever. Being smug and detached is cowardly, and this is the age for bold thinkers and even bolder doers. Instead, be genuine, thoughtful, and sincere. There is no need to mask how you feel or who you are. Express your true self—loudly.

Give up on unrealistic relationships that have never served you well. You do not have to maintain relationships just because you have known someone for a long time. You do not have to build a relationship with someone just because you have mutual connections. Maintain and build relationships that bring you joy and happiness.

Give up and keep on giving up until giving up becomes the most natural thing ever.

Have Zero Chill.

When something excites you, express it. When something offends you and your sense of self, express it. Act because you are delighted. March because you are offended. Support each other because it is key to our survival.

We must not normalize the mediocrity of being even keel and chill. It is okay to express feelings of happiness, excitement, sadness, or even disappointment.

Get in everyone's business

Do not mind your own business or stay in your lane. Support your friends and their passions. Invest yourself in causes important to the people around you. It will expand your worldview in a way that is personal and profound. When we care about something that someone else cares about, it increases our capacity for mobilization, empathy, and execution. It personalizes issues we might have previously overlooked. You build the muscle you need for a lifetime of community service and social impact.

Sweat the small stuff

Sweat the hundreds of tiny little moments that make up your daily experience. Focus on the things that no one else is because miracles live in minutia.

When we are young, we want to change the world, and when we get older, we realize that the only way to change the world is to change someone's day. See—and I mean really see—the people who make your day work: the baristas, the flight attendants, the parking lot attendants.

Figure out how to see them and acknowledge their contributions to you and the world.

Realize the divine is in the details. Sweat the small stuff on a project. Show your dedication to excellence. Be the person who pours over the proofing. Think about the invention of the modern-day computer or a complicated brain surgery. If one small piece is out of place, the whole system may fail.

And, when we sweat the small stuff, it is shocking how the big stuff falls into place.

"Borrow" from Your Friends

Borrow things that do not belong to you because your friends have valuables. They hold within their grasp the ability to make you better. The valuables you should "borrow" are the skills that come naturally to them—you know, the one thing you have admired most about them for as long as you have known them. Maybe someone is great at diffusing difficult situations or having tough conversations. Ask a friend to teach you and watch them transform your life.

Be Heard, Not Just Seen

Do not worry about being seen. Focus on being heard and lifting up your voice—and the voices of those who cannot reach the mic as easily as you. A person who cares about being heard is a person who focuses on ideas, on results, on lasting change. And ideas are more powerful than accolades.

***

When we flip the script and begin expressing ourselves at full volume, we can overcome society's expectations and achieve our wildest dreams.

20

Teh Bà Ta Hkèh Poo: **Sharing Stories**[1]

By Nathan Reddy, Eh Tha Yooi Lee, and Hserkaw Ler

"If you have come here to help me, you are wasting your time. But if you have come because your liberation is bound up with mine, then let us work together."

This quote is commonly attributed to Lilla Watson, a Murri (indigenous Australian) woman. She hates it when this quote is solely attributed to her since it was written collectively by an indigenous rights activist group of which she was a part in the seventies.

Teh Bà Ta Hkèh Poo (pronounced teh-bah-dah-thay-poo) means "sharing stories" in S'gaw Karen.

During my time as an undergraduate at Cornell University, I (Nathan) had the opportunity to participate in the Public Service Center Scholars Program, in which I was hired as a student educator for the 4H Urban Outreach Program, a youth-development program. I was more involved with the teenager program. The teenagers are Karen, and I don't mean they are entitled, middle-aged white women. The Karen (pronounced cuh-ren) people are an ethnolinguistic group from Burma who have been persecuted for centuries. The persecutor has changed roles, but the persecution has stayed the same. Most recently, it is the Burmese military that is committing genocide against them, from whom the teenagers (with whom I worked) and their families escaped. I have written in different publications about my transformative experience working with the Karen teenagers. In this chapter, I would like to foreground voices from their community itself.

What follows are interviews with Eh Tha Yooi Lee and Hserkaw Ler. Who are Eh Tha Yooi Lee (pronounced eh-thuh-yoo-lee) and Hserkaw Ler (pronounced chuh-cuh-law)? They are two of the Karen "teenagers" I

---

1 A revised version of this essay can be found in *Community Works Journal* on the following website: https://magazine.communityworksinstitute.org/teh-ba-ta-hkeh-poo-sharing-stories/.
The full version of the interviews is also available on that website.

worked with on the mural. Both initiated my own personal revolution of values that I will detail in an essay after their interviews. I put "teenagers" in quotes because—as I write this— they are no longer teenagers. Both are in college, with this being Eh Tha Yooi's last semester at the time of this writing. I will start with Eh Tha Yooi's interview.

Eh Tha Yooi Lee (ETY)
Nathan Reddy (NR): America has a lot of myths propping it up, one is in terms of immigrants—that we need to be grateful for America because this is the "land of the free," "home of the brave." We were rescued from the Third World, etc.

ETY: Yeah. That's what you were taught. I was taught that by my parents.

NR: As someone who has had the experiences that you have had, to what extent do you agree with these statements? How do you interpret these statements?

ETY: 'The grass is greener on the other side.' It's the same thing as that. When a group of people have been oppressed for so long and then have the opportunity to come somewhere that doesn't oppress them in the way that they were being oppressed, of course they are going to see that as a good thing. They are still being oppressed but not in the same way. For example, my people fled from the government—the Burmese soldiers. We have a history of genocide. Even though I didn't experience war firsthand, I grew up in a refugee camp and there were a lot of restrictions. If I were in Burma, I would also have a lot of restrictions.

When I was born, even though I was born in Thailand, I didn't have a citizenship of any country. My parents do not have citizenship of any country because if you're born Karen, you're not considered a citizen. If you are born in Thailand, you can't be a citizen because if your parents are not Thai citizens, you can't become a Thai citizen. When those families— like my family—come over to the US and it's considered the "land of the free," Statue of Liberty, of course they are going to think, "we are so free. We can do whatever we want." You can go outside in the States. In the camp, we couldn't even go out of our little area. Obviously, they're going to appreciate these "little" freedoms. Even though there is oppression behind it, and some people will say "go back to your country," they're still going to think "we're so free." Here, people can say whatever they want [freedom of speech]. In Thailand, there was a rule that you couldn't say anything against the royals. Here you can say whatever you want about any government officials. It's how you interpret it.

My parents' experiences are so different. Because I grew up here, I grew up with the mindset of someone who lived through all the flaws. I was aware of what I didn't have, but I wasn't so brainwashed to think that this was a good place. If you have had something bad for so long, a little light is going to be super important to you. A little hope is going to be like, "I love this." It's just like that. I think in some ways it is free, however you want to interpret "free." But there are limitations to where you can go. There are limitations to what you can say if you don't want to be hated. There's a lot of trolling on the internet. People are going to say, "go back to your country." They don't know my story; I can't go back to a country that didn't accept me in the first place. I go back to my parents because I see that as something so offensive. But my parents would just say "they don't know what they're talking about." They are just pushing it off. I think to most people, most Karen people, if you've been oppressed for so long, if you have been shut out from human rights for so long and then you actually have a little bit of human rights, you're going to be like, "oh my god this is great." It's like eating bad food and all of a sudden they give you decent food and you're like 'oh that's great.'

NR: I see exactly what you're saying.

ETY: Right? America is a terrible place for a lot of people, but you're not being governed in everything you do. They're not going to be like, "you're going out of Ithaca, let me see your ID." There are rules to protect us, and we feel protected. But racism, my parents are like 'what is racism?' My parents are starting to see it as they get older and they've lived here longer, but in the very beginning they didn't see it at all. Did I answer that?

NR: You answered it perfectly.

ETY: In the camps they had boards with pictures and stories on them. People would go in and read their stories and think 'this is legit now.' Just looking at it, it gives you hope. 'I can do this. I can do that.' That's the little light of hope that I was talking about. Once you do get there, you're like 'oh wow I can do this. I can go get food. Walk here and there. I can talk about this. I can...' As you grow older, you are going to see all the things that the US has to offer for white men and women. There are some things that my parents are starting to notice. But in the beginning, it was just light after darkness that they've been in. I don't blame them because that's what America commercializes itself as. They needed hope to survive to get where they are now. It's the US, they commercialized themselves as a happy place. Like Disney. New York City. LA. They commercialize themselves. You think that and then you come, and you're oppressed but you think it's good because your oppression before was worse.

NR: Something I'm taking away is that it's really complicated based on the experience of the person.

ETY: Yeah.

NR: There's a lot of different truths based on someone's experience. So, we're almost done. In your view, what does justice look like for the Karen people?

ETY: Justice is having a written history about the Karen people. I want a lot of things. That's something I want because I love the idea of telling a story. Preserving something that could have a story for the future. A lot of things were taken away from us, a lot of things were burned, written documents don't exist because we don't have a pen and a paper, we have guns and children, and pots and pans and clothes. Sometimes you don't even have clothes, you just have what you can carry and then you go into the woods. You don't have written things you only have stories. I'm encouraged by learning the Karen language as well so I can read my mom's diary in the future. She writes a lot, that lady writes too much.

NR: Oh, there's no such thing as too much writing.

ETY: She writes everything. My aunts, they write too. I just want to learn the language so I can read it again and know their experiences. My mom told me a lot of her experience fleeing from the soldiers. A lot of her friends died and a lot of them survived but the ones that are dead... it's just very hard for her to talk about... yeah... the people... it's so sad because they don't have gravestones so you can't really go back to them and have a final goodbye or anything. They're just there and then they get buried. I mean, it's sad to think about but that's most of the Karen people that have gone through the war. If you get injured... they just put you on the ground and you're dead. I see my mom's pictures with her friends, and I'll ask her, 'what happened to that one' and it's just so sad because he's not there and he didn't survive. She can't see him again because he died when they were in the rainforest so you can't really go back because you don't know. This is really hard... you can't have your final goodbyes. So, I don't know. It's just that, looking at my mom or dad's pictures, my dad doesn't have a lot of pictures, but my mom did and it's just very devastating. She has pictures from when she was fleeing. I was younger, and I pointed people out in the pictures. Some of them are here, but most of them are gone. They had known each other for a very long time. It's so... it's sad because when she talks about it, it's normal. It's the norm. 'It happens to everyone.' I didn't experience that... it's not normal to experience that. It's not. My mom shouldn't have to, but she did. I think justice for me, for my community is getting everyone who has passed, been killed, murdered, all of that, their names to be on a tombstone, or just a wall. Or anything that shows that they were alive and that they were killed. I don't know, something.

Hserkaw Ler (HL)
NR: You were born in Thailand and now live in America. Can you describe your journey to America?

HL: My journey to America was not an easy one. Growing up in the camp, life was very simple as there was not much you could do. In America, this was a complete contrast. There were many more opportunities that were available. Also, it felt freer to be able to leave the camp and live in a better place that has everything that I would only hear in stories. Life was better, but it definitely was not all perfect. Coming to a new country and trying to adjust to the new culture was difficult. It took a while before I could start to understand native English speakers.

NR: America is popularly known as the 'land of the free.' To what extent do you feel free in America and why?

HL: After residing almost fifteen years here in the United States, I experienced a lot of things. When it comes to freedom, I think it is a privilege for me since where I came from, freedom was limited. In the camp, we could not go outside unless we bribed the soldiers guarding the camp. Our entire life in the camp was restricted since there were not a lot of things you could do in the camp. We could go to school but the level of education we received was basic. Comparing my experience in Thailand versus America, it is safe to say that many people take freedom for granted. Personally, for me, freedom is a privilege. It is something I have learned to cherish and take full advantage of because back home, my family did not get to enjoy this type of freedom. With freedom came endless opportunities such as getting a quality education, having access to healthcare, being provided with a job, and much more. So, in that sense, I feel very free and wish that my people back home—some who are stuck in the camp and some still running away from the civil war—could enjoy the same freedom I am given. Of course, this is not to say that America is perfect. Although I enjoy being free, as an immigrant/refugee, we still had to face many challenges.

NR: What does justice look like for the Karen people and yourself?

HL: Honestly, I can't speak for every Karen person, but for me, I would say that justice will only be served if we are able to return to our homeland, free of persecution. Also, I would like to see the Burmese military held accountable for their actions. For about seventy years, this civil war has affected my people and other ethnic groups who are currently residing in Burma. Many lost their families and friends while having to flee because their villages were attacked and burned down. My family was fortunate enough to have escaped to Thailand where I was born and raised. I may not have experienced it, but my family has and overall, my ancestors. As much as I want to forgive them, I find it hard to do so because the killing is still happening today. Little has been done to stop the aggressions by the military. We can only rely on the brave soldiers of each ethnic group to stop the aggression. Even though many of us who reside in the United States want to help, there is not much we can do besides pray for our people back home. I may not know what my fellow Karens are thinking but I can confidently say that we all want this war to stop. We all want for the Burmese military to be stripped of their power and be held accountable for all the lives they have taken because of their selfishness to dominate other groups. Lastly, we all want to be able to one day return to a land that we can call home.

NR: You mentioned that you pray for the people back home in Burma and in the camps. Can you expand on your religious identity?

HL: I grew up in a religious community so most people in the camp identify or affiliate themselves with Christianity, which is probably an influence from when the Europeans colonized Burma (Myanmar). I do know that from a very young age, I was taught the Christian religion, and I attended church every Sunday. This is true even after moving to the United States. Although I identify as a Christian, my religious belief is not as strong as it used to be. Though when I find myself in need of help, I will pray to God to help guide me. As a Christian, I try my best to live according to his [*sic*] teachings and values.

NR: I know that you are studying to become a police officer. Why did you choose that path, and what qualities do you think a good police officer has?

HL: I honestly did not know what I wanted to do with my life. My dad brought me to America to get a quality education and to go to a university. Both he and my mom's goal for me was to graduate with a degree that would help me get a good paying job. Throughout my twelve years of education before entering a community college, I felt lost because I did not know what I wanted to do. Throughout my four years of high school, I was hoping that it would help me find an interest that could possibly help me discover a career path that I could pursue, but this was not the case.

By the time I entered college, I was still undecided on my future. I know I wanted to be there for my parents and for myself. I wanted to prove that I could amount to something since my parents did not have the opportunities like I have now. Two years went by, and I still could not decide what I wanted to do with my life. Nearing the end of my two years at a community college, I felt the pressure to decide on my future. One day, I sat down and thought about what I liked and did not like. I know for a fact that I could not see myself sitting behind a desk or doing work related to the STEM field. In the end, I ended up choosing criminology as my major. The reason is that I took some classes in this major and found that I quite liked it. The topic was interesting, and with the degree, I could use it to go into law enforcement. At first, the decision to become a police officer came from curiosity but as I took more courses in the major, I found myself more and more interested. I know that being a police officer is a risky job and it worried my mom at first, but as I became more determined, she started to show some support. I know that as a police officer, you must uphold the law and at the same time, be able to help people, resolve problems and establish a good relationship with the community. These are all important qualities.

NR: Last question. I wanted to ask about what growing up in the 4H program means to you? How did 4H shape you as a person? I would like you to also expand on what Ms. Cornell means to you (for the reader– Ms. Ramona Cornell is the director of the 4H Urban Outreach Program in Ithaca, who Hserkaw Ler has known since he started with 4H).

HL: In looking back at what the 4H program has done for me, I can say that it has done a lot. I believe that I have become the person I am today because of 4H. 4H has been part of my life since I was a child. It has helped me grow as an individual immensely. The support that I have received from Ms. Cornell and the tutors, like you, Nathan, has made me a better person. If it were not for 4H, I would have never dreamt of going to college. The education lessons that we were taught, the homework assistance, and the trips that we took were all fun experiences that taught me a lot. The person that I believe is at the heart of all of this was Ms. Cornell. Ms. Cornell is one of the most, or the most wonderful individual that I have had the opportunity to meet. She was like a mother to me and my friends. She taught us so much about life and the things we needed to know. She was always someone we could go to and she encourages us to go to college and has helped us with the process. For many years, she has continued to help our Karen community starting from the kids in grade school to us college students. She has impacted our life like no other person has. The things she has done, I can never thank her enough. Our community will always appreciate her kindness and willingness to help the kids of the Karen community grow so that we can all go to college and make a better life for ourselves.

Nathan: What They Taught Me

I would like to share the following story with you in the hope that it will deepen our shared humanity and our obligation to each other.

On a cool September night at Cornell University's college town in 2017, a Black student attempted to break up a fight. The appeal for peace proved to be an extreme affront to the white students who were fighting, and they closed ranks and called him a [racial slur] as he was departing. After he returned to confront them for using the slur, they started punching him as racial slurs rang in his ears from all directions. A South Asian student nearby who was witnessing the hate crime in progress was also called a [racial slur] for attempting to interrupt it, with one of the white assailants taking the time to explain that "You might be a [racial slur], but you're not Black."

As a South Asian myself, that explanation particularly weighs me down with thought. What was he saying? Was he saying, "you're not Black, so why do you even care about this Black student we're manhandling?" Or was he saying, "you're not Black, but we will attack you like you are if you come closer." Both the question and the warning upset me. They both also suggest the most tried and true strategy among the colonizers to maintain their rule over colonized people: divide and conquer. That strategy itself is strewn with contradiction. Even though white supremacy has divided us into distinct groups of color (Black, brown, red, yellow), we are oppressed, albeit in different and interconnected ways. An undifferentiated yet differentiated mass. This is how the white gaze sees us, and how it interrupts our seeing ourselves and each other. As I will relate, however, it is possible to interrupt the interruption.

I remember seeing and seething at the news. I was scrolling my social media account, and the article popped up in my feed. I felt a mixture of fear and anger, and my mind was racing. "This is big," I thought. And it was. Black Students United declared a state of emergency for Black students, and every student organization acknowledged it and affirmed their allyship with Black students.

Immediately, concrete actions to be taken were outlined by Black Students United, and many students — certainly not all students — made themselves available for them. Standing up to injustice is never a universal action, but the hate crime and the subsequent organizing of Black Students United enlisted a wide cross-section of students ready to give themselves to the cause. Both student activists and those who usually couldn't be bothered with issues of injustice were allied to support the BSU. What happened was just so heinous that something needed to be done. Black Students United decided that a hate crime clause must be added to the Campus Code of Conduct so that, going forward, racial slurs could not be protected by "freedom of speech." The University Assembly was expected to adopt the motion; nevertheless, both Black Students United and its allies — including me — showed up to their meeting to express our fervent support for it. We surrounded the space where the representatives sat and raised our fists in silence. I don't know how long we stood there with our fists raised, but for me, it felt like ten years.

A mixture of fear and rage went through me. One element of my fear was the prospect of being attacked in the way the Black student was attacked. Another was more complex. I was worried about whether I was being perceived as a "imposter" ally or authentic one. Was I perceived as someone who just showed up to showcase that they were an ally, or who showed up because they were actually an ally? Although the feelings I had are rarely articulated, as an Asian American, I can tell you that they are very common among us. Was I inauthentic? It was a question that I unwisely tried to answer simplistically and immediately, which was a mistake.

I was an opinion columnist for the *Cornell Daily Sun* at the time and explored my discomfort at the demonstration in my column for the week. I blamed "other" Asian Americans for the way I felt. I was embarrassed by the way I looked. I was embarrassed by other South Asians' attempts to be "white" (never mind that there were white students at the demonstration, let alone white people active in the Civil Rights Movement). Being South Asian made me be perceived as someone who didn't concern themselves with the struggles of Black people and instead busied ourselves with trying to be like white people, and that saddened me. As an "ally" in the struggles of the Black community, I dehumanized others as simply people who wanted to be white. It wasn't until later that I realized that to uplift others, you don't need to bring others down. Additionally, positioning oneself as the one doing the 'lifting' is a problem.

That same semester, I began work with the teenagers.

When I first met them, I had a very hard time connecting with them. They also seemed very wary of me, and I got the sense that it wasn't just me, but it was something they learned from past experiences with the college students who worked for 4H. We had something else in common in that we were both "Asian American." Many have criticized that label as something that is too broad to represent a very diverse community, and my relationship to the teenagers was a case in point. What did an upper-class Indian American Cornell student, who grew up in a lily-white suburb even have in common with a Karen high schooler? There was no common ground for us to stand on that first semester. Also, even though I was a "student activist" on campus saying things like, "Asian Americans are always trying to be white," I didn't have the courage to strike these sorts of conversations with the teenagers. I couldn't connect with them, but something I realized at this point was that the social justice conversations I was having on campus about Asian Americans' desire to assimilate into dominant white culture were disconnected from what the teenagers talked about: the immediate struggles of their daily lives, such as translating government documents for their families, or working extremely long shifts at Saigon Kitchen without bathroom breaks. These were struggles that I never personally experienced growing up.

Increasingly, it struck me that even being able to have abstract conversations about social justice and what it means to be an ally was a privilege among middle-to-upper class Asian Americans. Not only were these conversations filled with jargon, but they also positioned us as observers of society instead of as members of society. In a way, that was the case. The campus insulated us from community members of all races, and when I had a chance to leave campus, I left my "radical" spirit there too.

Something about being an activist where it actually mattered felt wrong to me, and that is worth deep reflection.

The second semester was better. We were tasked with doing digital stories of our lives (PowerPoint slideshows narrated by our voices as images of us growing up and our current lives flashed on the screen). Notice that I say "our" here. This was primarily a project for the teenagers, but my mentor suggested I do one too to get closer to the teenagers. It was a very good call. Upon seeing the teenagers' stories, I realized that characterizing all Asian Americans as wannabe whites was extremely reductive. "Wannabe whiteness," in their lived experience, was fleeing genocide in Burma, facing myriad other struggles that confront refugees like learning English, and genuinely believing that the United States presented novel opportunities for making their parents proud and making meaning of life. Is it fair to say this is an expression of internalized whiteness? It's not. In fact, many immigrants of color come to this country seeking new opportunities, mostly for their children. That's why my parents came here. It is simply a different perspective, a worldview shaped by experience that is not lesser or better than anyone else's. Finally, it was time to share my story. Even though the teenagers and I have lived and continued to live different lives, there were many similarities between our stories. There were things we could relate to such as having a tight-knit Indian or Karen community to rely on and share experiences with growing up and wanting to make our parents proud in this new country.

The teens and I also had the chance to hear a Black American's perspective on our stories. A prominent local Black activist watched the PowerPoints and was heartened by them, but also saddened. She said it is beautiful that we immigrants have come to this country seeking opportunity, but it's important to remember that Black people have been oppressed in the United States for centuries. Her courage to speak her truth taught me that what makes human relationships beautiful is that we can share our perspectives, built by our own experiences and identities, and learn from each other. She was a wise woman, so she didn't say we were all "trying to be white," she just wanted to share her story. She hugged me after she saw my story. Her comments within the context of the digital stories project made me reflect on what it means to be an ally to Black people.

Interestingly, I never conceived of myself as an ally to the Karen community. I became part of their community when we humanized each other by sharing our stories and connecting the dots between them, as well as noting where our stories diverged. We not only found common ground, but we also recognized that our coming together was yet another chapter of each other's story. Sharing our stories added to them. My story was woven with theirs and through this collective story, I learned that I shouldn't be an ally who sees someone else's struggle from a distance but consciously engages oneself in writing new stories with others that emphasize our shared humanity, thus humanizing each other and ourselves.

Initially, I dehumanized Asian Americans in my column, which extended to the Karen community who I barely knew at the time I wrote it. In time, however, through mutual humanization, I became more aware and conscious of the teenagers' struggles than I could have ever possibly imagined and was able to throw myself into working with them, not on or for them, to create a mural representing their community at the side of the local deli shop. They only accepted me into the mural project after I shared my story. After that, they saw me as someone who was worthy of being part of their story. Additionally, I learned so much from the teenagers even though I was formally designated as their "educator." Aside from teaching me that collective storytelling and writing are powerful forms of struggle, their bold identification as "Karen" in America encouraged me to explore my own Telugu roots ("Telugu" is an ethnolinguistic designation, much like "Karen"). I listen to Carnatic music on my walks and am learning the language under the instruction of my parents. We all have something to learn from each other, even people we thought had already taught us everything they know or people we wrote off from the get-go.

Recall the opening quote of this essay. Because of the story I share here and what I learned from it, I can infer the backstory that led that the group to write such a statement in the first place. Let us work together. Let us struggle together. What is it, exactly, we are struggling for? World peace. Hear me out.

What does world peace have to do with the critique of allyship I have just laid out? Allyship is an engine of the status quo, a status quo that yields to the inherently violent and interconnected triple evils that the leader of the Civil Rights Movement, Dr. Martin Luther King Jr., described: racism, economic exploitation, and militarism. The hate crime offered a masterclass in overt racism, but that picture of racism was complicated when I was confronted with the economic struggles of the Karen teenagers in Ithaca and understood that militarism, spurred centuries ago by British colonizers in Burma, led them to Ithaca in the first place.

That the Black student who endured a hate crime and the Karen teenagers are people of color is not a coincidence but a testament to the violent historical and present domination of white supremacy upon the global majority. If I only remained an "ally" to both, I would essentially be saying to each of them, "I see your plight and I will help you in your struggle." The fatal errors are in not recognizing that their struggles are different manifestations of one, and that struggle is mine, as it is yours, whether you are a person of color or not. "Your plight is mine. Let's struggle together." Making this shift from allyship with a particular struggle to being one with our struggle is key in defeating the triple evils. This is the case also in *how* we struggle. Being one with our struggle means understanding that violence, the root of the Black student's and the Karen teenagers' experience with oppression, must be vanquished altogether. Yes, there are Karen militant groups that sprang up because of their community being ethnically cleansed. Paulo Freire acknowledged that the violence of the oppressed, if it is expressed, was provoked by the violence of the oppressor upon the oppressed.

To interrupt this vicious cycle, however, we must be intentional and moral in our resistance. Working towards peace by peaceful means nurtures human solidarity, whereas violence emboldens difference and dehumanizes both the violator and the violated. It is not lost on me that part of the power of storytelling, sharing, and writing is that they are peaceful and collective treatments for the overwrought structural violence people of color live through. Violence cannot heal wounds wrought by it. If violence is what we face, confronting it with violence will result in just that: more violence. Likewise, peace begets peace. Nonviolent resistance is necessarily the answer, the struggle that will usher in the global "beloved community" that Martin Luther King Jr. envisioned.

One day at 4H the Cornell Asian and Asian American resource center staff came to teach the teenagers about Asian American history. The room was filled with "Asian Americans," but it promptly split between Cornell people and non-Cornell people. My friend who worked at the resource center beckoned me to go sit with her. "He's actually with us," one of the teenagers told her. Honestly, hearing that was one of the most liberating moments of my life. I was an ally no more.

Acknowledgments (Nathan): Thank you Nadinne Cruz, Hua Hsu, and my father, Shanker Reddy, who all offered very thoughtful feedback on earlier drafts of my essay. Thank you Eh Tha Yooi Lee and Hserkaw Ler graciously entrusted me with their stories. Finally, thank you to my mentor at Cornell, Amy Somchanhmavong, who connected me with the 4H program and engaged me in ongoing critical reflection sessions about my work with the teenagers, leading to the reflections I share with you here.

21

Out Here: Writing with the Unhoused

Christie Towers

People experiencing homelessness carry enormous burdens, literally and emotionally. They carry their belongings everywhere they go, lacking access to storage and to transportation, making it physically difficult to travel to places where they might receive care. They carry, too, the *previous* traumas that contributed to their homelessness, along with the *current* traumas of homelessness. Many are veterans suffering the traumas of war and moral injury.[1] Many have been victims of violence, sexual violence, and abuse from family members, caregivers, other people on the street, strangers, and law enforcement. Many are struggling with substance use disorders, mental illness, paranoia, and PTSD (Post Traumatic Stress Disorder), all of which can impact a person's ability to respond to the world around them as they are exposed to triggers, traumatic memories in mind and body, leading to unpredictable and changing moods that may not seem appropriate to the present situation. Many have been incarcerated and institutionalized. Many are experiencing concomitant traumas due to racism, xenophobia, sexism, homophobia, and transphobia. Some have developmental and/or physical disabilities.

All of them have broken relationships, with family, friends, caregivers, and systems of care. All of them have experienced the trauma of losing their housing. All of them experience the indignity and dehumanization of exposure and separation from normative society. All of them experience some level of social stigmatization. And, finally, all of them suffer

---

1 Moral injury refers to severe psychological, social, behavioral, and spiritual distress which occurs as a result of witnessing or participating in actions that go against one's values or moral beliefs. You might imagine it this way: when one is "following orders" that result in the death, murder, or injury of civilians, children, and even other soldiers, moral injury may emerge. Even if one does not participate directly in these actions, but is otherwise exposed to these things taking place, moral injury can occur. Moral injury is most commonly used to refer to the aftermath of war and combat, but, moral injury can occur in other settings where one's moral autonomy is compromised.

from a lack of resources to help manage and mitigate these past and present struggles. This lack of access to the most basic elements of safety and survival leaves people experiencing homelessness in a constant cycle of physical, emotional, and psychic trauma.

In working with a community of people who are—and have experienced being—homeless, I have learned that one of the most important foundations of care any person can receive is a sense of acceptance, belonging, and community. From this foundation, people can begin to find new ways forward, finding support, dignity, and a sense of worthiness. This foundation of support can help them as they navigate the challenges of lives lived in shelters, on the street, and in systems that are complicated, under-resourced and over stretched.

The community with whom I work, MANNA (acronym for Many Angels Needed Now and Always), is a community created by and for the unhoused and unstably housed community of Boston. It is not a social service in the usual sense in that MANNA does not provide case management for housing, substance use, or medical care. Instead, MANNA strives to bring people in from the margins and into community with one another and the wider world we share. Our primary focus is on relationship building and empowerment. One of the most profound ways we do this is through our writing program, The Black Seed Writers Group (BSWG). At the heart of this program is the desire to lift up and dignify those most in need of resources in our society: the unsheltered, the cast out, the strange, the brilliant, the addicted, the isolated. They are the beautiful beings who are so often pushed so far to the side that they can't be seen or heard by the world that rushes so quickly past them.

I admit, before my time at MANNA, I did not fully understand how I was complicit with that world that rushes past. I grew up in a semi-rural area on the Eastern Shore of Maryland and had only seen homelessness on school field trips to DC or other cities. When I moved to Boston to attend Emerson College in 2005, I found myself surrounded by it. A central shelter, St. Francis House, shares the same busy intersection as my class buildings. The Boston Common, a large public park at the center of downtown Boston, which I walked across every day to get to class and work, is the "living room" of many of Boston's unhoused. Having never lived in a city or interacted with people experiencing homelessness, I had very little understanding of what I was seeing every day.

In a way, my naiveté was a gift. The people gathered outside of the shelter were often rowdy and unpredictable, but I learned quickly how to navigate our shared sidewalk. When asked for a cigarette, or a light, I would give it freely and sometimes offered whatever snack I had lifted from the dining hall to those who asked for money or food. Sometimes, this would result in disappointment – people without dental care can't usually eat hard, crunchy things like apples or granola bars. Also, people sometimes just wanted money and my dining hall banana seemed like an insult. I didn't care what the money was for when I gave it, but I will always remember one man, crossing the intersection with me, yelling over the traffic, *I want money for DRUGS*. Fair enough, I thought, knowing perfectly well what many of us in college were planning to do with our extra cash later that night. Still, all I had was a banana. But I told him I appreciated his honesty.

And even with these little moments of interaction, of honesty I hadn't earned, of momentary camaraderie over an extra dollar or smoke, I must admit there were times I was afraid, judgmental, or thoughtless. These people were a part of my landscape and my world, but sometimes I avoided them, looked past them, or didn't acknowledge their greetings or inquiries. It was overwhelming, not knowing how to help or how to interact. I would see people in the throes of emotional meltdowns and psychosis. I would see people digging in trash cans, yelling at strangers, and nodding out on trains. I was sometimes nervous and afraid, and it was easy to miss the humanity I was witnessing—broken and wounded as it may have been—and instead lean into my own anxieties and fears. I didn't understand that some people aren't just "like that." I didn't understand that the world and the systems we have created have laid a heavy burden on the vulnerable and the outcast. People aren't yelling on the streets for no reason or because they want to – they are yelling because the world refuses to see them, to know them, and to care for them. They are yelling because sometimes this world is too much to bear.

At BSWG, writers lay down their burdens—their bags, their belongings, and their weary bodies—alongside the concerns and joys of their hearts through writing. Writing, though it may seem simply like a hobby, leisure activity, or a pursuit reserved for the educated and elite, is much more than that. And, it is not always easy; writing is a vulnerable activity. It poses a challenge to those who struggle with literacy and mobility issues. It opens up the interior world, a world that many on the street guard fiercely against the violence of the street and the systems of oppression and cruelty that keep them there. Writing, for anyone, can be scary – it opens us up to the world around us. It allows us to be known and seen for who we are as the deepest parts of ourselves become revealed on the page. It is a sacred act, this kind of sharing, and at BSWG, we work to honor each word shared as the sacred opening and act of trust that it is.

* * *

Do you feel like writing today? G rolls his eyes at me in dramatic slow motion, brows raised as he crosses his arms over his chest. *What do you think?* We go on like this for a few minutes, exchanging looks of mutual friendly exasperation, before he relents and offers me a seat beside him.

As we write together, G's arms unfold and his face relaxes, revealing a wide grin. He is telling me about his day in downtown Boston watching dancers and listening to beat boxers, his visit with his mother, his favorite Tyler Perry movies, and his thoughts on the Christian Gospel for next week. More recently, G has become a reviewer of local events, sharing his opinions on the latest production of Shakespeare on the Common and other public arts events. After some conversation, we get down to the business of writing. As he speaks, he pauses, waiting for my cramping hand to catch up. When we finish, he leans back in his chair, nodding along while I read back what he has composed.

I hear the elevator bell chime and look to see who has arrived. S bursts into the room like a hurricane, his sweet face twisted in distress. He slams his suitcase into a corner before slamming himself into a chair. He glares at me, a sort of heads up about his mood, and waves me over like a waiter. I let him know I've seen him, *Be there in a minute, S.* As we talk, he is almost in tears, his rage and terror too great for his body to contain. *I'm gonna die out here. I'm tired of sleeping in doorways like a dog.* I make a mistake, I offer, *I understand.* He points out how much I *do not* understand. And he's right. I've never had to sleep in a doorway, never had to wait outside for a shelter to open where, if I do get in, my sleep and safety are not guaranteed. I try again. *Would it help to write about it?* He scowls, but later he shoves a handful of pages into my hand. *Just don't mess it up this time*, he cautions me almost sheepishly, a smile forming around his eyes as he points to a few typos he's found in last week's writing packet.

M composes his poems in his mind, going over and over the words until they're just right. Sitting on the steps, his preferred writing spot, in the way of just about everybody, we huddle together and wait for the words to find their way. He tries out a few lines and asks me to read them back. We do this for as long as it takes. When we finish, he puts an arm around my shoulder and laughs, a few tears appearing before he recites his trademark closing statement: *Lord Jesus and Mother Mary, thanks for the love. To all my readers, God bless you and your family and me and mines.*

Taking a break from working the coffee cart, C settles into her writing for the week. She has a paragraph or so about the last few days, her worries about doctors' appointments, her children, her friends, a reflection about the places where she has found a sense of stillness in the busy week. *I'm stuck!* She shouts to me as I walk past, grabbing my arm. I read what she's got so far and ask a few questions, trying to draw out the details of what she's described, reassuring her that she's got this – she just needs a little bit more. And then, of course, her signature closing prayer, something she rarely gets stuck on. C is nervous about her reading and writing, but she is never nervous when it comes to God. She begins, *Hey God ...* as though she's writing to a close friend. I give her a quick pat on the back, my arm released as she dives deep, confident in where she's going, and leave her to it.

R comes through the door, open notebook flapping in hand, making a beeline for James Parker, his trusted long-time editor and the founder of BSWG, or me, if James is busy. *This is gonna blow your mind.* His latest poem, scrawled in his beautiful, drawling hand extends over four pages of his slightly soggy notebook does, indeed, blow my mind. I read it aloud, so he knows he's got my attention. "This city washed me out to where I'm at / on the highways and byways of Life."[2] Standing on the shore of this moment together, I get the feeling that we are in the break between waves, that there's a brief lull in the traffic of our lives, a beautiful—if cliché—cinematic moment where two people see one another from across the street just before the bus whooshes in and our next journey carries us away.

---

2 R., "Mystical."

* * *

This fleeting feeling of standing in the stillness of a storm is a sensation I have over and over during the course of the Black Seed Writers Group weekly hour and fifteen-minute meeting. When I first agreed to join the "faculty" as James now refers to us, his ever-growing cohort of staff and volunteers, I imagined something quite different. It was the fall of 2018, and I was entering my second year of a Master of Fine Arts (MFA) program in poetry at the University of Massachusetts Boston (UMass Boston). I had been in writing workshops for most of my life, throughout high school, college, and now again, almost ten years later, in this graduate program. Writing workshops like the ones I had attended don't prepare you for what is encountered at BSWG. Here, there is no "workshopping," no talk of who the "speaker" of this poem might be, no teacherly person walking around seminar tables, hands folded behind their back, while students quietly struggle over meter. Here, something else is happening entirely.

Tuesday mornings at BSWG have this electric, elemental feeling, the weather of the room shifting briskly from one corner, one writer, to another. The writers themselves are constantly in motion: blowing in and out of the room, town, getting into or losing their housing, spending time in prisons, jails, and hospitals, moving between varying degrees of health and illness, addiction and—often tenuous, but hard-won—recovery. Some writers have been with us for over a decade, others for a few months or weeks, and sometimes just one day. James calls this the "mystical body" of writers group – a reminder of how each of us who pass through this space become connected through the power of writing in community. Each writer we meet has left their mark, their word, some piece of their story, inscribed on the heart of this holy meeting place, this ever evolving and always moving body.

To accommodate this fluidity, we hold a simple but solid structure. Every Tuesday before the writers arrive, pens, paper, prompt sheets and a printout of the previous week's writings are placed on tables. Coffee and breakfast carts are assembled, and servers are assigned. Staff and volunteers gather to talk about the coming day, such as who might need a scribe, who might need a little extra care that day, and if there are any events, readings, or projects which might need preparation. Then, at

9:30am, the doors open, the writers enter, and for one hour and fifteen minutes, we write. At the end of our time, everything is collected, and the handwritten writings are photographed and sent out to a volunteer typing pool to prepare the coming week's printout. Every week, in blizzards, in blazing record-breaking heat, in sleet, rain and even in the depths of COVID-19, when every open door had closed to the unhoused and unsheltered, we met and we wrote. A miracle every time.

Writing, as one BSWG writer recently reminded me, *is* the miracle, a gift we give to others, freely, and forever. Writing is a portal to eternity, a place where our voices reverberate beyond the bounds of time and space. Writing is prophecy, witness, and protest. It's one way we stake our claims on reality, to say: *Here I am, friends, foes, neighbors, Mayor, and God. Here I am.*

* * *

You may be wondering why I am not referring to these writers by name. All of the writers' names are redacted, and I am deliberately not referring to things which might identify them specifically. An important part of this work is to protect community members' privacy. There are many reasons why someone in our community might not want to be identified and remain anonymous: some are in hiding from abusive partners and family members, others do not want to be identified by law enforcement for all kinds of reasons, and some feel the shame from the traumas of homelessness.

To give you a sense of who these writers might be, I will disclose generally our demographics: Our community is mostly cis men, mainly because many women and trans folks gravitate toward nearby programs designed specifically to support women and LGBTQ+ folks. many do, however, find their way into community with MANNA. Our community consists entirely of adults. There is a nearby program for teens where we refer teenagers who do occasionally come to us. We do not see many children or families, and when we do, we try to connect them to services supportive of their specific needs. Our community is, however, extremely diverse, and welcomes everyone. Our community is made up of folks of many "races,"[3] ethnic and religious backgrounds, beliefs, genders, sexualities, ages, abilities, and experiences. Class backgrounds vary, too. While people experiencing homelessness are, at the time of their homelessness and following it, experiencing some of the most vulnerable and precarious times in their lives, people from any class background may experience homelessness. In our community there are people who hold bachelors and master's degrees, people who went to expensive preparatory schools in their youth, and people who have led successful professional lives before their homelessness. However, most of our community members come from more marginalized or precarious class backgrounds and carry with them generations of poverty, scarcity, and financial and social instability.

MANNA is a place of empowerment and radical welcome. It strives to be a place of genuine belonging and flourishing. It's not easy— the work of love, reconciliation, and restoration is challenging work. It asks us to get uncomfortable, to get close, to put away our assumptions about others, and *meet* the person in front of us with openness and curiosity. All of the programs at MANNA work toward this mission, and BSWG is a place where this mission is, in some ways, most easily measured. As people begin to write, their identities as writers begin to inform other areas of their lives and days in meaningful ways.

James Parker calls me "the undermanager," and he has informed me that the reason is because I am attuned to things in the room that are not immediately in sight. This feels like a generous assessment of me. Whatever innate inclination or curiosity I may have, I have a unique vantage point which cultivates this attunement. I'm with the community throughout the week, in the other programs, occupying various roles. There's the pastoral, the pedagogical, the writerly, the preacherly, the food-"serverly," and all the human stuff in-between. I occupy many roles throughout the week, and the writers—in their many roles and shifting identities—are there with me.

The benefit of occupying these various roles—given the fluid and shifting nature of the room and community—is the opportunity to see the various ways that writing impacts the lives of community members inside *and* outside of that hour and fifteen minutes.

---

3 "Race" is a social construct, as the readers already know. We are one human race.

At a community meeting, a man who has refused to write, saying that he prefers simply to "be in the space and appreciate others," tells the group (with help from his Spanish language interpreter) that he has something published in the latest weekly printout. He says, *I don't write, I'm not a writer, but this girl* (a wonderful new volunteer, Eliza) *spent so much time talking with me last week. She asked if she could write down parts of our conversation. I said okay. So she did! And it's in the paper!* Although he continues to claim that he is "not a writer," it is clear from his body language that the experience of writing with Eliza is opening him up. He brightens as he speaks, and it is clear that writing is important to him. *It is like a prayer with your whole being*, he says, his body leaning further into the circle, a gesture so small, but indicative of something huge: a growing sense of belonging and presence in the community. As the weeks go by, he writes more openly, in Spanish and English, with volunteers and staff. He moves from isolation into connection, allowing his full self to be seen and appreciated as he sees and appreciates others.

Last summer, I received a call from a community member who had relocated to Montana. He says, *Hey, can you send me some of my books? These people need to know who I am – a writer.* He wanted his new case worker to have a copy, and had been writing while he had been away. He recited his work to me over the phone. From thousands of miles away he wrote a new book, and he sent me photos from his journey to illustrate the events described. When I sent him the new book he excitedly sent me photos of himself with it on the trail, at the day program, and in his new home. When he returned to Boston we met him at the bus station. Exhausted from days of travel in the heat and the anxieties and difficulties presented during the height of COVID, the first thing he did, after lighting a long-awaited cigarette, was to take out his notebook and insist on giving us a reading of his new work right there on the bustling downtown street.

During her time with us at the writers' group, one elderly woman had become unhoused and is now living in a shelter for the first time. She is working on a new book of poems, *Shelter Poems*, and has already designed the cover. Writing about her experience has helped her survive her circumstances. She says, *being here gives me purpose and meaning. It's kept me alive.*

Another community member, a housed man of middle age, came to us already a fairly accomplished writer. He has published in local journals and participates in readings in the area. His time with BSWG seems to have given him a sense of structure and stability. Recently, his subsidized apartment complex caught fire. This displacement caused him to suffer an incredible amount of anxiety and loss. Still, amid all of this, he came to writers' group to deliver his poems. This chaotic room has somehow become the calm center of his own personal storm.

One woman often blows through the doors like a storm. She's been kicked out of every shelter and program, every train station, every and anywhere. Everything has gone wrong; everyone is out to get her. When there is no place else to go, she returns to us and demands a notebook. Writing, she says, is the only thing that can calm her down. She puts her fury and terror to work on the page and leaves with a lightness in her step, shoulders lowered, face softened and laughing, ready to face whatever is next.

A man who cannot read or write on his own came in one day asking for help with a letter – he needed help explaining to his case manager why he needed a new one and one kind of person that new case manager should be. Together, we wrote a letter that helped him get the help he needed. And soon, after this immediate problem had been resolved, he became interested in other kinds of writing. Now, every single day he comes in, he asks if we could write a poem together. We sit together while he carefully composes his poems in his mind, asking me to read lines back as he revises, perfecting what he would like to say. He brings in new friends, strangers he has met out in the world who—he thinks–would like BSWG. At our public reading event this year, he stood proudly beside me as I read his poems to a large, rapt crowd, his eyes closed in complete and utter delight. He is working on his first book, a book that he tells me—while tears form in his eyes—*is for the world.*

Following the publishing of G's first single-author chapbook (we call them "broadsheets") under BSWG's own imprint, No Fixed Address Press, he began to open up in new ways. Previously, when asked to preach at Monday's MANNA Eucharist, he would need a lot of encouragement and accompaniment to even consider the slot. Now, he checks in with me almost weekly, *Christie … in two weeks I think I'll be ready to preach again!* Instead of needing someone to sit with him to read the sermon he's written, he reads it on his own, beaming proudly at his community gathered before him in the semi-dark sacred space. He checks in at meetings excitedly anticipating an upcoming BSWG reading at a local bookstore. He offers to read part of a community prayer to a crowd of over a thousand people at the annual Winter Walk, a walk to build awareness about homelessness and community. He checks in at community meetings about how many people are asking for copies of his book, remarking especially at how proud his mother is that his son is a writer. While writing is still difficult for him (he still requires the help of a scribe), it has become one of the most important and transformative parts of his life. He writes:

> *Writing is difficult.*
> *It is.*
> *'Cause sometimes I don't know what to say.*
> *Words just come out.*
> *I just say what's on my mind.*
> *Words just come out.*
> *I just say what's on my heart and whatnot.*
>
> *Sometimes it's difficult to come up with a topic.*
> *Sometimes it's difficult to figure out what to say.*
> *Sometimes it's difficult to have the courage to write.*
>
> *... James tells me to write down how I feel about things*
> *and that makes me feel like what I have to say matters.*
>
> *...Everyone here believes with me.*
> *...That's why people buy my books at the bookstore - because they believe in me.*
>
> *It is difficult to write, but when I start it feels really good.*
>
> *(Writing takes a lot out of you.*
> *Writing this piece took a <u>lot</u> out of me, just so you know).*[4]

---

4 G. "Writing is Difficult"

He's right. Writing can take a lot out of you. But like many things that can "take a lot out of you," writing can also be a place of incredible growth and expansion. My time with these writers has shown me just how powerful writing is. In my MFA program we talked a lot about the power of writing, but BSWG has made this power real. Writing can and does change the lives of the writer and the reader. It restores a sense of self, of voice, and of value. It helps us reshape our thoughts and our realities. It helps us feel worthy, known, and loved. It helps us navigate broken systems and challenge authority. It helps us notice the beauty of a moment, the pain of the past, and our own hopes for the future. It helps us, as G writes, believe *with* one another.

It's an incredible privilege to share in the stories and lives of people who are marginalized. It is powerful to give them a platform from which they can declare their own humanity, demanding dignity and respect as they tell their own stories in their own voices. And it is incredible, too, to see the impact this has on their entire being. It is beautiful to see the writers, even for a moment, drop their defenses and allow the world to meet them just as they are—brilliant and blazing in the fullness of their humanity. It is a holy experience to be with them in those moments of pure knowing and acknowledgement. It has changed them, and it has changed me. I am more open, more curious, more trusting, and more loving than I was before I knew them. They have taught me to be patient. They have taught me to understand what a gift it is to earn someone's trust and to give your trust to someone else. Person to person, soul to soul, these writers—I know—have the power to transform us all, our hearts, our minds, and our world.

BIBLIOGRAPHY

G. "*Writing is Difficult.*" Black Seed Writers Group Handout, March 29, 2022.

R. "*Mystical.*" Black Seed Writers Group Handout, March 29, 2022.

PART FIVE:
FICTIONS AS TRUTH-TELLING

22

Walter McMillian: Defeating the Powerful Hands of Death

Madeleine Moon-Chun[1]

Introduction

Walter McMillian, nicknamed "Johnny D" by his friends and family, spent six years on death row for a crime he did not commit.[2] McMillian was born on October 27, 1941, near the city of Monroeville, Alabama. The city in the deep South is famed as the home of Harper Lee, author of *To Kill a Mockingbird*. McMillian was a self-employed logger who lived much of his life in a small town eleven miles away from Monroeville.

In 1986, eighteen-year-old Ronda Morrison was murdered in a dry-cleaning store where she worked as a part-time clerk. The death of Ronda was a shock to her city. The Monroe County sheriffs searched in vain for suspects and evidence. After six months and still no leads, the town was getting impatient, and they craved revenge. Out of desperation, the sheriff's department turned their attention to McMillian, an innocent man with no evidence that pointed to him being the perpetrator and no prior criminal record, because they knew Monroeville was already angry at McMillian for the affair he had had with a white woman. They also knew the town would use anyone as a scapegoat and, by doing so, would trade any rationality and common sense for a false sense of security in the knowledge they believed they possessed.

From there, things began to spiral out of control. First, the sheriffs located Ralph Myers, a man accused of several crimes in nearby Escambia County. They used their power as sheriffs to bribe him, claiming that they would free him from death row. They pressed him until he resigned and gave them what they wanted: false evidence and accusations against McMillian. Under their scrutiny, Myers testified that he drove McMillian

---

[1] Madeleine wrote this when she was in Kendall Tappan-O-Connor's eighth grade humanities class. Thank you to Kendall for an excellent critical writing assignment.
[2] This is the account of a true story in Stevenson, *Just Mercy*.

to the scene of the crime in a "low-rider" truck and stayed in the parking lot of the dry-cleaning store while McMillian went in, shot Ronda, and took the money she had in her possession.

In 1986, Walter McMillian, aged forty-five, was accused of capital murder of a man he had never even seen before in his life. Even before his sentencing or conviction, McMillian was placed on death row by Monroe County Sheriff, Tom Tate. Though this plainly violated the Sixth Amendment, McMillian stayed on death row for over a year awaiting his trial. Fifteen months later, the trial began. Several people in the Black community—friends, family, and neighbors—testified that McMillian was at a family and church fish fry at the time of Morrison's murder. His jury even voted unanimously on a life sentence in prison, but his judge, Robert E. Lee Key Jr., ignored this and sentenced Walter McMillian to death. McMillian's trial lasted less than two days.

In 1988, a newly graduated student of Harvard Law School came to Monroeville and changed Walter McMillian's life. Bryan Stevenson, founder of the Equal Justice Initiative, saw the prison situation down in Alabama, and he was determined to help as many people on death row as he could—that included McMillian. Attorney Stevenson started off by uncovering new evidence McMillian's previous attorney had not. Stevenson and his co-worker, Eva Ansley, found a tape recording of Ralph Myers's testimony. This tape was something the police had tried to hide. On one side of the tape was a recording of Ralph Myers giving testimony that he was with McMillian when he killed Ronda. However, on the other side, there was a recording of Myers bitterly complaining that the police had been bribing him with freedom if he testified against McMillian. Additionally, they found out that McMillian's "low-rider" truck and been converted to a "low-rider" several months *after* the murder took place—not before, like Myers had previously testified. With this new evidence, Stevenson took McMillian's case back to court. The process took almost six years, but finally, in 1993, after another trial with the new evidence, Walter McMillian was free. He was one of the first to be exonerated from Alabama's death row after capital punishment was made legal again in 1976. It had been illegal for four years because of Furman vs. Georgia but became legal again due to another Supreme Court case called Gregg vs. Georgia.

After his exoneration, Walter McMillian worked tirelessly to educate the world about the evils of capital punishment. He spoke at a countrywide conference about his experiences on death row and being wrongfully convicted. McMillian's case became widely known across the country, and after he was freed, a movement began to free others who had been wrongfully convicted. On September 11, 2013, Walter McMillian passed away from early onset dementia, a result of the immense trauma from being on death row. This is why people often consider the death penalty "a double punishment." Inmates sit in their cells while knowing they have lived terribly in jail just to die at the cruel hands of the electric chair. McMillian once said, "From my [jail] cell, you could smell burning flesh. The smell of someone you know burning to death is the most painful and nauseating experience on this earth."[3]

Connections to *The Crucible*

In our modern society, race and social status are often used as a form of power just like Arthur Miller's dramatic play, *The Crucible* (1953), illustrates how people use their power to disadvantage others who they think are "easy targets." In *The Crucible*, Abigail Williams, a seventeen-year-old girl and niece of the reverend of Salem, is dancing and making love potions in the woods with her friends one night. When her uncle finds out, he is furious since there is no dancing permitted in Salem. Suddenly, her cousin, Betty, the daughter of Reverend Parris, will not wake up, and the townspeople are condemning witchcraft as the culprit. These people are confused, so they look to witchcraft to explain the things they do not fully understand. Similarly, the city of Monroeville immediately believed what the sheriff's department had said—that Walter McMillian was the murderer of Ronda Morrison—to blame someone they believed to be "inferior to them" and make themselves feel reassured in their knowledge. Additionally, when Abigail selfishly warns the other girls not to say a word about what really happened in the forest—that they made potions—she says she will "bring a pointy reckoning that will shudder you [them]" if they do.[4] Likewise, the Monroe County sheriffs bribed and threatened Ralph Myers until he resigned and gave them the lies they wanted to hear.

As the play, *The Crucible*, progresses, lies pile up in Salem. More people are accused by Abigail and the group of girls that follow her. These

---

3 Equal Justice Initiative. "Walter McMillian Was Sentenced to Death for a Crime He Did Not Commit," 2022. https://eji.org/cases/walter-mcmillian/.
4 Miller, *The Crucible*, 19.

girls make false accusations, yet they are revered and honored by their community. Their honesty is not questioned by the masses. Many of the accused are poor or women of color. Correspondingly, a disproportionate amount of people on our current day death row are financially destitute and people of color. What is more, the judges (in *The Crucible*) who determine whether someone is innocent or guilty of witchcraft do not acknowledge the other side of the argument. Even if someone were to be innocent, they are sentenced to a public hanging if they do not confess to the lies.

Similarly, Judge Robert E. Lee Key, Jr. only listened to Myers's accusation of Walter McMillian. He judged the other side of the story—told by multiple members of McMillian's family and several of his friends—as invalid. Because of the biases and racism in court, McMillian was sentenced to die for a crime he did not commit. False accusations due to abuse of power are still problematic legal practices of our society that create similar abuses of power between people who lived centuries apart.

This chapter is devoted to Walter McMillian because his story illustrates how deeply divided our society is in terms of the abuse of power because of someone's entitlement. In my drawing, I have a tiny man standing in the palm of a hand, pointing his finger at another man. The tiny man's expression is accusatory, and his stance is confident, but here (below), there is another hand holding up the strings of a marionette.

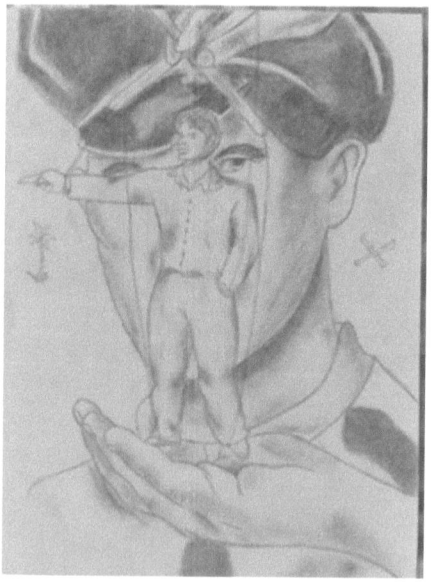

These strings are attached to the extremities of the man. Behind the man's body is the face of an officer to whom the hands belong. Adding strings to the body of the man in the palm of a hand illustrates how power can be an illusion: Although this man has the power to accuse someone, there are stronger forces that control him, and he seems small and insignificant in comparison. Additionally, the man who is being accused—Walter McMillian—has a keyhole near his heart. Oftentimes, hearts are symbols for life. By drawing a keyhole in his chest, I show how powerless this man is in prison with no rights. Because he is on death row, he sits in prison every day, smelling the burning flesh of his friends, all the while knowing he is living a terrible life just to die in the worst way. Next to him is a person's hand holding a key. The hand is holding the key loosely—just with two fingers right outside the prison bars. This key is supposed to symbolize the conniving power holding McMillian captive and the freedom that lies right outside the jail. At the same time, holding the key outside the bars demonstrates how far away freedom is because of how hard it is to get off death row. Furthermore, the key is held tauntingly loose to show the power McMillian lacks because of his race and social status. Above McMillian is a person sitting with their head down, and their arms are over their head as if they need protection from something. This is supposed to represent McMillian's soul and how helpless he feels. By sitting with their head down, this person conveys a sense of defeat and acknowledgment to the fact that they can play no part in gaining their own freedom because of the powerless feeling society has bequeathed to them.

Through the recurring theme of hands, these drawings further epitomize how power can be manipulated to benefit some people, depending on their place in society. There are many hands in these drawings because hands have played a large part in how people have built this modern world. Many times, hands are representations of amity, generosity, and protection. Hence the saying, "Lend a hand to someone in need." However, hands can also be tools for gaining power. For example, our hands, and our brains, are what helped change our world—for better or for worse. Having a cupped hand holding up the accuser and another hand controlling the marionette strings of the tiny man represents the immense power this person—to whom the hands belong—possesses to be able to control another. Although the bottom hand seems to be helping the tiny person, the top hand is manipulating this same person. This signifies how power can be twisted to profit the people who hold this power. For example, in *The Crucible*, Abigail uses her hands to point and accuse many people of being witches—everyone except herself, that is. Abigail's hands are what brought her to power. Abigail's hands are also what brought other people down, just so she could rise to power. Another important aspect of these drawings is the fact that nothing is in color. I chose to use just charcoal and pencil because these can very easily be erased from the page. In the same way, life is very ephemeral, and, despite how people think they are perfect, no one—regardless of their power or respect—knows what comes next in life. We are all vulnerable to death. Additionally, charcoal is very easily smudged. Making the edges of the drawings fuzzy exemplifies how helplessly McMillian lived for six years with the prospect of execution hanging over his head. Conclusively, these illustrations of Walter McMillian's experiences embody the pros and cons of manipulative power brought on by racism and unjust social status entitlement.

BIBLIOGRAPHY

Equal Justice Initiative. "Walter McMillian Was Sentenced to Death for a Crime He Did Not Commit," 2022. https://eji.org/cases/walter-mcmillian/.

Miller, Arthur. *The Crucible. A Play in Four Acts*. Reprint. London: Penguin Books, 1976.

Stevens, Bryan. *Just Mercy: A Story of Justice and Redemption*. Reprint ed. New York: One World, 2015.

23

Life In a Three-Day Loop

Leenah Safi

Senior year of high school has felt like it's made up of basically three kinds of days. There are the "yesterdays," containing those big things that have already happened and that make me who I am at any given moment. There are the "todays" that are somehow both precious and mundane, in which I am running to simply keep up, and ironically, also trying to make meaningful so that they can stand on their own. And then there are the "tomorrows," where I lay my hopes down to rest until we can meet.[1]

"Yesterday"

I unpacked my school bag while Baba was getting ready to head to his evening shift, I thought his face looked thinner than usual.

"Baba, are you okay?"

"Hm, what did you say habibity?"

He was distractedly looking at a newspaper—we had many lying around but he seemed fixated on the date at the top.

"You look tired Baba; can I make you some coffee to take with you?"

"Coffee? Oh yes, that would be great. Like I always say, you make the best coffee in town. I tell my buddies—they take one whiff of the cardamom and their eyes light up. I tell them, my daughter, her name is Selma, she hooks the coffee up for me."

Baba always had something sweet to say. His height seemed to shoot up like a thin but tall tree among us. I would guess at his full height he would be about 6'2." He didn't have much meat on his bones, but today his back seemed to bend a bit with gravity, and his cheek bones protruded. I was put off by the look of him.

---

[1] "The life of this world is made up of three days: yesterday has gone with all that was done; tomorrow, you may never reach; but today is for you so do what you should do today." Al-Hasan Al-Basri.

My younger twin brothers, Abood and Rayyan, were playing before dinner. I went upstairs to greet Mama before coming back down to get them started on their homework. When I got to the top of the staircase, I was surprised to find her door ajar and that she was laying down. This was unlike her. I knocked hesitantly, and when I walked in, I could see that her eyes were red. She must have been crying for a while. A steady stream of tears moistening her cheeks. "What's wrong Mama?" I tried to hide the fear in my voice.

"Come sit down Saloom, there is something I need to talk to you about," she said, sitting up and gesturing for me to sit next to her.

Still at the doorway, my stomach was doing back flips at the seriousness in her voice, and I could feel my toes turning cold.

"Your Baba is sick." I hesitated a bit as her words filled the air, I scrunched my toes to find feeling in them and see if my feet would move with me to sit on the bed,

"We got the phone call from the doctor a few days ago. They told us what we were most afraid of, it's probably spread too far already…but we are going to take *whatever* they can give us, and I have been working really hard to get referrals for whatever treatment is available. I want to try everything. He deserves that, we deserve that. I had a feeling something was wrong, but he refused to get a checkup. He kept insisting on putting it off and going to work instead…."

The more she talked, the more upset I became. My head felt like a heavy block of concrete, balancing on my neck, threatening to fall and break apart, making a mess all over the floor. When I thought of this potential mess, I concentrated all of my will power to keep everything in place. But the room seemed to be spinning, so I shut my eyes tight and heard myself ask plainly just to stop the flow of information from coming at me.

"Is Baba dying?" I asked.

Mama let out a sob, and that was the surest response I could get.

"How long do we have?"

"We don't know for certain, but he has an appointment tomorrow that I need you to take him to after you get home for school. And he is *insisting* you go to school first even though I told him I barely got him in for the last possible appointment…"

"Why isn't *he* the one telling me this?" I could hear the anger in my own voice now.

"Susu, habibity" her voice was pleading now for my understanding. I know you love your Baba a lot. Don't be upset with him. He didn't know how to say it, he just couldn't find the right time...."

I got the gist and didn't need to hear any more about how or why they willingly kept me in the dark. The gravity in the room was only getting heavier, making it harder to hold my head up. I went to lay in my own bed and didn't come down later that evening when the boys shouted with excitement that we were having pizza for dinner.

"Today"

My eyes were sore when I tried opening them this the morning. No doubt the shortest night of sleep of my life—had I actually slept at all, or just dozed off? Either way, the realization that morning had broken without regard for the night made me feel both defeat and relief. The day would start regardless of whether my life as I knew it had been shattered. With that thought, being at school was a welcome reprieve to what was going on at home.

I opened my notebook in between classes, to add "Pick Baba up after school to take him to his appointment" under my agenda for the day. The "must get done" list marked **urgent** had been the same for a few weeks now:

Finish FAFSA application
Call the registrar back and ask about which college at the school offers the closest thing to an American studies program
Ask about school's financial aid and out of state tuition

I slammed my notebook shut in frustration and rushed to my locker when I heard someone say,

"Hi Selma"

I turned around to see Ahmad standing just about a foot away, his books falling out of his arms.

"Oh, hey Ahmad, do you need some help?"

His face turned red.

"This is not the ideal hallway meeting."

I smiled in his general direction and bent down to the floor to help pick the books off the floor.

"Is there an ideal *hallway* meeting?"

Ahmad's family had made his interest in me known to my family, but I didn't know what to make of him.

"Uh, yes. It's called a 'meet cute.' Hey quick, I know class is about to start, but I was wondering if you'd like to review college applications together some time. I was told to have someone look over my statement before submitting it, and you're so good with this sort of thing...." He was starting to sound as self-conscious as he looked.

"Sure, I can read it but I haven't even written mine yet."

"Alright now, Selma, Ahmad, you're going to be late for history, hurry up please." The principle always stood at the head of the hallway, to make sure no one lingered—and especially that mingling between boys and girls was minimal.

On the bus ride home, I pulled my notebook out. I started doodling around my forever to-do list and suddenly found my thoughts fixated on why in the world I had said yes to working on school applications with Ahmad, rather than what I really wanted to say in the middle of that hallway. I should have shouted——MY LIFE IS RUINED. I should have been crying, knees to the ground, as dramatically as possible—anything at all to call attention to the volcano erupting inside of me. But I couldn't even get the words out now. Besides, who could I talk to without divulging the secret? Does anyone else *in the family* even know? Probably now. Mama and Baba have always been the ones to look after everyone else. They were the eldest in their families and the first ones to come to the United States. They had a great sense of duty and pride about helping their siblings. Getting them involved would jeopardize too much.

When we finally got home, I left the twins in the living room and ran upstairs to change, I could hear Baba and Mama in their room, a conversation turning into an argument.

"I told Selma a few days ago that she had my permission to apply for University of Chicago as we had been saying...." Baba spoke.

"What? Why would you do that, Na'im?! You should have been steering her to stay home and apply to schools nearby."

"I know that's what you and I talked about last, but I think she deserves exposure to more than what she has been getting at Islamic School and living in that city has been a dream of hers...."

"I can't understand why we are talking about this right now when you need to be getting ready to leave...."

There was a break in the conversation. I pressed my ear to the wall, and the unexpected sound of Baba's sobs caught me by surprise. I didn't know how much his encouragements of my college plans over the last few weeks were requiring him to sacrifice.

"The best thing I can do is show Selma that I believe she has a bright future. She is going to be the first college graduate in the family. That is always what I have wanted for her. And she will need your help, Samar, to...."

Snapping before he could finish making his request, Mama lamented, "I can't Na'im. I can't be on the phone with the doctors right now and think about how Selma can get into a school out of state. I am sorry, habiby. I can't. But I will promise you not to get in the way of your dreams for her. If Selma gets into a school out of state with financial aid and wants to go, then I don't know.... We will cross that bridge when we get to it. But I just don't think focusing on achieving that is a priority right now"

My heart sunk. I didn't want them to fight about me. But I also didn't want my graduation plans to not be a priority anymore. I wondered, what would happen to me in all of this?

Ping

A notification on my phone, an email from Ahmad...

"Salam Selma,
Sorry we didn't get the chance to finish our conversation earlier
I attached my statement draft for State. If you wouldn't mind taking a look, I'd really appreciate it.
Is there anything I can do to be of help as you do your applications? I am sure you will apply to more than one place.... It would be cool if we wound up going somewhere similar.
Sincerely,
Ahmad"

I was flustered reading his email; this wasn't the right time. I threw jeans and a t-shirt on and knocked on my parent's door, as it was time to head out.

I gripped the wheels of Baba's silver 2008 Toyota Camry tightly. I had learned to drive in this car and found the sturdiness of its wheel in my fully clenched fists comforting. I thought of the many days driving around supermarket parking lots when I was too small to reach the peddles, Baba would work the peddles and I would steer in circles.

My stomach was empty. I didn't have an appetite all day and its gurgling only reminded me of how nauseated I felt. Baba sat slightly reclined, clutching his abdomen in discomfort. I looked at him and asked, "Baba, how badly is your stomach hurting you?" "Just a little, baba. Not much more than yours—from the sound of the grumbling." I smiled. I would come to measure how bad things were by whether or not he could lift the pain in the air with a caring acknowledgment of those around him.

It was a twenty-five-minute drive to his chemo appointment and baba's discomfort officially made me an anxious driver. I wanted to think about something that would distract me from our current predicament, Ahmad came to mind. Maybe the hand of God was involved in bringing us together so I could have someone help me get through all of this. Maybe this is what *naseeb* looks like…The idea that this should be fate brought a smile to my face. If it were to be my fate, I could accept it.

When we arrived, I jumped out of the car and went over to the passenger's side. Baba was slow to get up, but he insisted he could make the walk over. I looked at this brick clinic attached to a major hospital with some gratitude, at least we wouldn't get lost and have to walk endlessly to get to the front door.

I sat Baba down in an empty waiting room, remembering Mama tell me that we had the last appointment of the day. I was grateful not to have to wait in a line, which meant we could see the doctor quickly. I turned toward the reception desk only to hear Baba call my name, and I turned back around to see him heaving. I looked frantically for a bag, and I'm not sure how I got one, but I rushed over to him and sat him down and held the bag to his mouth as he vomited.

I could not understand what was making him sick. I looked over at the nurses and they were not in a rush to get to me. I called over to one, and when she came, quite bothered to have left the chart she was working on, sternly said, "What's wrong?"

"I don't know... umm.. he has cancer... and he just started throwing up. Can't you give him something to help?" I gestured to the obvious fact that he was vomiting.

"You will have to wait until someone can check him in, and we will have to wait for a doctor to see him before we can give him anything."

I gripped Baba's shoulders tightly and felt a lump in my throat—sadness I think, with some self-pity over our situation. But most of all, helplessness. Baba tapped my hand after a short while and said, "Selma, it's going to be alright."

Finally, we made it to the back, and Baba said, "It's a big comfy armchair, Selma" A genuine smile of relief spread on his face, as he sank into the softness of the chair. "Not like the one in the waiting room."

Before I sat down, I made a point to draw the curtain around us, and the sight of other the patient's sitting alone reminded me that I was there for a reason. I could ask good questions. My Dad wasn't alone.

A middle-aged nurse with pink scrubs came in first. I was grateful that she seemed friendly. Her braids were tied up in a bun and she wore a paisley pink top.

"Hello Mr.—umm, you're going to have to help me learn how to pronounce this..."

I said, "Dabaji, its pronounced Duh-bah-jee"

"That's a pretty name. It is Mediterranean?"

"Umm, yes, its Arabic. My name is Selma, I am his daughter," I replied as I pointed to my dad.

"Oh good, it's so important to have children supporting in this."

"I couldn't agree more," Baba said looking up.

"And how are you Mr. DUH BAH JEE?"

"I am doing just fine thank you, but we didn't get your name."

"My name is Samantha, and I will be looking after you today. Anything you need at all, it's my job to take care of you. I love my patients and absolutely believe that good care makes a difference."

"I don't know if you heard, but my dad was throwing up in the waiting room just now. Are we still able to go ahead with treatment today?"

"Yes, I did hear about that. That's a symptom of the cancer he has—so nothing to worry too much about. We are going for treatment today to try and counteract the potency of the cancer in his system. But, as I hope was explained to you already, the treatment may have its own adverse side effects, and vomiting may be one of them"

A somberness seemed to come over Baba as we listened to this. I wanted to ask him what he was thinking once the nurse left, but he closed his eyes and seemed to doze off. At least he wasn't in pain anymore, I thought.

When we got home, I joined Mama in the kitchen.

"Mama, treatment was really hard."

"Oh, what happened?"

I didn't know where or how to start. Baba was resting on the couch within ear shot.

"They were just very cold, as Baba was throwing up in the waiting room."

"Yes, he has been for a few days. He's been trying to hide it from you. I'm so glad they still gave him the treatment."

She went on cooking.

"Mama, have you talked to Khalty recently?"

Mama looked taken aback at the mention of her sister.

"What made you think of her right now?" She said with some suspicion.

"Well, I was thinking maybe she could help…like with the twins or—"

There was a heavy pause.

"I haven't told her about what we are going through. But help with the twins is a good idea—maybe I can send the twins there."

My heart dropped.

"Oh, I was thinking maybe Khalty could come here, having the twins away means we would miss them"

"Of course, we would miss them, but then I would have more time to follow up with Baba's appointments and things. Plus, they'll be around your cousins, the twins will have fun and give Baba more opportunity to rest during the day"

I held back tears. This is not what I intended.

"Mama…."

"Habibity, it's a good idea. It will give you time to do your schoolwork. We don't want you failing your senior year.

"Can you at least ask if Khalty will come here first before sending them away???" I was imploding now.

Mama shot a disbelieving look at me but presumably for Baba's sake, she didn't go off. She kept on cooking....

Noting my tears, she patted my hand

"This way you will get what you want. You'll be able to apply to Chicago. If they stay home, you will have to look after them. You wouldn't be able to do what you have to do," she said, like it was a matter of fact.

"Mama, I am not sure that's what I want." Finally, she put the food down and looked right at me.

"What makes you say that?"

"It doesn't make sense that's what I wanted before knowing Baba was sick, and now knowing that he is sick...I don't know—shouldn't that mean I choose to stay close to home?"

She reached out for an embrace, and I was glad for the acknowledgment that what I said was important, but I worried, that the embrace was also an unspoken agreement that a decision had been made.

"Tomorrow"

The next morning, I awoke to a quiet house. Mama was already at work- she sent me a text saying my aunt was on her way and that I should get the boys ready for their stay at her house. Baba was still sleeping. I pulled my phone up and went to re-read Ahmad's email and skim his statement. Wow, the letter was good. And I felt a twinge of bitterness. People in my class would go on with or without me—and I wished that things could just stop for just a little while.

Dear Ahmad,
So, I am not sure how to say this, but my dad is pretty sick. I am not sure I will even be able to apply to schools this year. Please don't tell anybody.

Ping

"Selma,
I am so sorry to hear that your dad is sick. You should definitely still apply. My dad was sick in freshman year, and I didn't think I would be able to make it to school, but he pulled through. And I am so happy I didn't my fear get in my way. I heard from a shaykh I was listening to on YouTube

that really helped me at the time, that if you say this particular Du'a with conviction, it would heal any sickness. All of the nurses and doctors that were caring for my dad said his pulling through was a miracle. Share it with your dad, too. He is an amazing man, my dad misses seeing him at fajr at the masjid. No one could have managed to pray fajr at the masjid for as many years as your dad did without being a great believer. I attached the Du'a and some other inspirational quotes below."

I opened the document and read through the prayer, and promptly closed it and put my phone down with some annoyance to be given an extra task. I grabbed the twins' suitcases from the back of the closet, and started packing some of their things: pajamas, changes of clothes, school stuff, they wouldn't need toys or books as the cousins would probably have some. I checked my phone again, and Mama had sent me an address where to meet Khalty with the kids. We did a quick breakfast, and I peaked in Baba's room before heading out

His room was dark, but he was awake, "Selma, hurry back, I want to talk to you before Mama comes home."

We met Khalty in a parking lot. We kissed and hugged. She and I tried not to make a big fuss so as not to give the boys any indication that this was something more than a fun sleepover for a few days. "Selma, your parents need you now more than ever." I nodded that I knew this. "But they will also worry about you. Especially Baba. Dad's will always want to make sure their girls are okay." I felt the tears coming on. "Whatever happened to that Ahmad boy? I remember your mom saying something a few months ago about his parents calling to express their interest." This was not something I wanted to discuss—so I said something like, "Oh, um, yeah he's fine, we talk." "You should not turn that opportunity away! Being supported is very important, and there will never be a perfect time. You may not have a chance like this again. In the future, it will be harder without your dad." We both stopped at the harshness of those last words. "Oh habibty, I am sorry! I didn't mean it like that. I just meant; you are a smart girl, and you have look out for your future."

When I returned home the house was quiet. Baba was sitting on the couch in the living room. He was praying. I went into the kitchen to wait until he was done

"Selma, baba, come here"

I sat next to him inching closer until our knees were touching.

"I want you to pray for me, habibity"

This felt both somehow trivial and burdensome at the same time.

"Pray for what Baba?"

"About everything. Big things, little things, always make the *istikhara* prayer."

"Oh, I thought that prayer was only for marriage."

He smiled.

"Yes, most often that is when people turn to it. But you should understand it as a sincere request you make to Allah for help when you have to make a decision. Whatever comes to your heart when you are before Allah that you feel anxious about, say the prayer."

"Baba, when the nurse was explaining what we should be expecting with treatment, you seemed sad..."

He looked down.

"Either way, I am dying habibity."

He held both of my hands in his now.

"I can't say this to your mom, but I think I can say it to you."

"Things will never be the same, no matter how much treatment I get. Going back to how things were, is not the goal. Do you understand what I mean? Don't let others, no matter how much they may pressure you, convince you into thinking that."

We were quiet for some time.

When Mama came home, Baba and I pretended like we were having a lighthearted moment. After the three of us shared a light dinner, I went to my room. I faced the *qibla,* thinking I would make the *istikhara* prayer about Ahmad, what my aunt said made me feel like I must resolve to take action to secure my own future. And making the prayer was a sure way to take my future with him seriously. But it wasn't until the closing of the prayer that I realized I had asked about something else:

Allahumma, I seek [guidance] from your Knowledge and your Ability, because You know and I do not, and because You are capable and I am not, and you are Knower of the layers of Unseen. If you know seeking treatment for Baba's cancer to be good for him, in this life and the return of his affairs, then make it so, and put blessing in it. And if you know seeking treatment to be bad for him, in this life and the return of his affairs, then turn it away from us,

and turn us away from it, choose what is best for us, and allow us to come to terms with it...
End

Reading Questions
- What themes does this story highlight?
- What are some messages Selma is receiving about her future and about her dad's illness?
- Are there instances where Selma expresses expectations that she has about how things will go?
- Do any of the feelings Selma identifies strike you or resonate with you?
- What are moments of connection between Selma and her parents? What about moments of disconnection?
- Considering the main characters in this story, how does each of them begin responding to the crisis? And does that seem to change later in the story?
- Were you curious at any point in the story and would have liked Selma to elaborate more on something that she said?
- Are there any characters that are mentioned but we do not hear from? How might they be impacted?
- What are some of the cultural and religious elements that you noticed, and how are they informing the ways that Selma is navigating life at home, at school, and at the hospital?
- Are there any characters you can relate to or identify with in this story? If so, in what ways? And if not, what perspective do you think may be missing?

24

Dreams That Hold Power

Madeleine Moon-Chun[1]

It is almost midnight, but I can't sleep. I am in a room with whitewashed walls and big windows, smelling of disinfectant. I look at the small shape of my little sister lying curled up on the bed next to my chair. I have never noticed how small Aonani looks without her big personality to fill her up. I tear my gaze away from her and walk to the window. I open it and lean my head out to feel the breeze. I can see the parking lot. The cars and buildings look like toys I used to play with when I was younger. The sky is clear, so I try to count the constellations to distract myself. It was something Aonani and I used to do on warm nights, sitting together on the porch.

I have always thought of my life as a remote mountain—a mountain that I had to hike up like a lonely wanderer—always walking, unable to turn back, even in the rain and snow. When I was a child, my backpack was light, and I was in no rush. There were places with gentle slopes and vibrant trees, fresh air, and beautiful views. Even in winter, I was content, so I didn't notice the bitter cold. But now, as the years pass, my backpack grows heavier with every step I take.

The slope grows steeper, rockier, and the air is too thin for even the toughest of trees.

"Tell me a story," Aonani begged me. *We lay on her narrow bed side by side, our bodies making the shape of closed parentheses.*

"Alright," I had said. "What kind of story?"

"The happy kind," she whispered, holding out her tiny hand for me to take. I took it in my own calloused one and gave it a gentle squeeze.

---

[1] Madeleine wrote this when she was in the eighth grade for Tom Painting's creative writing class. It won a Gold Key Award for flash fiction in the Regional Scholastic Writing Award.

"Once upon a time," I began, "in a place full of love, there was a girl who believed that dreams were powerful things...."

That was one year ago, before Aonani was diagnosed with bone cancer. In one year, she has changed far more than I could have imagined. Her eyes have become dark and bottomless, and I know she is climbing a steep mountain of her own—with a backpack far heavier than mine.

And yet her bright smile never wavers. Our parents picked her name wisely. It means "beautiful light." Every day she asks for a story, and every day I tell her the same one. I think about that night—the night when I first told her that story—a lot. But it makes my heart hurt because I know she used to be so happy.

For a long time, this story had fueled her and had given her the energy to smile through another day. But now, I can see her fight is waning. She sleeps a lot now, sometimes almost for a whole day. I still tell her the story, whether she can hear it or not, for it gives me strength and hope.

I am so lost in my memories and thoughts that I don't hear Aonani call out until the second time.

"David?" she whispers. I rush over and take her hand. "Can you tell me a story?"

"Of course," I say. "I know just the one."

"Once upon a time, in a place full of love, there was a girl whose name meant 'beautiful light.' She believed in dreams because knew they could be powerful things—if one believed in them hard enough ...."

Afterword
Teaching and Learning Through *Konbit*

Cécile Accilien

So many of the people and places that I love are literally being annihilated at this moment because of injustice, inhumanity, greed, and unwillingness to share power. As I write this, I feel the pain and suffering of people in my home country of Ayiti (pronounced **A-yee-tee**),[1] where I grew up until the age of twelve, and Burkina Faso, where I lived and taught for about a year. A friend suggested that I do some *tonglen* breathing, which consists of inhaling sorrow and anger and exhaling compassion and presence. Tonglen is a Tibetan term that means "giving and taking." The idea behind the practice is that we are transforming our anguish into a positive force: as we exhale, we share light and well-being with everyone who needs it at that moment. To me, this aligns well with the concept of *konbit* (pronounced kon-beat), one of my favorite words in my maternal language of Haitian Creole. Konbit refers to a communal harvest whereby individuals come together to help each other. We also see konbit during Vodou ceremonies, in which individuals work with one another to invoke the spirits. Vodou, a religion that does not proselytize, often creates a space where everyone is welcome. In Ayiti, konbit is everywhere.

The essence of konbit is community; it is being present for one another, supporting one another, and living in community. Its tenets include the following:

1. We bring all our strengths and power together for the greater good.
2. Diversity, Equity, Inclusion, and Belonging exist because we recognize everyone's humanity regardless of gender, class, race, and/or ability.
3. We have mutual aid so we can sustain one another.

---

1 Another alternate spelling is Hayti.

4. We have ubuntu, a Zulu concept that means "I am because we are" and an African philosophy that lets us know that we only exist in relation to one another.
5. We promote healthy co-dependency.
6. We have mutual respect.
7. We are socially responsible for one another.
8. We dialogue with one another.

I recently traveled to Kigali, Rwanda, with a nonprofit organization called WAKE Tech 2 Empower, which helps women social entrepreneurs based in the United States share knowledge and skills with women in international communities, offering resources to help them succeed as leaders while they work to eradicate gender-based violence, illiteracy, and poverty. In Kigali, we met with leaders from the Nyamirambo Women's Center and learned about the ways in which the government subsidizes milk, water, gas, and other basic items to ensure that they cost the same for everyone. The work that the Nyamirambo Women's Center is doing to empower women in their community is a form of konbit. How I wished that some of my students could be there to see a different Rwanda from the one they probably know through stereotypical media representations.

We also visited the Kigali Genocide Memorial.[2] Walking around the walls of graves, thinking about the atrocities that happened here a mere twenty-eight years ago, left me with few words. The dehumanization of the Tutsis, the media propaganda, the masterminds behind the genocide—all seemed incomprehensible. There were rooms such as the children's memorial that I could not visit. It is so hard to comprehend how human beings can on the one hand create so many beautiful things, and at the same time commit so many horrific crimes in the name of power, greed, and fear. The date of my visit was September 11, and it was not lost on me how the world responded to September 11, but not to the Rwandan Genocide. It is clear whose lives matter in our society. I remember exactly where I was during that genocide. I was living in France. Luckily two of the people in the group were close friends, so I was able to talk through things a bit with them. But how do you talk through such horrors?

---

2 See Kigali Genocide Memorial website, https://kgm.rw.

Contemplating this history, I felt deep sadness and anger, but I also felt hope. What is hopeful is the intentional ways in which Rwanda is working on ensuring that such an atrocity never happens again. For instance, every Rwandan child must take a course on "Peace Education" to learn about the genocide and ways to cultivate empathy, critical thinking, and personal responsibility. "Trauma Healing" classes include a forgiveness workshop. Sustainable livelihood communities are working towards finding ways to deal with issues that can create conflict, including climate change, which can and does lead to a lack of food, and therefore to hunger. Where there is hunger, young people are vulnerable to radicalization, joining armed militias, and becoming victims of sexual exploitation.

When survivors explain what the Kigali Genocide Memorial means to them, one says, "The Memorial is a place where I feel whole again. Where we can be with our loved ones again. It's our home." At the memorial I learned about *umuganda* (community workspace), where people in the community, especially young people, are intentional and conscious about working together to live with one another in peaceful harmony. I also learned about *ubumuntu*, which means kindness, humanity, or greatness of heart in Kinyarwanda. After the visit, to process my emotions, I wrote the following:

Ubumuntu helps us remember in order not to repeat these horrible, inhumane, unimaginable, horrific acts of violence. Ubumuntu invites us to share power. There is enough for ALL of US! The world said "Never again" after the Holocaust. Yet they allowed the murders of over one million Tutsis. One people, one culture, one language. Divided by colonial greed, capitalism, fear, religion, and power. The church, the government, the media bonded together to support and empower the extremists as they massacred their sisters and brothers. It was never about anything else except greed and power. When you start to see your neighbor, friend, colleague as "Other," as Inyenzi (cockroach); you can easily convince yourself that they bring fear, that they do not deserve to exist, and then the genocide is simple. Family, friends, and neighbors tear at one another out of fear. Felicien Ntagengwa notes: "If you knew me and you really knew yourself you would not have killed me."[3]

---

3 Quote at the Gisozi Genocide Memorial in Kigali, Rwanda.

As I reflected on the meaning of konbit during my journey to west Africa, I understood that it brings together the concepts of ubuntu, ubumuntu, umuganda, and sawubona, the Zulu greeting that means "I see you." This word is more than a simple hello. It is an acknowledgment of each other's dignity, humanity, and presence. It is an invitation.

This book is a konbit. When we educate through the lenses of konbit, we can eradicate some of society's major ills, including oppression, lack of healthcare for all, homelessness, food insecurity, racism, sexism, ableism, and other "isms." We allow ourselves to co-create knowledge; we question the "traditional" European and US–centric model of education and learning as "*the*" way to learn. We understand that the classroom in whatever form it takes is a sacred space where we encounter souls. We embrace the notion that, as the late feminist scholar bell hooks reminds us, "The classroom remains the most radical space of possibility in the academy."[4] We decolonize our syllabi in whatever ways we can. In this way, we educate to liberate. In this way, we have konbit.

We only exist through our common humanity. Real freedom and stability can only be achieved when we work together. Yolande Mukagasana wisely reminds us of the importance of compassion, community building, and forgiveness when she states, "There will be no humanity without forgiveness. There will be no forgiveness without justice. But justice will be impossible without humanity." In the name of justice, humanity, and *urukundo* (love), let us become whole by working together to educate for peace.

---

4 hooks, *Teaching to Transgress*, 12.

Consuming Africa

I love Africa but please don't let me interact with Africans

I want to see the gorillas, mountain monkeys, lions, etc. but don't ask me to learn how to say please and thank you in the native language

Murakoze Asante sana is too hard to learn

I want to come and explore Africa but how dare you ask me to buy a visa. After all I have an American passport! And a European passport

I want daishikis, local coffee, African color, fabric but don't let me interact with those "poor" children

I love Africa. I want to consume Africa while living as if I were in the US, Canada, or Europe.

I want to explore Africa on my terms

I want Africa without the Africans. I want Africa without having to think about history of colonization as well as my own power, privilege, and positionality

After visiting the Kigali Genocide Museum
9/11/2022

Ubumuntu and Umuganda

Ubumuntu helps us remember—in order not to repeat this horrible, inhumane, unimaginable, horrific, unforgettable... acts of violence.

Ubumuntu invites us to share power. There is enough for ALL of US!

The world said 'Never again' after the Holocaust. Yet, they allowed the atrocious murders of over one million Tutsis.

One people, one culture, one language. Divided by colonial greed, capitalism, fear, religion and power.

The church, the government, the media bonded together to support and empower the extremists to massacre their fellow sisters and brothers.

It was never about anything else except greed and power

When you start to see your neighbor, friend, colleague as 'Other' as *Inyenzi* (cockroach), you can easily convince yourself that they bring fear, that they do not deserve to exist, and then the genocide is simple.

Family, friends, neighbors tear one another out of fear. Felicien Ntagengwa notes: "if you knew me and you really knew yourself you would not have killed me."

Umuganda strengthens us and create hope for the future. Real freedom and stability can only be achieve when we work together. Yolande Mukagasana reminds us wisely of the importance of compassion, community building and forgiveness. She states: "There will be no humanity without forgiveness. There will be no forgiveness without justice. But justice will be impossible without humanity."

In the name of justice, humanity, *urukundo* (love), let us become whole by working together to educate for peace.

Ubumuntu= goodness and humanity
Umuganda= community workspace

BIBLIOGRAPHY

hooks, bell. *Teaching to Transgress: Education as a Practice of Freedom.* New York, NY: Routledge, 1994.

www.ingramcontent.com/pod-product-compliance
Ingram Content Group UK Ltd.
Pitfield, Milton Keynes, MK11 3LW, UK
UKHW041304180426
11947UKWH00009B/683